AMERICA
A Regional COOKBOOK

MARY BRANDT KERR

CHARTWELL BOOKS, INC.

A QUARTO BOOK

Published by Chartwell Books Inc.
A division of Book Sales Inc.
110 Enterprise Avenue
Secaucus, New Jersey 07094

ISBN 1-55521-075-9

This book was designed and produced by
Quarto Publishing Ltd
The Old Brewery, 6 Blundell Street
London N7 9BH

Senior editor Jane Laing

Art editor Nick Clark

Editorial Susie Ward

Designer Hazel Edington
Design assistant Ursula Dawson

Illustrators Vana Haggerty Mick Hill
Photographer John Heseltine

Consultants Scott Ewing Barbara Croxford
Indexer Viki Robinson

Art director Alastair Campbell
Editorial director Jim Miles

Typeset by Text Filmsetters Ltd, London
Paste-up by Mick Hill
Manufactured in Hong Kong by Regent Publishing Services Ltd
Printed by Leefung-Asco Printers Ltd, Hong Kong

CONTENTS

THE REGIONS

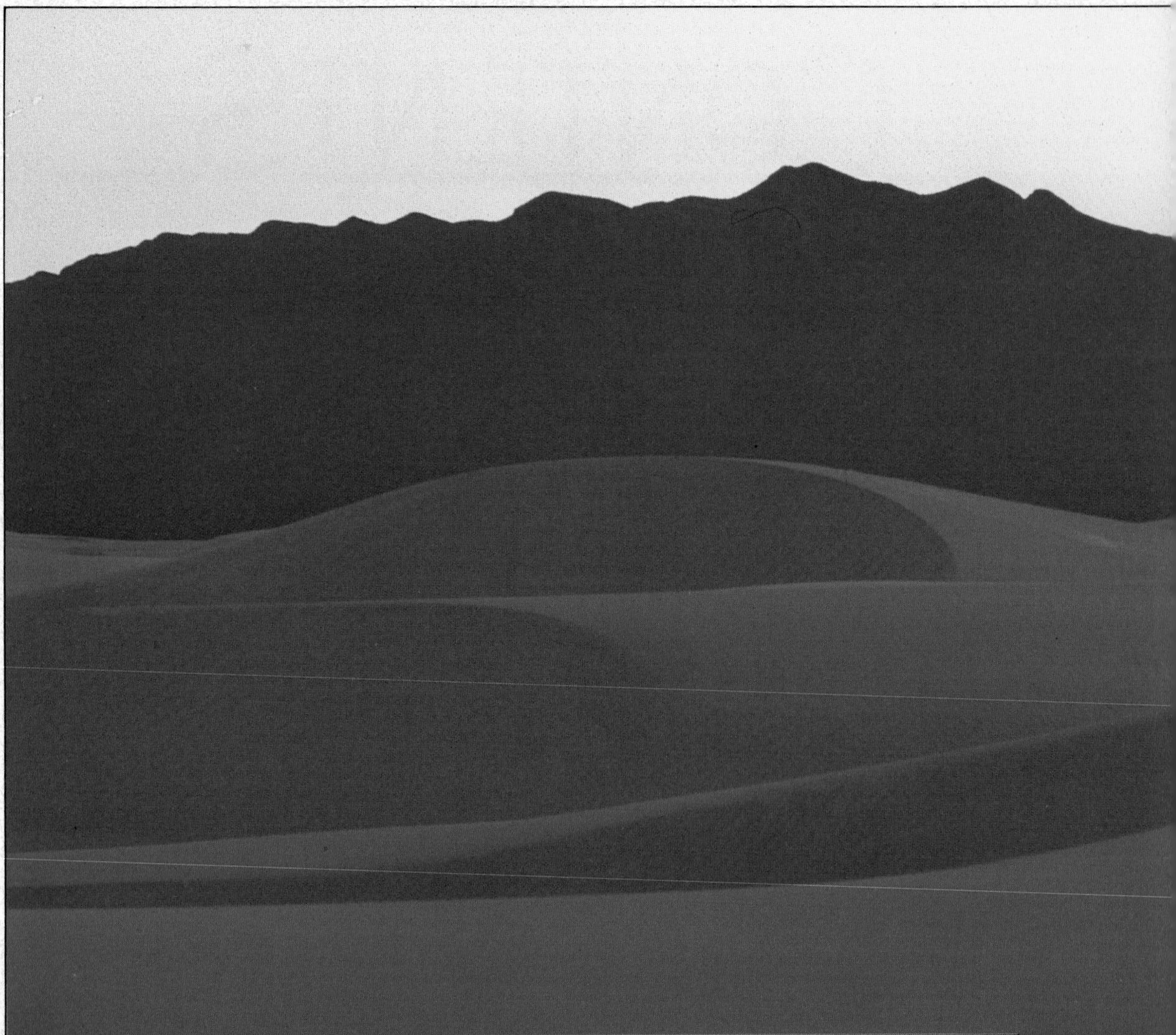

INTRODUCTION

American-style cooking has been evolving since the beginning of the new nation. A good ethnologist with a willing palate and a hearty appetite might identify as many as thirty culinary traditions in the United States, all transformed by New World ingredients into versions uniquely American.

Much of our nation's classic recipes owe their foundation to the early settlers, or to the Indians with whom they intermarried. It is certainly true that many of the cooking techniques – particularly those of the Western, Midwestern and Pacific Northwestern states – evolved from the open-fire methods of the Indians, trappers and cowboys. The barbecue, whose popularity has spread to Europe and Australia, is probably the leading symbol of this culinary tradition. What is more "typically American" than a perfectly char-broiled steak or a plump hamburger on a sesame bun, heaped high with all the requisites – lettuce, tomato, onion, pickle and one of a codebook of "secret" sauces? Typical, too, are the planked King salmon of the coastal Indians, the tortillas and chili basting sauces of Texas and the Southwest.

Yet barbecuing is only one cornerstone of American cuisine. What of the European traditions and techniques that continued to develop in the new land, using the strange new foodstuffs: the breads and the bean stews, incorporating molasses; the pies and savory dishes made from pumpkin or squashes.

Some communities, such as the Italians, Chinese, Polish and Scandinavians, have kept their ways proudly, while inventing pizzas, chop suey, pickles and cheeses unknown to their kin across the seas. Other groups have contributed their culinary heritage more indiscriminately, so that now every supermarket in the country boasts a huge range of sausages, cold meats, cheeses, jams, pastries and mixed salads. To generations, America has been the New Testament version of the Promised Land – and milk and honey were only the beginning.

The States of the Union
Except for the outlying states of Alaska and Island Hawaii, the United States fits snugly in the middle of the North American continent between Canada and Mexico. It is possible to go round the world simply by sampling the dishes in the fifty states, and the country is often divided into seven regions, each with its own culinary traditions. The regions are:
New England Maine, Vermont, New Hampshire, Massachusetts, Rhode Island and Connecticutt;
The North Atlantic Seaboard New York, Pennsylvania, New Jersey, Delaware, Maryland and West Virginia;
The Deep South Virginia, Tennessee, North Carolina, South Carolina, Mississippi, Alabama, Georgia, Louisiana and Florida;
Texas and the Southwest Texas, New Mexico, Arizona, Utah, Nevada;
California and Hawaii;
The Pacific Northwest and Alaska Oregon, Washington and Alaska;
The Midwest and Mountain States Idaho, Montana, Wyoming, Colorado, North Dakota, South Dakota, Nebraska, Kansas, Oklahoma, Minnesota, Iowa, Wisconsin, Illinois, Missouri, Arkansas, Michigan, Indiana, Ohio and Kentucky.

THE CULINARY

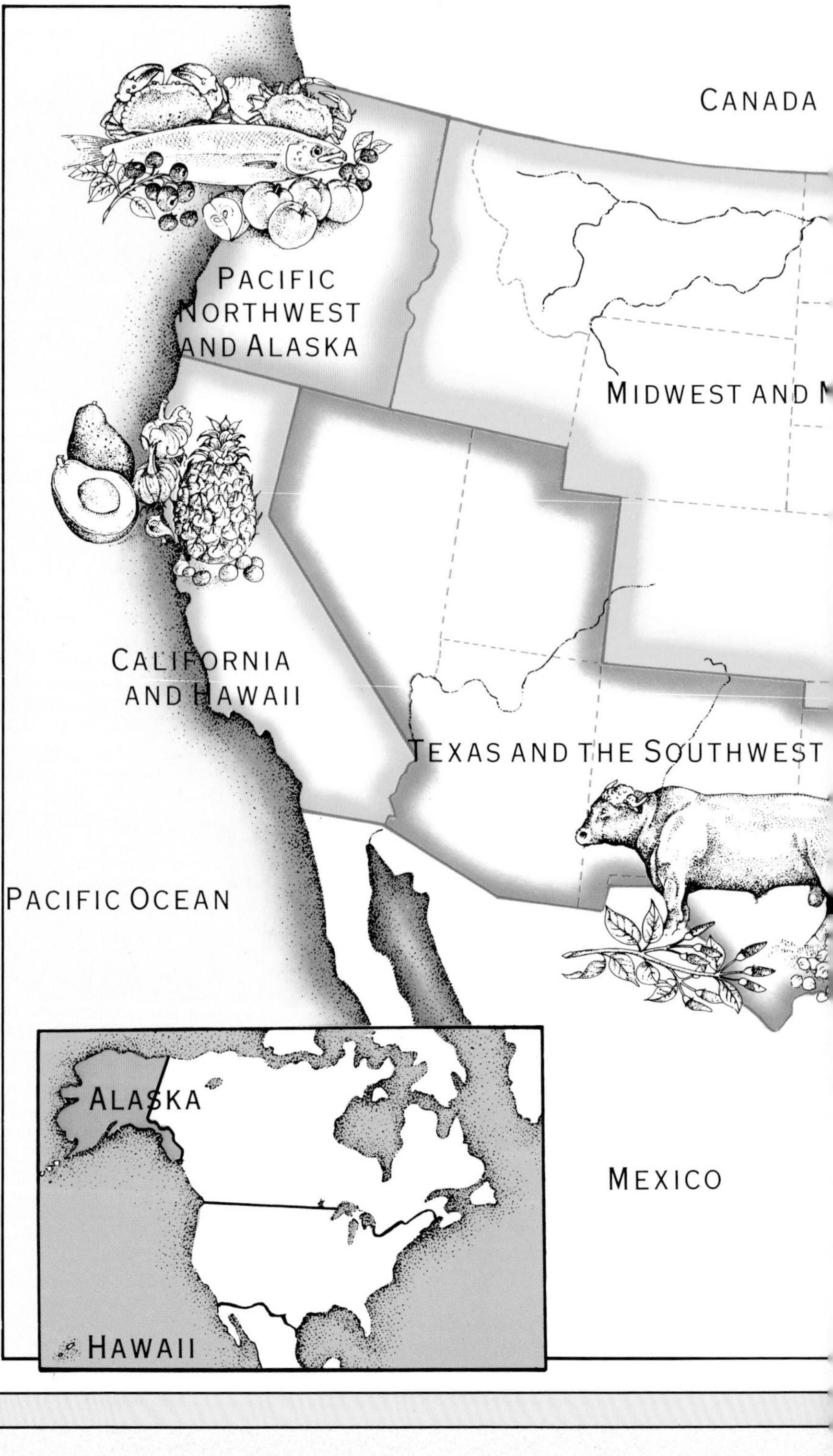

CANADA
PACIFIC NORTHWEST AND ALASKA
MIDWEST AND
CALIFORNIA AND HAWAII
TEXAS AND THE SOUTHWEST
PACIFIC OCEAN
MEXICO
ALASKA
HAWAII

EGIONS OF AMERICA

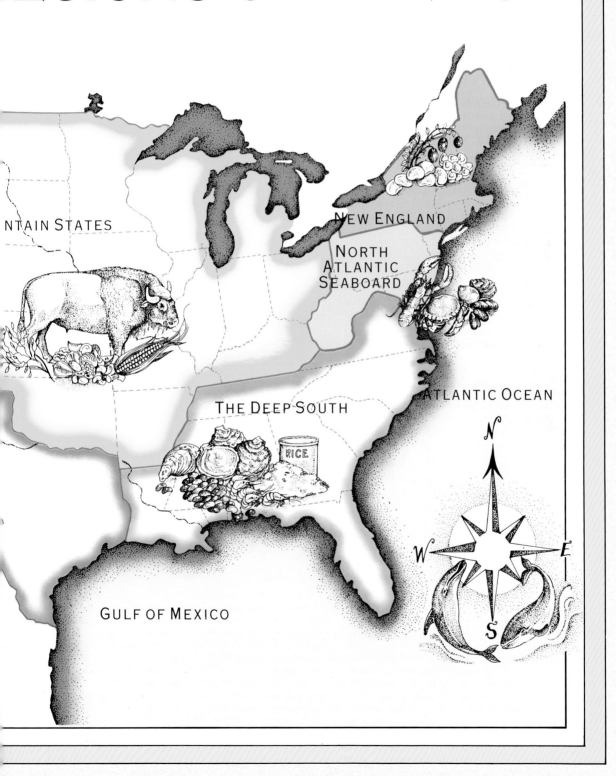

NTAIN STATES

NEW ENGLAND

NORTH ATLANTIC SEABOARD

THE DEEP SOUTH

RICE

ATLANTIC OCEAN

N

W

E

S

GULF OF MEXICO

NATIVE INGREDIENTS

Eclectic and fresh are the bywords of modern American cooking. The new American cuisine is predicated on American ingredients and cooked with American flair, with a subtle infusion of classical preparations, but it is still essentially an ethnic melting pot.

CORNMEAL

Cornmeal, in all its manifestations (blue cornmeal is the current favorite), has always been the staff of life in the Americas. A good example of cultural diffusion, cornmeal was part of the everyday diet of the Indians before Columbus landed. The Hopi tribes of the American Southwest had a rainbow of cultivated corn, which they roasted and ground into flour.

The earliest Pilgrims chanced upon an abandoned Indian store of corn, which helped them through their first terrible winter, and by the next spring they were planting corn in earnest. They learned the Indian method of planting: a seed kernel was poked into the ground and a dead fish added for fertilizer. Cornmeal dishes quickly became ubiquitous on the daily menu of early colonists. Later, cornmeal sustained the slaves in the Southern plantations and the settlers making the great westward trek.

By the mid-nineteenth century, such huge quantities of corn were grown in the United States – both for human consumption and for use as animal fodder – that the Great Plains states began to be referred to as the "cornbelt." Today, Iowa is the largest producer of corn in the US.

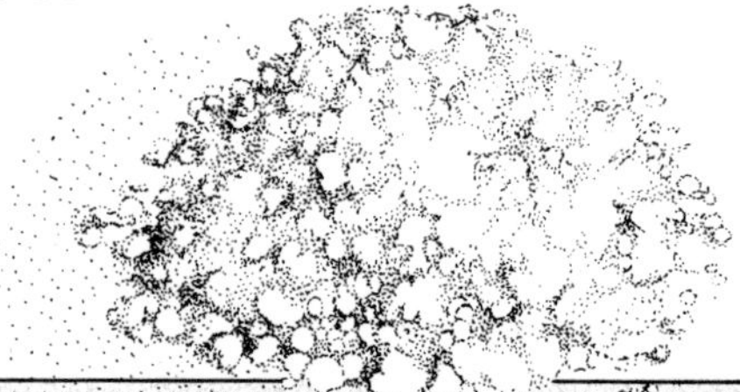

HOMINY

Hominy is simply hulled corn. The hulls are removed by scalding shelled corn in water and wood ash or lye until the outer skin can be removed. If it is then boiled whole it can be used to accompany a meal in place of potatoes. If it is finely ground, it is known as grits, much used in Southern recipes. Originally an Algonquin dish, hominy was one of the first New World foods to be adapted by the white pioneers.

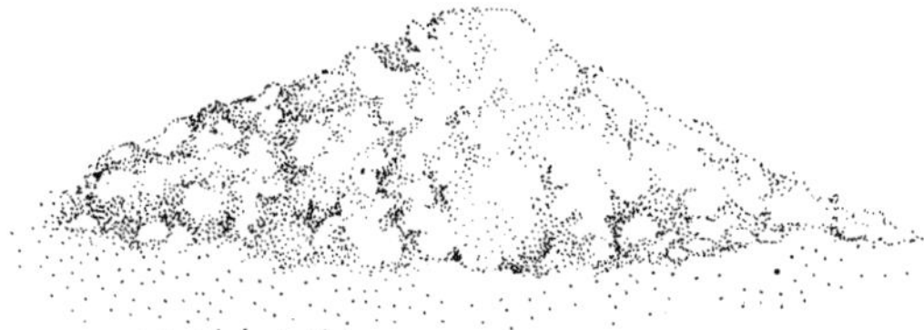

TABASCO SAUCE

Tabasco sauce is made from a type of chili known as tabasco, which is indigenous (via Mexico) to Louisiana. Tabasco sauce is made and bottled in Louisiana. To make the sauce, tabasco chilies are first mashed, allowed to ferment for three years, then combined with vinegar and salt. It is a prime ingredient in a Bloody Mary cocktail and is used to spice up everything from shellfish dishes to baked, stuffed potatoes.

BLUEBERRIES

Native to North America, these deep blue-colored berries are often confused with huckleberries. Cultivated all along the eastern heartland, from Michigan south to the Carolinas, the delicately sweet berries are delicious when eaten raw but are most often incorporated into pies, jams and syrups. A form of blueberry vinegar – a sweet vinegar – it is intended to be diluted and served as a refreshing, cooling drink, although it is rarely served these days.

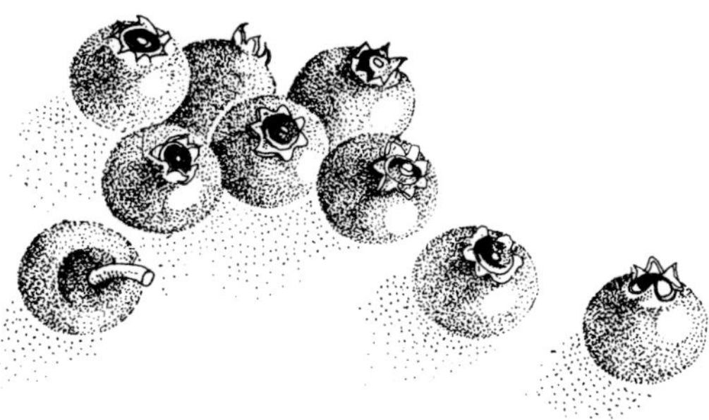

CHILIS

Chilis are very hot red, yellow or green fruit, native to tropical America. The term chili, also known as chillie, chile and chilly, is derived from the Mexican Nahuatl tribe. The size of a chili can range from a foot long to something as small as a pea. And color is no clue to a chili's hotness: some are scalding, some are mildly sweet. Chilies are also ground into powders – cayenne and paprika are the most common. Chilies are important ingredients in many Southwestern dishes, particularly in the Texan dish, chili con carne (literally "chilies with meat"). Of course, chilies are also important in the Mexican-American dishes found in California, Arizona, New Mexico and Texas – also the major American growing areas for chilies. The most common varieties used in the US include the California (long, green and mild), the jalapeño (green, approximately two inches long and hot), ancho (dark red and mild, usually sold in dried form), and the Fresno (green, cone-shaped and fairly hot).

One word of caution: wash your hands thoroughly after handling chilies – any chili on the fingers causes intense and painful burning if the eyes are rubbed accidentally.

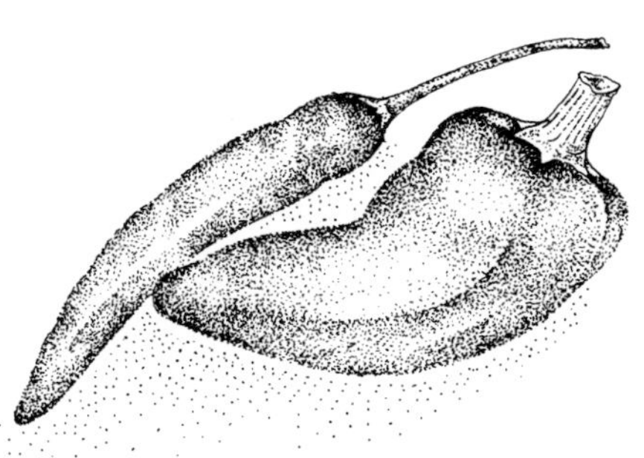

SQUASH

Squashes include the native American pumpkin, zucchini, and gourd – three of the most commonly recognized varieties – as well as melons, cucumbers and gherkins. In parts of Europe, the large variety of summer squash is called vegetable marrow, the small version (zucchini) is known as courgette. The word squash derives from the Narragansett Indians who lived in Massachusetts. Again, the squash was probably first cultivated in Mexico and through cultural diffusion found its way into the diet of North American Indians.

Summer squashes include crookneck, zucchini, pattypan and spaghetti (so called because the flesh is long and stringy). Winter squashes include hubbard, turban, butternut, acorn and, of course, pumpkin. Squashes are most commonly baked, stuffed, or hollowed out and used as soup tureens

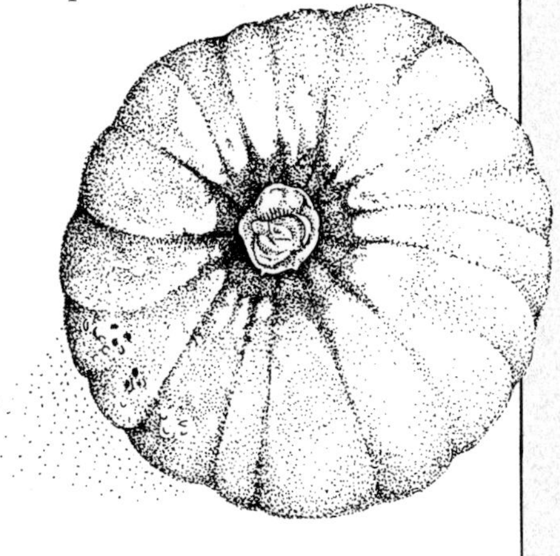

MASA FLOUR

Masa is the Spanish word for dough. Masa flour is made from hulled corn that has been simmered in lye and is used to make tamales, tortillas and enchiladas. It is sold in Mexican-American markets, in both blue and white form, as masa harina.

WILD RICE

Also known as Indian rice or Tuscarora rice, wild rice is not a rice at all but the grain of a tall, aquatic grass found in the northern section of the American Midwest, notably Minnesota. It grows wild in shallow lakes and ponds, although commercial rice paddies are now found in parts of Minnesota. Wild rice is harvested by hand, which accounts for its often prohibitive price. It is a traditional stuffing for Thanksgiving turkey and baked fish throughout the Midwest.

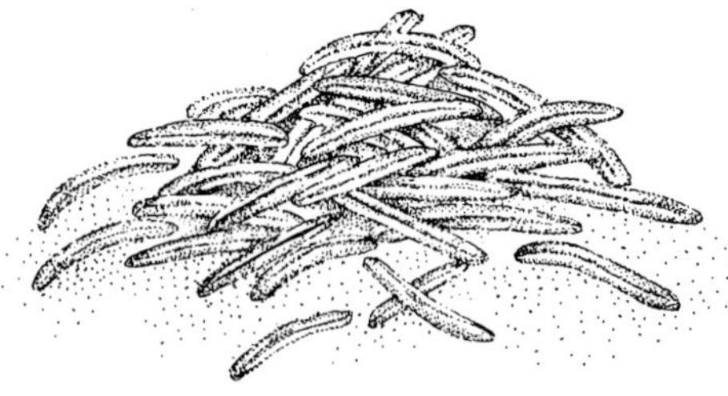

MACADAMIA NUTS

Native to Australia, and therefore also known as "Queensland nut," macadamias are one of Hawaii's most important crops. Hawaii is also the largest commercial producer of macadamias.

The creamy sweetness of this nut make it ideal for snacks, but it is also popular roasted and salted, when it is used to accompany salads, meat and fish dishes.

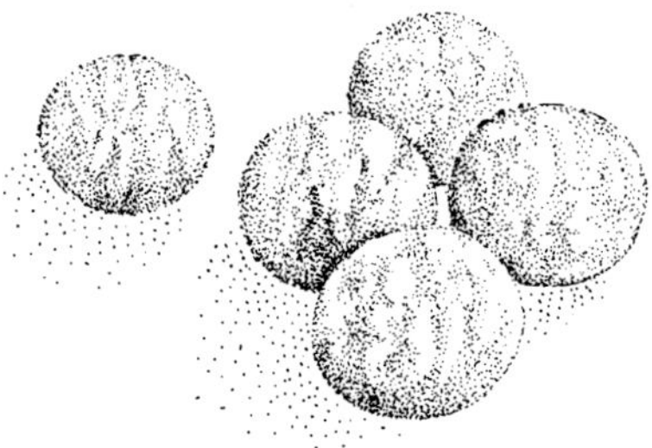

AVOCADO

Also known as avocado pear and less commonly as alligator pear, the name is from the Nahuatl word meaning "testicle" because of its shape. There are more than five hundred varieties of this fruit worldwide.

The Aztecs were the first to eat avocados, but because the fruit was considered too bland to be really enjoyable, it didn't catch on until the first half of the nineteenth century, when the first trees were planted in Florida (hence the name, alligator pear). It wasn't until the 1950s that this fruit became an often used salad ingredient. Today, California, Hawaii and Florida are the major avocado-producing states.

Guacamole is a popular dip made from avocados and chilies, with sour cream an optional addition.

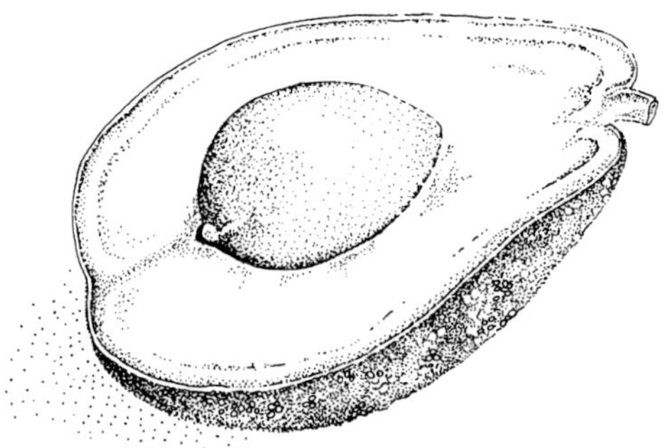

FILÉ POWDER

A vital ingredient in Creole and Cajun cuisine, filé powder is made from sassafras leaves, which are ground into a powder. It has a very slimy, sticky quality and a hot, spicy flavor.

BUFFALO

When is a buffalo actually a bison? When it's the American version – as distinct from the Asian or African oxen. American buffalo are shaggy-haired, hoofed members of the cattle family, characterized by a large head and massive hump. These lumbering animals, which can weigh as much as 2,500 pounds, once numbered in excess of sixty million. The Indians' absolute reliance on the buffalo for food, clothing and shelter was the cause of their demise. A particularly creative federal general, dispatched to clear hostile tribes out of the way of white immigrants, figured that Indians were difficult to catch and hit upon the novel idea of eradicating their food source. He and his cavalry troops were so effective that by the middle of the nineteenth century buffalos were nearly extinct. Today, approximately 30,000 of these animals are protected and range in such areas as Yellowstone National Park.

Buffalo meat tastes remarkably like beef. Buffalos have been successfully cross bred with Herefords to produce a hybrid called "beefalo" which, to no one's surprise, also tastes remarkably like beef.

POTATO

A member of the deadly nightshade family, this popular tuber is native to the South American Andes. The Spanish conquistadores thought potatoes were a kind of truffle. Its association with Ireland is due to Sir Walter Raleigh's explorations along the coast of Virginia. Both the Germans and the Irish planted the crop to prevent famine – although it was disdained by many people as potentially poisonous. Irish immigrants brought potatoes to New England during the nineteenth century.

BEANS

There is a wide variety of beans available in the States. Fresh beans include green beans and string beans – slim, green and delicious on their own or in mixed salads; lima beans and butter beans – kidney-shaped beans, good on their own and in salads and soups. Dried and canned beans are also common, and include navy beans – small, pale flageolets used in classic Boston baked beans; pinto beans – speckled and used in a variety of Southwestern dishes; garbanzo beans (or peas), made popular both by health-food recipes and by the ethnic influence of Italians and Greeks; and kidney beans, the staple of chili con carne.

PINEAPPLE

This sweet fruit, dubbed "pina" (pine cone) by the Spanish because of its appearance, grew originally in the tropical forests of South America. In 1790 the English explorer, Captain

James Cook, introduced pineapples from the tropics of South America to Hawaii and today Hawaii is the largest commercial producer of pineapples. The advent of canning methods helped put pineapple in all its various forms on the nation's market shelves as early as the turn of the century.

CORN ON THE COB

Corn on the cob has become indelibly associated with hearty country eating – almost a symbol of clean and simple American fare. This is because corn, or maize, is still mainly cultivated in Europe as animal feed, and the fresh, cooked cob on the table is rarely seen. As every schoolchild knows, corn was one of the discoveries made by the early explorers of North and South America.

OUTDOOR COOKING

Barbecuing may be a legacy of our ancestors – whether from a century past as pioneers, or from dinner in a cave thousands of years ago – but today it has become a fully-fledged rite of summer. Glowing coals, sizzling meat and that unmistakable smell means a party – for two or twenty!

The word barbecue comes from the Caribbean word "barbacoa" – the green-wood grill used by the indigenous West Indians to cook their meat above smoldering coal pits. Although Europeans were well-used to the concept of outdoor cooking, they had never encountered charcoal used as the cooking medium before. Columbus and later explorers passed this discovery on to their troops and followers and, by the time of the American colonists, a variety of techniques were in use for outdoor cooking, from clambakes to charbroiled pigs and oxen. Charcoal burners, too, could be found – those dark, ragged men who made their homes deep in the forest and spent their days inside a stone bunker, slowly burning down ripe wood into blackened lumps.

A hundred years ago, hoe-downs, barn-raisings and other community get-togethers would always include a barbecue – whole roasted livestock were turned and basted by the men, while the women assembled a wondrous assortment of cole slaws, breads, salads, vegetables and put-ups. Today, the Basque sheep farmers of Nevada hold great lamb barbecues, which have become celebrated events, attracting people from all over the state.

For most of us, a barbecue means a meal out – in our own back yard. On summer evenings, at lunchtimes, on weekends or during the week, a barbecue turns an ordinary meal into something special. The food tastes and *smells* different – watch those envious neighbors – and everyone can join in the cooking, unless it's the one culinary talent the man in the family prides himself upon!

Another reason for the barbecue's popularity is that there is very little that it can't handle. From steak to hamburgers, lobster to sardines, turkey to quail, potatoes to mushrooms – it is

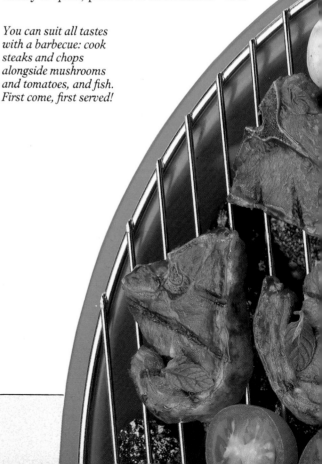

You can suit all tastes with a barbecue: cook steaks and chops alongside mushrooms and tomatoes, and fish. First come, first served!

eminently adaptable. Top-grade cuts have their juices sealed in and are exceedingly tender; lesser-quality meats benefit from the smoky flavor and fun, informal recipes – from kebabs to marinated slices.

Barbecues are also easy on organization. No family silver, linen napkins or fine china, no matter how large or how grand the company. Just cardboard plates, cups and paper napkins – lots of those! You'll need them, since barbecued food tastes so much better eaten with the fingers, Henry VIII-style! Informality is the keynote; eat when the food is ready, don't wait for the next man. Cold barbecued spareribs are not so appealing. Help yourself to the salads, the garlic bread and ash-roasted potatoes, and settle down to a feast. That's the fun of a barbecue – it's selfish, but at the same time tremendously convivial. Keep some extra bits on the side; if unexpected guests show up (like that neighbor with the sensitive nose!) or if friends arrive late, it couldn't matter less. The mottos are "the more, the merrier" and "better late than never."

Variety is also at your beck and call, a mixed grill at the flick of a spatula. If you have a guest who hates meat, together with a team of hearty beef-lovers and a troop of youngsters, what could be easier than a grilled trout, several thick steaks and a ream of hot dogs – all cooked at the same time? You don't need ingenuity to solve that problem – you need a barbecue!

Barbecuing quickly turns from an experiment into a hobby, and from a hobby into an addiction. A known relaxant, the only threat it poses is to your kitchen range. So don your apron, grab your spatula, and make burgers while the sun shines!

Choosing the right barbecue is half the battle in successful outdoor cooking. If you have the space, materials, and expertise, a built-in barbecue may provide the answer. Always ready to do service at any break in the clouds, never requiring the sometimes annoying inconvenience of setting up, nor suffering defeat by rust or burn-through. Its only drawback is its immobility. However your outdoor entertainment requirements may change through the years you are stuck with it where you put it. On the other hand you may be tempted to use it more often, simply because it is there.

Most people, however, choose a manufactured barbecue, both for ease of assembly and for portability. There are many kinds to choose from. Points to keep in mind when deciding on your barbecue include:

Sturdiness: heavy-gauge metal or cast iron is long lasting, though heavy. Lighter metals are better if the barbecue is to be used for camping or back-packing.

Placement: can it be lifted easily? Does it have wheels? Will it need to be moved often? Where will it fit?

Size of grill: how many people are you likely to be cooking for at one time? Remember that a round grill can accommodate more than a similar-sized rectangular grill.

Other features: will you require a spit for whole roasting? Would a mechanical spit be adequate or would you prefer a more expensive battery-operated version? Windshields and hoods provide protection from winds. How useful would they be to you?

The picnic barbecue (below) *is quick to assemble, the legs and windshield slotting easily into place. A set of forks, turners, tongs, skewers and broilers* (right) *are essential implements for the barbecue enthusiast.*

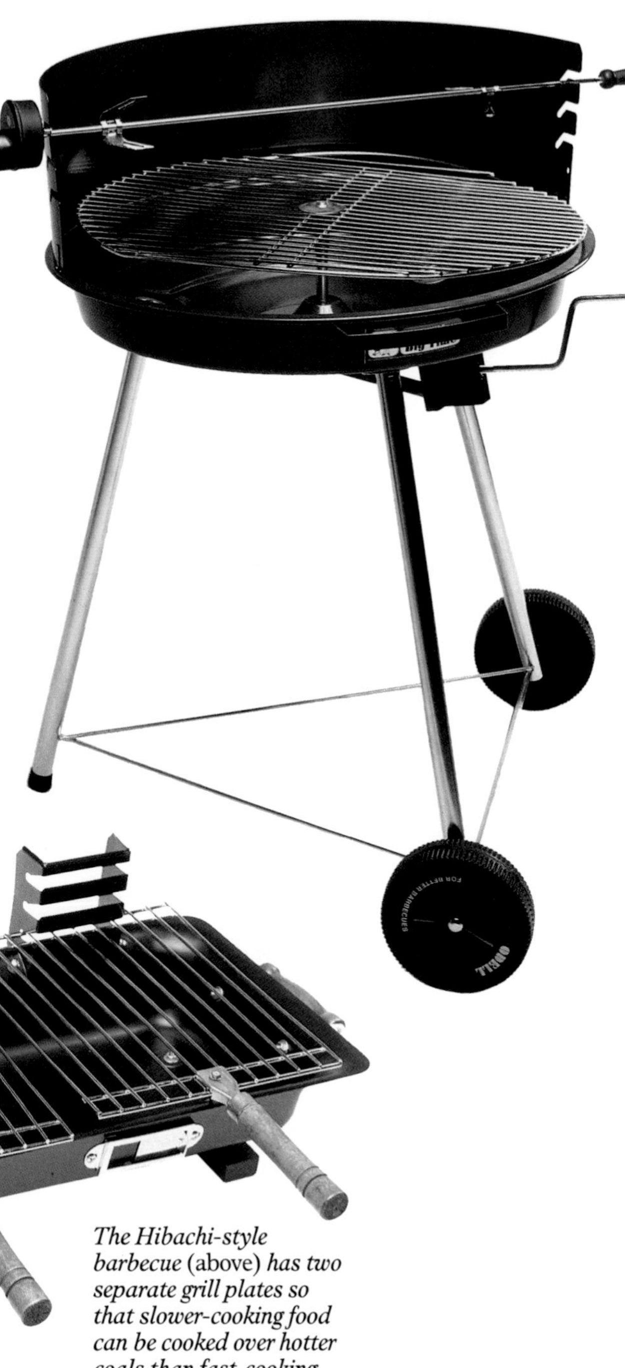

The Hibachi-style barbecue (above) *has two separate grill plates so that slower-cooking food can be cooked over hotter coals than fast-cooking food.*

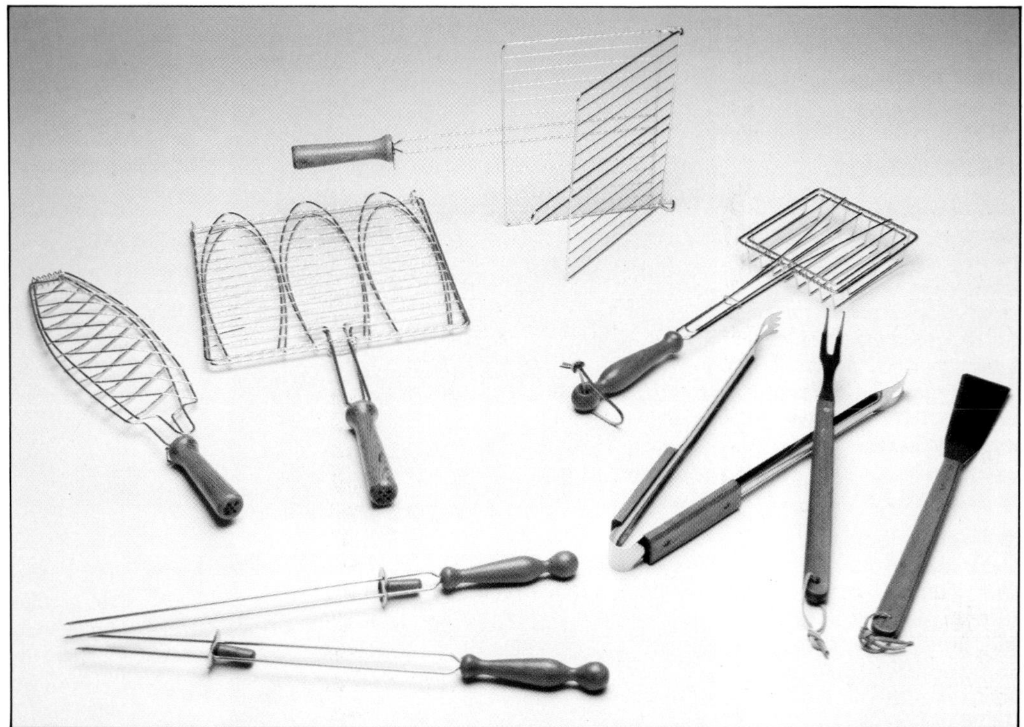

Types of barbecue

The following are the most popular kinds of barbecue available. Each has its particular uses and good points.

Brazier barbecues These stand on legs, sometimes with wheels. The coals are placed in a shallow tray below the usually circular grill. This grill can be raised or lowered to regulate cooking heat and speed, and can often be revolved for easy access to the food. There is usually a spit attachment, either hand-turned or battery-powered.

Picnic barbecue These are lightweight, basic versions of the above, often designed to be placed on a table. They are portable and will usually cater for only a small number of people – about four.

Hibachi These have become particularly popular during the last decade or more, for several reasons, including the low price, easy portability, and toughness of their cast-iron bodies. Hibachi is Japanese for "fire-box": the charcoal rests in the box underneath the grill. There are draft controls on the side to help with lighting and heat control. The most common form is rectangular, though there are some round versions. The former come in single- double- and triple-grilled options; these allow slower-cooked food to be switched over hotter coals with a minimum of fuss. There is no spit.

Half-hooded barbecues These are more extravagant versions of the brazier barbecue, often rectangular in shape. They tend to be quite large, allowing you to cook for up to twenty people at a time. The hood acts as a wind and rain guard and as a support for a spit. It may also have a rack to keep cooked food warm.

Kettle barbecues These are the aristocrats of the backyard set, efficient, usually globe-shaped, and made of weather-proof porcelain-enameled steel, with a deep fire-bowl for the coals. All barbecuing is done with the lid down: this tenderizes and browns the meat and is particularly useful for large joints and birds. Both fire-bowl and lid have vents for air and heat control. These barbecues are also very effective smokers when used according to the manufacturer's instructions.

Accessories

A working barbecue is very hot, so long-handled implements are a must. It is also important not to prick certain meats, etc, while they are cooking, so tongs and turners and spatulas are advised. Finally, vegetables, fish, sausages and frankfurters can often be awkward to turn over without breaking or dropping, so tailor-made, double-sided grids, which enclose these items are useful, if not obligatory, accessories.

LIGHTING THE BARBECUE

Intense heat without flames is the secret to the perfect barbecue fire – the kind that produces perfect, cross-hatched steaks, not the charred and petrol-flavored apologies for steak often served up. Good fuel and good technique are required to achieve the desired results.

● **Fuel** There are two kinds of charcoal: lump and briquette. Lump charcoal contains no additives and is irregular in shape. It is less dense than briquette charcoal and therefore easier to light, but it burns twice as fast. Briquettes are easy to arrange and do not smoke and flare up as lump charcoal may. Briquettes are therefore the better choice for home barbecuing.

● **Mesquite,** bay and grape vine twigs are among the woods that can be added to produce a delicious flavor to food cooked on a barbecue. Prepared packets of herbs also add a distinctive flavor. All these "additives" should be sprinkled on the coals when they have turned gray, so that their smoke permeates the meat, poultry or fish being cooked.

● **Firelighters** Since briquettes are very dense, they can be quite difficult to set alight. A gas or electric lighter is a highly efficient way of lighting a fire, and does not impart the alien flavor that

1 Place kindling or firelighters on base of fire bowl. Pile charcoal into a low pyramid, slightly larger in area than the food to be cooked. You will probably achieve better results if you use charcoal sparingly.

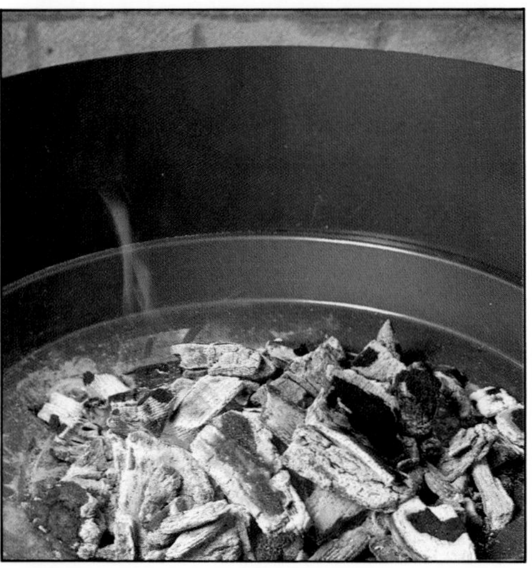

2 Put a match to the kindling or firelighters. The flames will flare up, then gradually die down. Adjust vents and windshield so that coals catch light.

3 Let charcoal burn undisturbed for about 15 minutes, until edges of briquettes turn gray. As the fire takes hold, spread briquettes out slightly to form a solid, flattish mass. All coals must touch.

purists object to from firelighters. These latter, however, are very convenient, and some brands claim to be ordorless. They can be bought in the form of blocks or granules to be broken up and/or mixed with the briquettes, or in a paste to be squeezed among the coals before lighting. Never use petrol or paraffin to start a barbecue; they are highly dangerous.

● **The fire** Follow the steps on this page to light the fire. To judge whether the coals are hot enough to begin cooking, hold your hand at meat level above the coals. The temperature must be hotter for grilling than for spit-roasting: you should be able to hold your hand above the coals no longer than 2 minutes for the former (about 325°F), or 4 minutes for spit-roasting (about 275°F). If the fire cools at any time during cooking, raise the grill, prod the coals, and blow gently with a bellows. If the coals are too warm, raise the grill or spit while cooking.

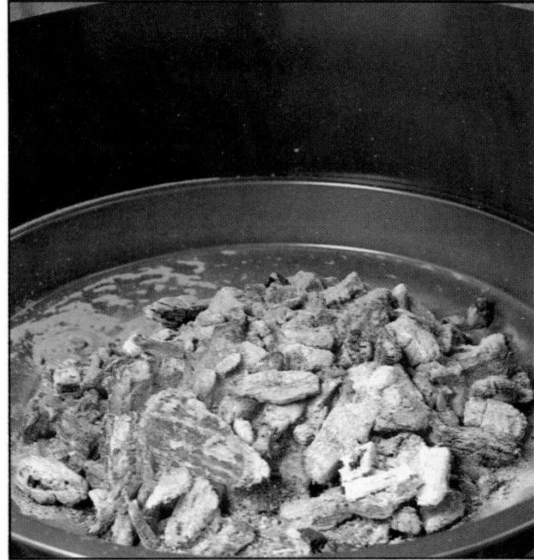

4 Let coals lie for another 15 to 25 minutes, until covered with white ash and flames have died out.

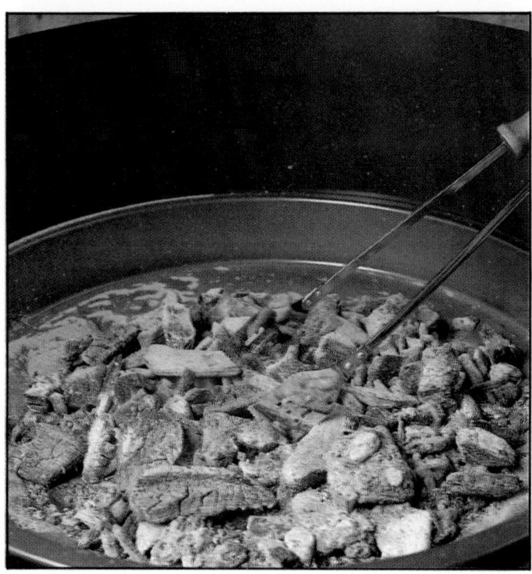

5 Turn coals over and spread out to a single layer. If necessary, add fresh charcoal around edges. Position grill for cooking.

BARBECUING STEAK

A char-broiled steak is for many the epitome of barbecuing. However, although the method is very simple, getting the steak just right requires practice. Two basic techniques are used to produce the perfect steak – all-over searing and a lower-heat finish.

● Choose your steak with care. The finer cuts – rib, fillet, porterhouse and sirloin – can be put directly on the grill after trimming off excess fat and cutting through the remaining thin border of fat at 3-inch intervals: this will keep the meat from curling. Other, tougher cuts – rump, chuck, skirt – profit from an overnight marinade.
● An ideal thickness is somewhere around 1½-2 inches. This will allow the outside to sear first while the inside cooks more slowly. Searing should take no more than about 5 minutes; including this time, the steak should spend no longer than 8 minutes per inch for rare, 10-12 minutes for medium, and 18 minutes for well-done steaks. Make a cut near the bone to test for interior color, when you feel the steak should be done.

1 Rub grill with reserved piece of fat cut from the steak, to prevent meat from sticking while cooking.

2 Place steak in center of grill, where heat is hottest. Steak should be trimmed of all excess fat, as this causes coals to flare up, singeing the meat. Sear steak on edges of both sides to seal in juices.

3 Use tongs or a spatula to turn steak over. Do not use a barbecue fork, as piercing the meat will cause it to lose flavorful juices, which will in turn cause the coals to flare up. After searing, continue to cook steak over less intense heat by dispersing coals or moving steak to side of grill.

BARBECUING FRANK-FURTERS AND SAUSAGES

Frankfurters and sausages are at the other end of the scale from steaks; they are the barbecue food for the people – and kids! Country-style sausages can take the place of hot dogs for a welcome change – that bit more adventurous and spicy. What a difference there is between a boiled frankfurter or a broiled sausage and their barbecued counterparts. They have the taste of the great outdoors!

● Because both hot dogs and sausages tend to roll about and are difficult to turn over once they have cooked – and curled – on one side, it is helpful to place them in a hand-held grid or basket, which can be left on the grill until you need to turn the sausages over. Using a grid also keeps the sausages or franks over the same heat, allowing similar cooking time; keeps the skin free from pricking – which causes the fire to flare; and makes lift off and serving one easy movement.

1 Place sausages or frankfurters within wire grid and lower top half, securing them. They should not be touching.

2 Place grid on grill rack over the hot coals. This saves having to hold grid during cooking.

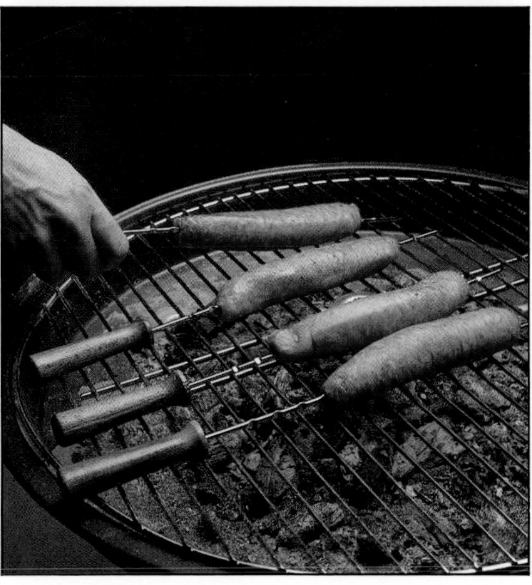

3 If a grid is unavailable, skewer the sausages. This enables them to be turned easily and prevents them from curling while cooking. They can be slid from skewer onto plate or into bun when ready.

SPIT-ROASTING A CHICKEN

Spit-roasting brings back the traditions of great-grandma's day! It is a bit more work than grilling, but the taste of a whole, spit-roasted bird is sensational.

● The chicken should be cleaned and trussed and the legs and wings tied close to the body. When skewered, the bird should be evenly balanced, so that it will turn easily on the rotisserie.

● If the chicken is done over a barbecue, the coals should be covered with white ash and glowing when the bird is placed over them. If the roasting is done in a fireplace, the warm coals from a *wood* fire should be just behind and below the skewered bird, which should have a drip or basting pan underneath it.

● The chicken should be started off with no seasoning. An ordinary-sized bird will take about 2½ hours on a barbecue (unless it is a kettle barbecue, in which case the time will be much less). After the chicken has been on for about 1 hour, begin basting it liberally with left-over marinade or sauce. The juices of the chicken should run clear when done.

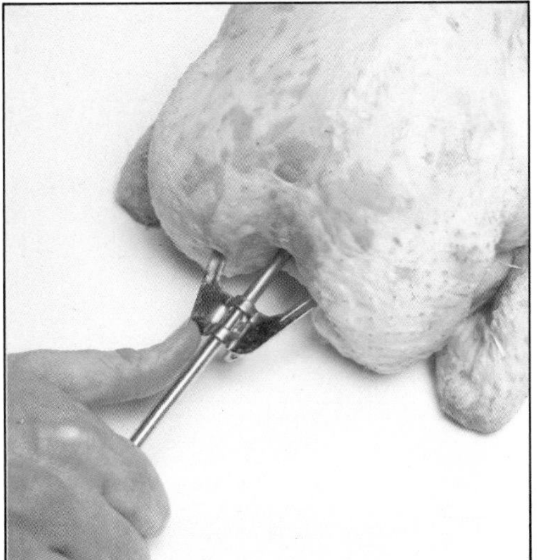

1 Put skewer through cavity, positioning bird in center of skewer. Push prongs of forks into bottom of either breast and secure.

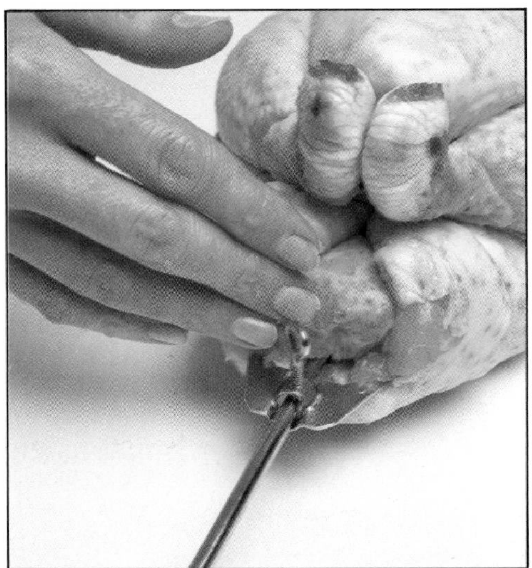

2 Slide on other fork and push prongs into top of breasts and secure. Screw forks down tightly. Push tail-end firmly into cavity to prevent loss of cooking juices.

3 Baste bird frequently during second half of cooking time.

BAKED BEANS

These beans are a traditional Boston dish, but they have been adopted by barbecue enthusiasts everywhere as a perfect complement to practically any barbecue dish.

Serves 6–8

4 cups dried navy beans
1 onion
1/2 pound salt pork
1/2 cup firmly packed dark brown sugar
1/3 cup molasses
1 tablespoon salt
1 teaspoon dry mustard

1 After soaking beans overnight in 12 cups cold water, drain, add new water and cook until tender (about 1 hour). Drain beans and place 1 cup in a bean pot or heavy casserole. Add onion and cover with remaining beans. Score salt pork to rind and push down among beans until it just shows through the top.

2 Combine brown sugar, molasses, salt and dry mustard in a small bowl. Pour mixture over beans and mix gently. Add enough hot water to fill pot and bake in 200°F oven for at least 8 hours. The juice should bubble at the top continuously. Add more water if necessary during baking. Check beans every hour or so.

3 Serve beans and salt pork directly from the pot.

BARBECUE SAUCE

There are several "classic" barbecue sauces, to which every barbecue enthusiast will have added his own special touch. This is one popular version – rich, slightly spicy, slightly sweet-sour, and a real hit on steaks, chicken, hamburgers and spareribs.

Makes about 1/2 cup sauce

2 tablespoons olive oil

1 onion, chopped

2 garlic cloves, chopped

1 1/2 pounds very ripe tomatoes, chopped, or 1 pound canned tomatoes, drained

2–3 sprigs thyme or 1 teaspoon dried thyme

1 bay leaf

1/2 teaspoon chili powder

1/2 teaspoon dry mustard

1 tablespoon Worcestershire sauce

2 tablespoons brown sugar

4 tablespoons vinegar

1/8–1/4 teaspoon Tabasco sauce

salt and pepper

1 Heat oil in a heavy-bottomed skillet over low to medium heat. Sauté onion and garlic until they are soft and slightly brown, stirring occasionally.

2 Add bay leaf, thyme, tomato and onion and simmer over a low heat, uncovered, for about half an hour.

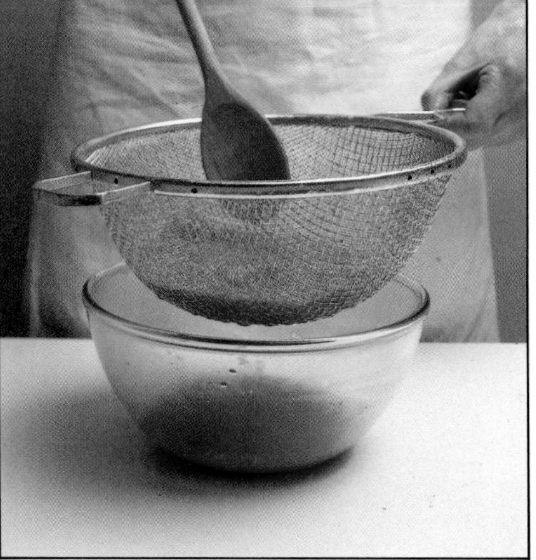

3 Press the pulpy mixture through a sieve using a wooden spoon. Discard solids.

4 Return purée to pan. Add spices, Worcestershire sauce, brown sugar, vinegar, Tabasco and seasonings and simmer for about another 30 minutes.

5 The sauce is ready when it is thick enough to coat a spoon.

SPIT-ROASTING FISH

As the early Indians appreciated, there is little to compare to a succulent fish baked over an open fire. The Indians used various techniques – planking, skewering, grilling and cooking over hot stones – but for a whole salmon, one of the prizes of the Northwestern frontier, no recipe surpasses spit-roasting.

● Today, our method varies little from the traditional Indian way, although our skill as fishermen is sadly lackluster, and fish straight from a river or inlet and onto the fire is one joy that most of us will not experience. However, modern methods of transport mean that a selection of fine fresh fish is available to many, so spit-roasting should be attempted by anyone who loves barbecuing *and* fish.

● Spit-roasting ensures the even cooking of the fish and an attractive presentation unthreatened by the hazards of turning and adjusting on a grill. The stuffing gives the fish both flavor and support as it rotates on the spit. Choose a stuffing, such as the one used here, which is complementary to its delicate taste. Steamed, chopped sorrel or spinach would make another lovely stuffing. Alternatively, you may

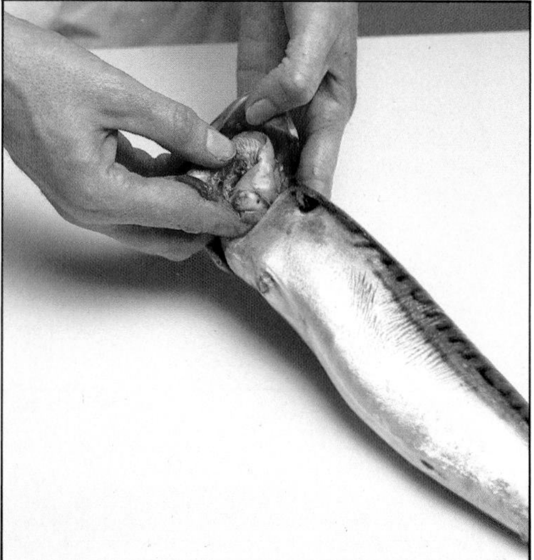

1 Cut off tail and fins of fish. Pull out entrails through the gills. Reach into cavity to ensure that you have completely gutted the fish. Rinse under cold running water and pat dry.

2 Mix a stuffing of sautéed onions, garlic and mushrooms, combined with breadcrumbs, lemon juice, an egg and herbs. Mix with your hands and season carefully with salt and pepper. Add enough breadcrumbs to make mixture comfortably moist but not wet.

3 Hold fish by the head and push stuffing through gills into belly of fish. Fill cavity loosely; do not overstuff.

simply wish to fill the cavity with a selection of fresh herbs – choose from thyme, marjoram, chervil, parsley, dill or coriander.

● The fish most suitable for spit-roasting are salmon, bass, pike, carp, some of the larger trout and some manageable-sized sea fish. Plain melted butter or perhaps butter flavored with garlic makes the best basting sauce.

● To serve, remove the skin and fillet the fish neatly, accompanying each slice of succulent flesh with a tablespoon of the stuffing.

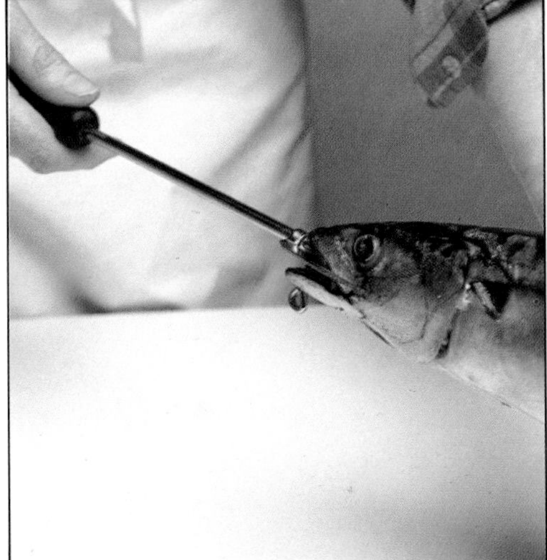

4 Slip one of the holding forks onto the spit and push it down toward the handle end. Pass other end of spit through mouth, and skewer actual flesh of fish just above backbone; spit should come out through tail.

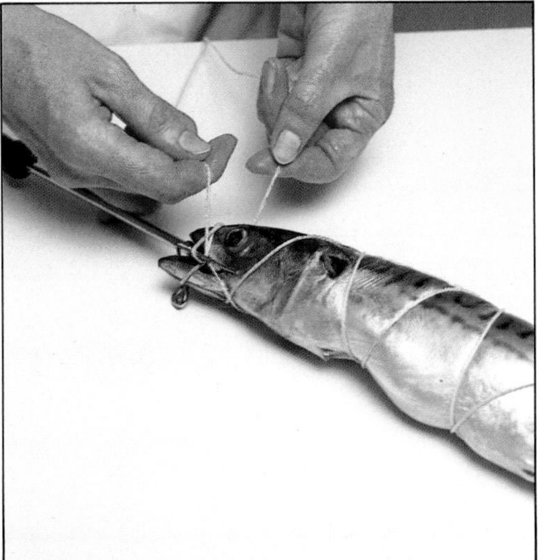

5 Screw prongs of forks securely into fish. Cut a long length of string; tie middle to tail fork. Wind string around fish, working toward the head and criss-crossing string over and under the fish several times.

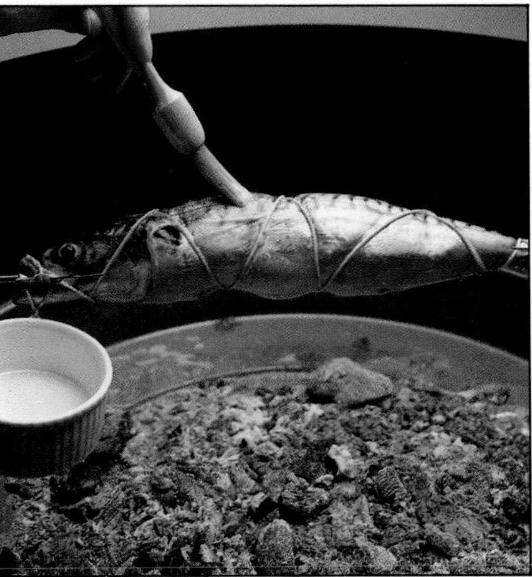

6 Barbecue fish about 7 inches above the coals and begin turning immediately. Allow 10 – 12 minutes per pound for a stuffed fish. Rotate spit constantly and baste fish frequently with melted butter. When a knife inserted behind the head shows opaque flesh, the fish is done.

TORTILLAS

Tortillas, the bread of Mexico, are best when fresh but can be kept frozen for weeks if well wrapped. Even the stalest tortilla will, when cooked on a lightly greased griddle or skillet, taste deliciously nutty. Masa harina is available in some parts of the country from supermarkets, while in others it is available in specialist food shops.

Makes 8 to 10 tortillas

2 cups masa harina (fine corn-starch)

1½ tablespoons salt

1¼ cups water

lard

1 Mix the masa harina and salt in a mixing bowl. Gradually add 1 cup water. Knead dough until it can be gathered into a ball.

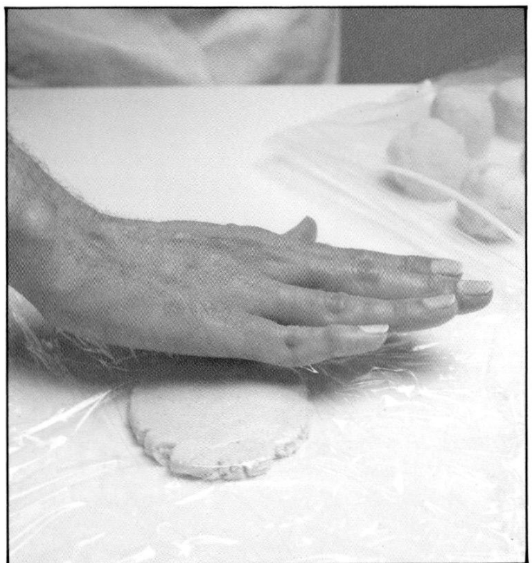

2 Divide dough into several small pieces. Form into walnut-sized balls and place in a plastic bag. Take one ball at a time from the bag and flatten between two sheets of waxed paper, using the palms of your hands.

3 Using a rolling pin, continue to flatten and shape the rounds until they are thin discs.

4 Lightly grease a skillet with lard and place over a medium heat. Add tortillas, one at a time. Cook on one side for about 30 seconds. Turn with a spatula and cook on other side for about 15 seconds. Stack tortillas between pieces of waxed paper as finished.

BABY POTATOES

Like baked beans, potatoes are a traditional accompaniment at a barbecue. One time-honored treatment is to wrap them individually in foil (the Indians did without!) and throw them in among the coals. Less dirty is the way they are done here – baby potatoes neatly skewered and basted with butter or oil. This method makes them easy to serve and results in a delectable, less brittle skin.

● Serve them with a generous helping of sour cream and chives. Alternatively, pass a sauceboat of melted garlic and chili butter, and offer a heaped bowl of cheese and chopped green onion to sprinkle on top.

1 Position 4 or 5 scrubbed potatoes, one after another, on a skewer. Place skewer on grill above coals.

2 Brush potatoes occasionally with melted butter throughout roasting time.

THE REGIONS

There is no single, identifiable American cuisine: there are as many variations as there are immigrant groups. Native Americans – the "Red Indians" – also stirred the culinary melting pot, adding many indigenous vegetables and wild game.

There are many old, "classic" American recipes, derived from the Indians and to be found in all parts of the States: from the tightly knit Cajun and Creole communities in Louisiana and Alabama to the rich merchants of the North Atlantic seaboard. But there are newer classics too, products and recipes traceable to the Depression and Prohibition; to the great nineteenth-century hotels of New York and San Francisco; and to the ethnic cook-ups and church socials that are an important part of heartland America.

Today, many of these baronial or rib-sticking creations have been replaced by lighter fare, inspired by ever-fresher ingredients and by the new wave of health-conscious eating which has swept from California across the American map, and now permeates the rest of the world. Today's "new American cuisine" offers real American food, made with American ingredients, prepared the no-nonsense American way. Ostentatious French sauces and elaborate titles are out. In their place, few frills and fussy descriptions. Low salt, minimal fat and no sugar are the rallying cries of this culinary renaissance.

Despite, or perhaps because of, their puritanical roots, Americans in the 1980s can relish the diverse pleasures of a national table that is bounteous without being a calorific calamity. Here begins a cook's tour of the United States, with the nation divided into seven broad regions, based on local history and development. Open the following pages – read, cook, experiment and enjoy.

NEW ENGLAND

New England is famous for its fall foliage, taciturn people and plain, homespun cooking. It still reflects the Puritan tenets of its early wives – few sauces, an economical use of ingredients, and a penchant for pickles, jams and other "put-ups"

The men and women of New England are as solid as the granite that dots the landscape: California may lead the country in wildly creative ideas, but New England anchors the nation with sensible, forthright thoughts and actions. Comprised of six states, Maine, New Hampshire, Vermont, Massachusetts, Rhode Island and Connecticut, it is a hilly region, studded with granite outcrops cloaked in forests of oak, maple, birch and dark fir, threatening to take over the carefully cleared pastures.

The earliest Yankees were the Puritans, evicted from England and characterized by at least one historian as "religious nuts." This hardy band of nonconformists were thoroughly dismayed when their small, frail craft landed at the tip of Cape Cod in 1620. They had planned to land the *Mayflower* further south in the Hudson River Valley, or Virginia, where the landscape and climate were more hospitable. Undeterred, these early colonists, numbering about one hundred souls, quickly established themselves in a deserted Indian camp. Naming this first settlement Plymouth, in honor of the English port from which they had set sail, the Puritans settled in for the winter.

The New England winter came as a nasty surprise. The biting cold and wind caught them completely unprepared, and half the population of the colony died during the first winter. A young Indian warrior named Squanto took pity and befriended the starving survivors. British educated, Squanto taught the settlers how to recognize and eat indigenous foods. He also introduced corn to the Puritan diet, which, together with beans, became the mainstay of their survival.

Although the soil was (and still is) stony and the terrain rugged, the lakes, forests and

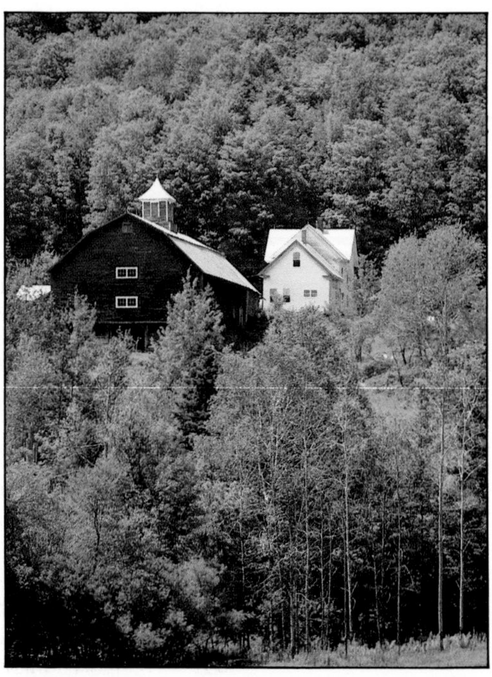

Green spring peace on a New Hampshire farm

seashores were teeming with edibles when the Puritans landed. Five of the six New England states face the sea and over two hundred kinds of fish, both freshwater and saltwater, were abundant. Unfortunately, the Puritans were poor, or disinterested, fishermen. After their first disastrous winter, however, their interest increased and scrod, salmon and cod were added to the menu. Huge lobsters, weighing as much as a hefty thirty pounds, populated the bays, but the Puritans preferred eels (the tradition carried on into this century that "proper" individuals did not eat lobster and in fact pieces of lobster were used as bait to lure the more prized codfish).

Plentiful game stalked the dark forests but most meat – moose, bear and venison – was provided by the Indians. The Puritans were also apparently bad shots. Indigenous crops, besides corn and beans, were limited. Cranberries grew wild in sandy bogs along the shore and were eaten both raw and cooked. A kind of bean tuber – known as ground nuts but distinct from peanuts – was abundant, tasting vaguely of roasted chestnuts (they are nearly extinct today). And it was their Indian friends who also introduced potatoes to the Puritans – not the later Irish immigrants.

Not intent on "going native," the Puritans had successfully imported most British crops and meats, from mutton to flour, within a generation of the first arrivals. The first English cows were landed in 1624.

Primarily middle class, the Puritans' plain, dour beliefs were reflected in all aspects of their way of life and are carried on today. The earliest settlers brought with them their plain, unimaginative English cooking. But what, ask modern Yankees, needs to be added to fresh softshell crab served with freshly picked beach plums? Similarly, venison served with cranberries is a truly indigenous meal – unadorned and delicious. The Puritans disdained "French trickery" and rich sauces. Everything was fried, boiled or stewed, and this is still largely true of New England cooking.

Importantly for their recipes, the early settlers quickly turned some of their acres of timber into sailing vessels. Their trading efforts brought teas and ginger from China, wines, brandy and raisins from the Mediterranean, and molasses – that staple of New England cooking – from the West Indies.

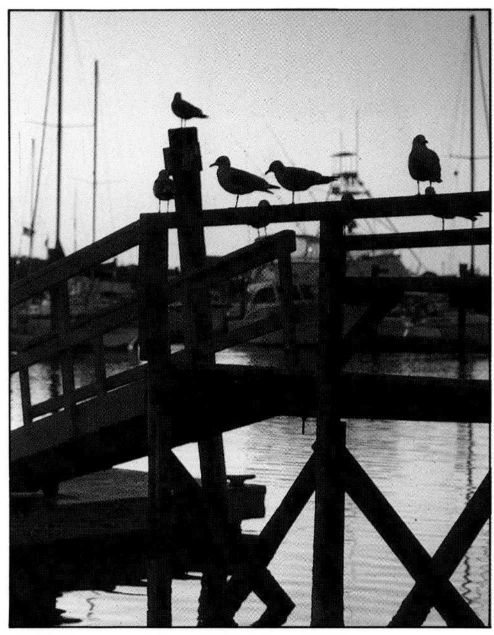

Seagulls await a Cape Cod dawn

It is the winters that dominate life here and New England culinary traditions reflect this fact of life. The emphasis is on preserving, storing and "putting by" for the long, dark winter months. Surplus meat was stored in a salt barrel. Accordingly, salt pork, salt cod and corned beef became the heart and soul of colonial meals. Pies, both meat and fruit, were eaten at every meal and good colonial wives could turn out as many as fifty at a time for winter storage (a heavy sugar syrup warded off bacteria).

In addition to an artless style, the Puritans valued frugality in all things. Baked beans with obligatory salt pork and Boston brown bread became a regional favorite. It is still a compliment to any Yankee hostess to remark upon the fine economy of her meal planning.

Good sense and hard work have always been the cornerstones of success in New England. True Yankees can proudly trace their lineage to the Mayflower Charter. Italians and Irish, so strongly identified with Boston (and to a lesser extent Hartford), arrived with the teeming hordes in the nineteenth century. Portuguese immigrants settled along the coast, establishing bustling fishing fleets. But the culinary tradition was already established by the time these later settlers arrived – a culinary tradition that is purely Yankee in style and flavor.

NEW ENGLAND
CLAM CHOWDER

Chowder is a simple method of cooking fish and while it is thinner than soup, it is considered a meal in itself. Some Yankee stalwarts insist that chowder is improved in flavor when it is allowed to "rest" away from the heat for about an hour, and then reheated just before serving.

Serves 6 to 8 as a main course soup

1 quart hard-shelled clams
1/2 pound salt pork, diced
3 onions, finely chopped
2 cups boiling water
3 potatoes, peeled and finely diced
1/2 teaspoon black pepper
3 cups milk
2 cups heavy cream

Scrub and open clams, reserving juice. Chop clams and save juice. ★ Sauté the salt pork in a large pot until half-cooked; pour off most of the fat. Add onions and sauté until brown. Add boiling water, potatoes, black pepper and clam juice. Cover and cook over a medium heat for 20 minutes. ★ Add clams, milk and cream, stirring gently. Cook over low heat for 15 minutes, being careful not to let the soup boil. Season to taste. *Picture page 40*

FRANCONIA POTATOES

The Franconia range of the White Mountains in New Hampshire gives this dish its name.

Serves 4 as a side dish

1 1/2 pounds new potatoes, well scrubbed
1 cup melted butter
salt to taste
black pepper to taste

Cook potatoes in a large pot of boiling salted water until just tender, about 20 minutes. Drain well. ★ Preheat oven to 400°F. Place potatoes in one layer in a baking dish and pour over melted butter. Sprinkle with salt and pepper and bake until browned, about 20 minutes.

HARVARD BEETS

The name of this dish comes from the red of the beets, which is supposed to represent Harvard's color – crimson.

Serves 6 as a side dish

- *2 pounds beets*
- *½ cup brown sugar*
- *1 tablespoon cornstarch*
- *⅓ cup red wine vinegar or cider vinegar*
- *½ cup water*
- *2 tablespoons butter*
- *1 tablespoon chopped fresh parsley*

If beets have already been boiled, peel and cut into ¼-inch slices. If uncooked, boil beets in their skins for about 45 minutes, until tender, then drain (reserving some cooking liquid), peel and slice. ★ In a saucepan, stir together sugar and cornstarch. Add vinegar and water (or beet cooking liquid, if possible), bring to a boil, then reduce heat to a simmer and cook, stirring for about 5 minutes, until lightly syrupy. ★ Remove pan from heat, add beets, stir gently to coat and let them sit for about 30 minutes. Return pan to a moderate heat, bring liquid back to a boil, stir in butter, then transfer to a heated serving dish and top with parsley.

SCALLOPED TOMATOES

Long suspected of being poisonous, tomatoes did not move from their ornamental plant status to become a garden vegetable until the mid-nineteenth century.

Serves 4 to 6 as a side dish

- *½ cup butter*
- *1 medium-sized onion, chopped*
- *2 cups chopped fresh or canned tomatoes*
- *1 teaspoon salt*
- *1 tablespoon sugar*
- *½ teaspoon black pepper*
- *2 cups breadcrumbs*

Preheat oven to 375°F. Melt 2 tablespoons butter in a skillet. Add onion and cook until translucent but not brown. ★ In a mixing bowl combine cooked onion, tomatoes, salt, sugar and black pepper. Butter a baking dish. Place a layer of tomato mixture in prepared dish, followed by a layer of breadcrumbs. Repeat, alternating layers and ending with a layer of crumbs. Dot with remaining butter. Bake for 30 to 40 minutes.

GREEN PEAS
AND NEW POTATOES

This dish is traditionally served with poached salmon on the fourth of July.

Serves 4 as a side dish	*8 small new potatoes*
1/4 pound sliced salt pork or bacon	*2 cups cooked peas*
2 small onions, chopped	*1 cup heavy cream*

In a small skillet fry pork or bacon slices until crisp. Remove meat from skillet and add onions. Cook until onions are lightly browned. ★ Scrub but do not peel potatoes. Place in a saucepan, add pork or bacon, onions and just enough cold water to cover. Cook over a moderate heat, covered, for 20 minutes. ★ Remove pork or bacon slices. Add peas to potatoes and onions. Pour cream over vegetables and simmer until well blended. Do not let cream boil.

CRANBERRY-STUFFED
MACKEREL

Fish stuffed with berries was a traditional dish of the early Indian tribes, using the fruit and fish of the wilderness.

Serves 4 as a main course	*4 tablespoons butter*
2 mackerel, totalling 3 pounds	*1 teaspoon anchovy paste*
1/2 pound cranberries	*salt and pepper to taste*
4 tablespoons breadcrumbs	*1/8 teaspoon cayenne pepper*

Preheat oven to 350°F. ★ Clean and wash mackerel. Split down the spine and remove bones. ★ Chop cranberries coarsely. In a mixing bowl, combine cranberries, breadcrumbs, butter, anchovy paste, salt, pepper, and cayenne. ★ Stuff each mackerel with the cranberry mixture. Wrap the fish in aluminum foil and place in a buttered baking dish. Bake for 30 minutes. Carefully remove foil and serve. ★ If gooseberries are available, substitute them for the cranberries.

Picture page 41

CODFISH BALLS

DEEP-FRIED

The English explorer Bartholomew Gosnold gave Cape Cod its name in 1602 for the great abundance of codfish in the waters there. In 1640, Pilgrim colonists exported more than 300,000 dried codfish.

Serves 6 to 8 as a main course

- *1 pound salt codfish*
- *2 cups mashed potatoes*
- *3/4 teaspoon black pepper*
- *1/2 teaspoon grated nutmeg*
- *4 eggs, beaten*
- *1 1/2 cups vegetable oil*

Soak codfish for 4 hours in enough cold water to cover, changing water after 2 hours. Drain fish, place in a pot, cover with fresh water and bring to a boil. Drain and flake fish. Combine with mashed potatoes, pepper and nutmeg. Add eggs and mix thoroughly. ★ Heat oil in a heavy skillet until very hot (375°F). Drop fish mixture by teaspoons into oil making codfish balls, and fry until golden brown.

BROILED COD

IN LEMON BUTTER

The fortune of one of the great New England families, the Cabots, was based on the humble cod. George Cabot was captain of a codfish schooner when he was just 18, in 1770.

Serves 4 as a main course

- *2 pounds codfish fillets*
- *6 tablespoons melted butter*
- *3 tablespoons lemon juice*
- *1 teaspoon salt*
- *1/2 teaspoon pepper*
- *2 tablespoons soft, fresh breadcrumbs*

Preheat broiler to highest temperature. In a baking dish, mix melted butter, lemon juice, salt and pepper. Dip cod fillets in mixture to coat both sides. Arrange fillets in one layer in dish. ★ Broil fish 3 to 4 inches from heat for 5 minutes. Baste fillets with pan liquids. Sprinkle breadcrumbs over fillets and broil for a further 5 minutes, or until fish flakes easily. Serve fillets at once with pan liquids poured over them.

YANKEE POT ROAST

The ingredients and style of cooking in this recipe are exactly as they were in colonial times. Because it is made from a cheaper meat it also embodies the true New England value of thrift.

Serves 6 as a main course
- *3 pounds bottom round, chuck or rump roast*
- *2 tablespoons flour*
- *½ teaspoon grated nutmeg*
- *3 tablespoons bacon drippings, lard or butter*
- *2 cups cranberries*
- *1 cup apple cider*
- *2 tablespoons brown sugar*
- *1 cinnamon stick*
- *6 whole cloves*
- *1 teaspoon salt*

In a small bowl combine flour and nutmeg. Rub mixture into meat. In a large, heavy pot or Dutch oven melt bacon drippings and add meat, browning well on all sides. ★ In a saucepan combine cranberries, apple cider and brown sugar. Bring mixture to a boil. Simmer over a low heat until cranberries are tender, about 8 minutes. Pour mixture over meat. ★ Put cinnamon stick and cloves in a cheesecloth bag. Place bag in pot with meat. Sprinkle meat with salt. Cover pot and simmer for 2 to 2¼ hours, or until meat is tender. To serve, remove spice bag and place meat on a serving platter with sauce.

NEW ENGLAND SALT PORK
WITH MILK GRAVY

Salt pork was the heart and soul of early colonial cooking. Salting was an efficient and safe way to store and preserve meats for the long New England winters. Milk and dairy products were highly prized in the new colonies – the first three cows didn't arrive until 1624.

Serves 4 as a main course
- *2 pounds salt pork, with streaks of lean*
- *4 tablespoons flour*
- *2 tablespoons lard*

Milk gravy:
- *¼ cup salt pork drippings*
- *3 tablespoons flour*
- *2¼ cups milk*

Cut salt pork into ½-inch slices. Soak slices in enough warm water to cover for 4 hours, changing water 3 or 4 times. ★ Pat pork slices dry. Dredge each slice in flour. In a skillet greased with lard, cook pork slowly, turning occasionally, until slices are a rich crusty brown. ★ To make the milk gravy, remove pork slices from skillet. Remove skillet from heat and drain off all but ¼ cup drippings. Stir 3 tablespoons flour into drippings. Blend thoroughly and add 2 tablespoons milk. Stir until smooth. Add 2 more tablespoons milk. Mix well. Gradually stir in remaining 2 cups of milk. Cook over a low heat, stirring constantly, until mixture thickens. Serve salt pork with gravy.

BOILED DINNER

Developed by colonial wives who had to cook over wood fires and usually in just one pot, this meal is generally served with vegetables arranged around the centerpiece of meat.

Serves 6 to 8 as a main course

5 to 6 pounds corned beef brisket
½ pound salt pork
8 carrots
8 parsnips
8 small white turnips, peeled
1 medium-sized onion
8 medium-sized potatoes
1 medium-sized head green cabbage, cored and quartered

Place corned beef in a large pot and add enough cold water to cover. Simmer, covered, for 2 hours. Add salt pork and continue simmering for another 2 hours. ★ Skim pot carefully and add carrots, parsnips, turnips and onion. Cover and cook for 30 minutes. Add potatoes and cabbage. Cover and continue cooking until potatoes are tender, about 30 to 40 minutes longer. ★ To serve, place meat in the center of a large platter. Surround with drained vegetables.

Picture page 45

NEW ENGLAND CLAM CHOWDER

Recipe page 34

CRANBERRY-STUFFED MACKEREL

Recipe page 36

ROAST TURKEY

WITH SAUSAGE AND SAGE DRESSING

The turkey is a native American bird of remarkable stupidity. It was domesticated very early by the Indians of the Southwest and the Aztecs; other Indians found the bird easy to capture in the wild. It is uncertain whether turkey was served at the first Thanksgiving held by the Pilgrims in 1621, but ever since the holiday was made official in America by President Abraham Lincoln in 1863, turkey has been the traditional main course.

Serves 12 to 15 as a main course

- *1 14-pound turkey*
- *2 small loaves stale bread*
- *milk*
- *2 large onions, finely chopped*
- *3 celery stalks, finely chopped*
- *4 tablespoons butter*
- *2 pounds fresh pork sausage*
- *1 teaspoon salt*
- *1 teaspoon black pepper*
- *3 teaspoons dried thyme*
- *6 parsley sprigs, finely chopped*
- *3 teaspoons dried sage*
- *18 stoned black olives, chopped*

Preheat oven to 450°F. Rinse turkey and pat dry with paper towels. Set aside. Cut stale bread into small cubes. Put in a large mixing bowl and add enough milk just to moisten. Set aside. ★ Melt butter in a large skillet. Add onions and celery and sauté until soft but not brown. Add to bread cubes. ★ Remove sausage filling from casings. In same skillet, brown filling, breaking it up into small pieces. Drain off fat and add sausage to bread cubes. Add salt, pepper, thyme, parsley, sage and black olives. Blend well. When you are ready to roast turkey, stuff cavity of turkey with mixture. (Never stuff a turkey in advance.) Sew cavity closed or close with skewers and truss bird securely with kitchen twine. ★ Place turkey in a large roasting pan and roast for 15 minutes. Reduce heat to 350°F and continue to roast, basting often with pan juices, until juices run clear when a fork is inserted into turkey's thigh. This will take about 20 minutes per pound, or 4-5 hours.

SUCCOTASH

This dish, introduced to the Pilgrims by the Narraganssett Indians of Massachusetts, was probably served at the first Thanksgiving in the New World.

Serves 6 as a side dish

- *1 1/2 cups fresh lima beans*
- *1 1/2 cups fresh corn kernels*
- *2 tablespoons butter*
- *3 strips lean bacon, cut into 1/4-inch pieces*
- *1/2 cup whipping cream*
- *1/2 teaspoon salt*
- *3/4 teaspoon black pepper*
- *2 tablespoons chopped fresh parsley*

Bring a saucepan of water to a boil. Add lima beans and cook for about 10 minutes; add corn and cook for about 5 minutes more, until vegetables are tender. Drain well. ★ Melt butter in a skillet over a moderate heat. Add bacon pieces and sauté for 3 to 5 minutes, until they just begin to crisp. Stir in vegetables and remaining ingredients and cook for 3 to 5 minutes more, until sauce is hot. *Picture page 45*

RED FLANNEL HASH

A classic example of early American thriftiness, this dish is traditionally made from the left-overs of a New England boiled dinner.

Serves 4 as a main course

- *1 1/2 cups cooked chopped corned beef*
- *1 1/2 cups cooked chopped beets*
- *3 cups cooked chopped potatoes*
- *1 small onion, finely chopped*
- *salt to taste*
- *black pepper to taste*
- *1 teaspoon Worcestershire sauce*
- *light cream or half-and-half*
- *1/4 cup bacon drippings*

In a large bowl combine corned beef, beets, potatoes, onion, salt, pepper and Worcestershire sauce with enough cream or half-and-half to bind the ingredients together. ★ Melt bacon drippings in a skillet and add meat mixture, spreading it evenly. Cook over a low heat. Loosen hash around edges with a spatula and shake skillet occasionally to prevent the bottom scorching. When a crust forms on the bottom, flip hash over and brown on the other side. Remove from skillet and serve on a platter.

BOILED DINNER

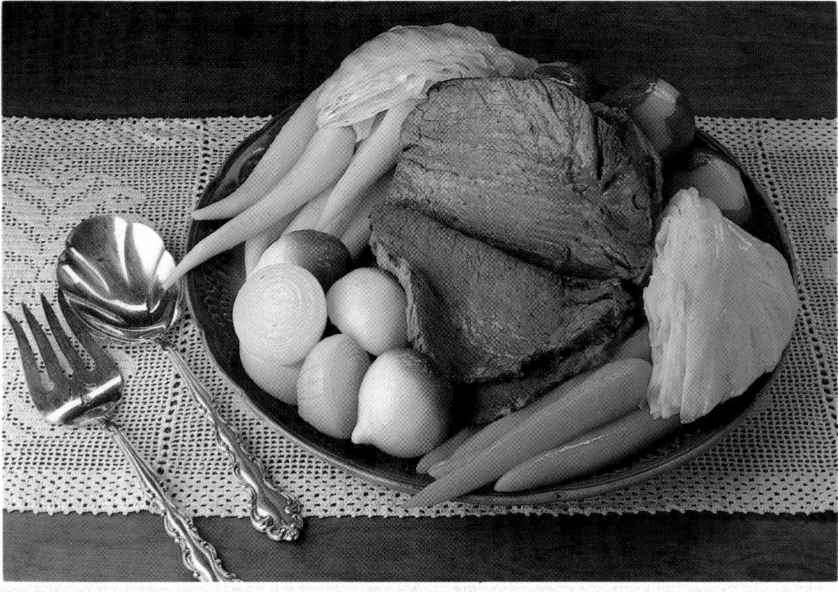

Recipe page 39

SUCCOTASH

Recipe page 43

INDIAN PUDDING

Not really an authentic Indian dish, this recipe got its name because early settlers called sweet corn "Indian corn."

Serves 6 as a dessert

- *½ cup yellow cornmeal*
- *4½ cups milk, scalded*
- *¾ cup molasses*
- *3 tablespoons butter*
- *1 teaspoon salt*
- *½ tablespoon cinnamon*
- *¾ teaspoon ground cinnamon*
- *¼ teaspoon nutmeg*
- *2 eggs, beaten*
- *1 cup cold milk*

Stir cornmeal into scalded milk in the top of a double boiler and cook for about 20 minutes. Stir in molasses, 2 tablespoons butter and seasonings. Gradually stir in beaten eggs. ★ Preheat oven to 350°F. Grease a shallow baking dish with remaining butter. Pour cornmeal mixture into dish and pour cold milk on top, without stirring. Bake pudding for about 1 hour, until topped with a deep golden crust.

MAPLE BAKED APPLES

Abundant maple trees all over New England still yield maple sugar and maple syrup. The Algonquin Indians of Massachusetts taught the colonists how to collect the sap from the tree by cutting a slash across the tree trunk. Maple sap "runs" in March.

Serves 6 as a dessert

- *6 large red or green baking apples*
- *6 teaspoons coarsely chopped walnuts*
- *6 teaspoons raisins*
- *6 tablespoons maple syrup*
- *6 tablespoons sweet butter*
- *ground cinnamon*
- *ground allspice*
- *grated nutmeg*
- *1 cup heavy cream*

Preheat oven to 375°F. Cut cores from apples, but take care not to cut through the bottoms. Place apples in a shallow baking dish. Put 1 teaspoon each walnuts and raisins into each apple. Pour 1 tablespoon maple syrup into each apple, and top with 1 tablespoon butter. Add dashes of cinnamon, allspice and nutmeg to each apple. ★ Pour ½ inch cold water into the bottom of the dish to keep apples moist, and bake until soft, 25 to 30 minutes. Transfer to serving bowls and drizzle the apples with cream.

EASY PIE CRUST

"Easy as pie" is this simple pastry dough, equally delicious for berry and fruit pies and for single-crust meringues.

Makes enough dough for a double-crust 9-inch pie

2 cups all-purpose flour

1/4 teaspoon salt

2/3 cup unsalted butter, cut into pieces

3 to 4 tablespoons ice water

In a mixing bowl, sift together flour and salt. Add butter and rub into flour with your fingertips, or cut in with a pastry blender or a pair of knives, until mixture resembles a coarse meal. ★ Gradually mix in just enough water to make dough stick together. Knead briefly with your hands until smooth. Gather dough into a ball and wrap in plastic wrap. Refrigerate for 1 to 2 hours before use.

PUMPKIN PIE

This recipe can also be made with other yellow- or orange-fleshed winter squashes.

Makes 1 9-inch dessert pie

2 cups cooked pumpkin (fresh or canned)

2 eggs beaten

1 cup brown sugar

1 cup half and half

1/2 cup milk

1 tablespoon brandy

1 teaspoon vanilla extract

1 teaspoon cinnamon

1 teaspoon ground ginger

1/2 teaspoon nutmeg

1/2 teaspoon allspice

1/2 recipe Easy Pie Crust (see above recipe), with 1/2 teaspoon cinnamon and 1/4 teaspoon nutmeg

1 cup whipping cream

Preheat oven to 425°F. Stir together pumpkin and eggs, then stir in sugar, half and half, milk and brandy. Add remaining flavorings and stir well. ★ Roll out pie dough to a circle large enough to line a 9-inch pie plate. Line plate with dough, gently pressing it into bottom and sides. ★ Spoon pumpkin filling into pie shell and spread evenly. Bake pie for 15 minutes. Reduce oven temperature to 350°F and bake for 20 to 25 minutes more, until a thin knife blade inserted into the filling comes out clean. ★ Let pie cool to room temperature. Whip cream and spoon generously over pie before serving. *Picture page 51*

WALNUT-TOPPED BROWNIES

Brownies are as all-American as you can get.

Makes 25 brownies for dessert or snacks

3 ounces unsweetened chocolate
6 tablespoons sweet butter
1 cup sugar
1/4 teaspoon salt
2 large eggs, lightly beaten
1 1/2 teaspoons pure vanilla extract
1/2 cup sifted flour

Topping:

1/4 cup sweet butter
1/4 cup sugar
1/2 cup firmly packed dark brown sugar
2 tablespoons flour
2 large eggs, lightly beaten
1 1/2 teaspoons pure vanilla extract
3 1/2 cups coarsely broken walnut pieces

To prepare brownie base, melt chocolate together with butter in a heavy saucepan over a very low heat. Remove from heat and stir until well blended. ★ Add sugar and salt to chocolate mixture. Stir until smooth. Add eggs and vanilla extract. Stir until well blended. Add flour and fold in until thoroughly incorporated. Spread batter evenly in a buttered 9 × 9 × 2-inch baking pan. Refrigerate for 2 hours. ★ Preheat the oven to 350°F. To prepare the topping, melt butter in a heavy saucepan over low heat. Add sugar and brown sugar. Cook, stirring constantly, for 1 minute. Remove from heat. ★ Add flour and eggs to butter mixture and stir to blend well. Return mixture to heat. Cook over low heat, stirring constantly, for 3 minutes or until thick and light in color. Be careful not to overcook or the eggs will curdle. Remove from heat. Add vanilla extract and walnuts. Stir until walnuts are evenly coated. ★ Remove brownie base from refrigerator. Spoon topping over base and spread evenly. Bake for 40 to 50 minutes or until top is dry and a cake tester inserted into the center comes out barely dry. ★ Remove from oven. Cool in pan on a wire rack. Cover pan and let set overnight. Cut into squares.

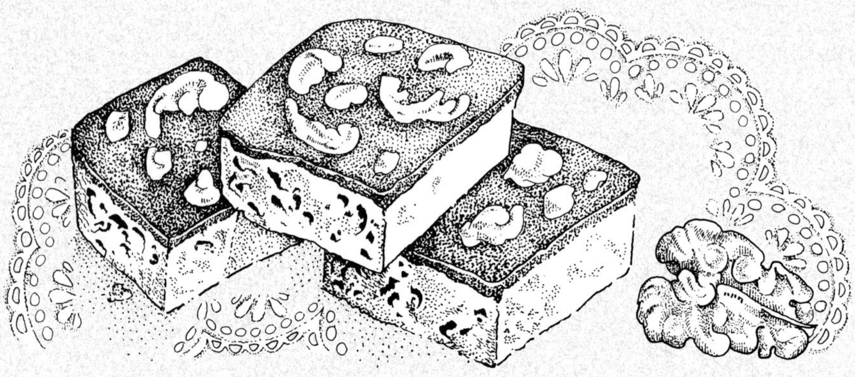

FUDGE FROSTING

Fudge frosting sets off all kinds of cake – yellow, chocolate or white.

- *4 ounces unsweetened chocolate*
- *1 1/2 cups milk*
- *4 cups confectioner's sugar*
- *1/8 teaspoon salt*
- *4 teaspoons light corn syrup*
- *1/4 cup butter*
- *2 teaspoons pure vanilla extract*

Place chocolate and milk in a heavy saucepan. Cook over a low heat, stirring constantly, until well blended. ★ Add sugar, salt and corn syrup. Stir until sugar is dissolved. Boil mixture over a very low heat, stirring occasionally, until small amounts dropped into cold water form soft balls. This will be when mixture is approximately 234°F to 240°F on a candy thermometer. ★ Remove saucepan from heat. Add butter and vanilla extract and mix well. Cool mixture to lukewarm and then beat until creamy. ★ To frost Wellesley Fudge Cake, place one layer top-side down on a cake plate. Spread with approximately one-third of frosting. Place second layer on top, right-side up, and spread sides with approximately one-third frosting. Then spread top of cake with remaining frosting. Smooth frosting and swirl with a knife. Let set before cutting cake.

POPOVERS

Popovers pop when the steam that forms inside them expands as they cook. If your popovers don't pop, it is probably because the oven isn't hot enough or the batter doesn't have enough eggs in it.

Makes 12 dinner popovers

- *1 cup flour*
- *1/2 teaspoon salt*
- *2 to 3 eggs, beaten (use 3 if small)*
- *1 cup milk*
- *1 tablespoon melted butter*
- *butter*

Preheat oven to 450°F. Combine all ingredients in a large mixing bowl. Beat with a spoon or mix in a blender until batter is completely smooth. ★ Fill each cup in a well-buttered preheated muffin pan one-third full. Bake popovers for 15 minutes. Reduce heat to 350°F and continue baking for 20 to 25 minutes. Serve hot with butter.

PUMPKIN PIE

Recipe page 47

TOLL HOUSE COOKIES

Recipe page 56

OLD-STYLE JOHNNYCAKES

FROM RHODE ISLAND

The name johnnycake is said by some to derive from "journey cakes," the idea being that travelers took them along. However, there is a good chance that the name comes from the Indians who taught the settlers how to cook cornmeal – the Shawnees.

Serves 6 as a breakfast or dinner bread

1 teaspoon salt
1 tablespoon butter
1 cup yellow cornmeal
1 cup boiling water
1/4 cup milk
2 tablespoons bacon drippings or butter

Preheat oven to 475°F. Put cornmeal, salt and butter in a mixing bowl. Pour boiling water over cornmeal. Stir immediately. It is crucial that the water is actually boiling when poured. Add milk and stir until well mixed. ★ Melt bacon drippings in an 8- or 9-inch round cake pan. Grease sides of pan and pour in batter. Place pan over heat until batter begins to bubble around edges. ★ Place pan in oven. Bake for about 30 minutes, or until golden brown. After first 10 minutes, dot top with butter if desired.

DOUGHNUTS

Why do doughnuts have holes? One day half the crew of a New England fishing boat fell overboard after eating doughnuts and sank like stones. The captain was so annoyed that he punched holes in the doughnuts with a belaying pin to make them lighter. After that, he never lost a man!

Makes 6 to 8 doughnuts

1 cup milk
1/3 cup sugar
1 egg, beaten
4 tablespoons butter
1/2 teaspoon baking powder
1 to 1 1/2 cups flour
vegetable oil for frying

In a large bowl combine milk, sugar, egg, butter, baking powder and flour. Mix together well, knead gently, and add more flour, if necessary. Knead about 8 times and then roll dough out onto a lightly floured surface. Cut dough with a doughnut cutter. ★ Heat oil to 370°F in a deep skillet. Add doughnuts and fry on both sides until brown and light. Drain doughnuts on paper towels.

COLONIAL SPICE-AND-VINEGAR PIE

This recipe goes back to the very earliest colonists in New England.

Makes 1 9-inch dessert pie

1/2 recipe Easy Pie Crust (see page 47)
4 egg yolks
2 egg whites
1 cup sugar
1/4 cup flour
1/2 teaspoon grated nutmeg
1/2 teaspoon cinnamon
1/2 teaspoon ground cloves
1/4 teaspoon salt
1 cup sour cream
3 tablespoons melted butter
3 tablespoons cider vinegar
1 cup chopped walnuts or pecans
1 cup raisins

Bake pie crust in a preheated 450°F oven for 10 minutes. Remove from oven and set aside. Reduce oven temperature to 400°F. In a small bowl, beat egg yolks. In a separate bowl, beat egg whites until stiff but not dry. Fold sugar into whites and mix with yolks. ★ Combine flour with nutmeg, cinnamon, cloves and salt in a large bowl. Add alternately with sour cream to egg mixture. Add butter and vinegar. Fold in nuts and raisins and stir to distribute evenly. ★ Pour batter into pie crust. Bake for 5 minutes, then reduce heat to 350°F and bake until filling begins to get firm, about 15 minutes. Remove pie from oven. Cool and serve topped with whipped cream.

CHOCOLATE FUDGE

Fudge was first made in the mid-1800s by students of the famed women's colleges of New England.

Makes 1 pound of candy

2 cups sugar
2 tablespoons corn syrup
2/3 cup evaporated milk
3 tablespoons butter
1 teaspoon pure vanilla extract
1/2 cup chopped walnuts

Combine sugar, corn syrup, evaporated milk and butter in a saucepan. Bring to a boil over a moderate heat until mixture reaches 236°F on a candy thermometer or until a small amount of it forms a soft ball when dropped into a bowl of cold water. ★ Pour mixture into a buttered shallow pan. Stir in vanilla and chopped walnuts. Spread mixture evenly in pan. Let cool and cut into squares.

MAPLE POPCORN BALLS

The Indians first introduced popping corn to the colonists by heating it over burning embers.

Makes about 3 dozen balls	*1 cup sugar*
1/4 cup vegetable oil	*1 cup maple syrup*
2 cups unpopped popcorn	*1 cup unsalted roasted almond*
3 tablespoons butter	*halves, pecans or walnuts*

Heat oil and 3 or 4 popcorn kernels in a large pot over a moderate heat. When kernels pop, add remaining popcorn and cover pot. When corn begins to pop, shake pan continuously until popping stops. Remove from heat and reserve. ★ Melt butter in a saucepan over a moderate heat. Add sugar and maple syrup and bring mixture to a boil, stirring frequently. Reduce heat and simmer mixture until it registers 244°F to 248°F on a candy thermometer, or can be molded into a firm but pliable ball when a spoonful is dropped into ice water. ★ Add nuts to popcorn and use a wooden spoon to stir in syrup. When mixture is cool, grease your hands and mold popcorn into 3 dozen balls.

HERMITS

This recipe owes its origins to early Yankee trading with the West Indies – which brought molasses – and the Mediterranean – which yielded raisins.

Makes 72 cookies	*1 teaspoon cinnamon*
1/2 cup sugar	*1/2 teaspoon grated nutmeg*
1/3 cup butter	*1/2 cup dark molasses*
1 egg	*1/2 cup buttermilk*
3 cups flour	*1 cup raisins*
1/2 teaspoon salt	

Preheat oven to 350°F. In a mixing bowl cream together sugar and butter until light and fluffy. Beat in egg. ★ Combine flour, salt, cinnamon and nutmeg in a small bowl. Mix molasses with buttermilk in another small bowl. Add molasses mixture alternately with flour mixture to creamed sugar and butter. Stir in raisins ★ Drop dough by teaspoons approximately 1 inch apart on to a greased cookie sheet. Bake for 8 to 10 minutes, or until lightly browned. Cool on a rack.

WELLESLEY FUDGE CAKE

Named after the famed New England women's college, this cake was served in village tearooms on Wellesley Square.

Makes 1 layer cake

- *4 ounces unsweetened chocolate*
- *1/2 cup hot water*
- *1/2 cup sugar*
- *2 cups flour*
- *1 teaspoon baking soda*
- *1 teaspoon salt*
- *1/2 cup butter*
- *1 1/4 cups sugar*
- *3 eggs*
- *1 teaspoon pure vanilla extract*
- *2/3 cup milk*

Preheat oven to 350°F. Combine chocolate and hot water in the top of a double boiler. Cook over simmering water until chocolate is melted. Add 1/2 cup sugar and cook for 2 minutes longer. Set aside. ★ Sift flour, baking soda and salt on to a large piece of waxed paper. Sift together twice more and set aside. ★ Cream butter in a mixing bowl. Add 1 1/4 cups sugar and cream together until light and fluffy. Add eggs, one at a time, beating well after each addition. Add vanilla extract. Add flour alternately with milk, beginning and ending with flour, beating well after each addition. Add chocolate mixture and blend well. ★ Pour batter into two greased and floured 9-inch square cake pans. Bake for 25 to 30 minutes or until a cake tester inserted into the center comes out clean. Cool pans on racks for 10 minutes, then turn out and continue to cool. When cool, frost cakes with Fudge Frosting.

TOLL HOUSE COOKIES

The famous Toll House Inn in Massachusetts was established by Ruth Wakefield. This is her personal recipe for the original chocolate chip cookies, developed in 1930.

Makes 24 cookies
- *1/2 cup butter*
- *1/2 cup sugar*
- *1/4 cup firmly packed light brown sugar*
- *1 egg, beaten*
- *1 teaspoon pure vanilla extract*
- *1 cup flour*
- *1/2 teaspoon baking soda*
- *1/2 cup chopped walnuts or pecans*
- *6 ounces semisweet chocolate bits*

Preheat oven to 375°F. In a large mixing bowl cream butter until soft. Gradually beat in sugar and brown sugar, beating well after each addition. Beat in egg and vanilla extract. ★ Add flour and baking soda to mixture. Stir until smooth. Stir in nuts and chocolate bits, making sure they are evenly distributed throughout batter. ★ Drop batter by scant teaspoons 2 inches apart on to lightly greased cookie sheets. Bake for 8 to 10 minutes or until edges begin to brown. Cool on racks.

Picture page 51

SNICKERDOODLES

Another favorite cookie – worth serving for the name alone!

Makes 36 cookies
- *2 eggs*
- *2 cups water*
- *1/2 cup butter, softened*
- *1 teaspoon pure vanilla extract*
- *4 cups flour*
- *4 teaspoons baking powder*
- *1 teaspoon salt*
- *1 cup milk*
- *1 cup raisins, chopped*
- *1 tablespoon sugar*
- *1 teaspoon cinnamon*

Preheat oven to 350°F. Beat eggs in a mixing bowl, gradually adding sugar. Stir in butter and add vanilla. ★ Combine flour, baking powder and salt in a bowl. Add flour mixture alternately with milk to egg mixture. Beat well after each addition. Stir in raisins. ★ Drop dough by teaspoons about 1 inch apart on to greased cookie sheets. Combine 1 tablespoon sugar with cinnamon in a small bowl. Sprinkle mixture generously over cookies. Bake for 20 minutes or until cookies are golden. Cool on racks.

JOE FROGGERS

It's amusing to try this recipe just so you can tell your unsuspecting guests you're serving them "Joe Froggers."

Makes 48 to 68 cookies	*2 teaspoons baking soda*
1 cup butter	*2 cups dark molasses*
2 cups sugar	*7 cups flour*
1 tablespoon salt	*1 tablespoon ground ginger*
3/4 cup water	*1 teaspoon grated nutmeg*
1/4 cup dark rum	*1/2 teaspoon ground cloves*

Cream butter and sugar together in a mixing bowl until light and fluffy. In a small bowl dissolve salt in water and mix in rum. In another small bowl, add baking soda to molasses. ★ Combine flour, ginger, cloves and nutmeg. Add flour mixture alternately with liquid ingredients to creamed butter and sugar. Stir well between additions. The dough will be sticky. Chill overnight in refrigerator. ★ Preheat oven to 375°F. Flour a counter and rolling pin. Roll dough out to 1/2-inch thickness. Cut into shapes and place 2 inches apart on greased cookie sheets. Bake for 10 to 12 minutes or until golden. Cool on racks.

GRAHAM NUT BREAD

The Reverend Sylvester Graham was a nineteenth-century dietary reformer from Boston, whose belief in the virtues of whole wheat flour is shared by many today. His name lives on in graham crackers.

Makes 2 loaves	*2 cups whole wheat or graham flour*
2 tablespoons butter, melted	*1 2/3 cups white flour*
1/2 cup sugar	*1 teaspoon salt*
1/2 cup molasses	*1 teaspoon baking powder*
2 teaspoons baking soda	*1 cup chopped walnuts*
2 cups buttermilk	

Preheat oven to 375°F. In a large bowl combine butter, sugar and molasses. Mix well. Dissolve baking soda in buttermilk and add to molasses mixture. Stir until well blended. ★ Combine whole wheat flour, white flour, salt and baking powder in a bowl or on a large piece of waxed paper. Add to molasses-buttermilk mixture. Stir in nuts. ★ Pour batter into two 9 × 5 × 3-inch greased loaf pans. Bake for about 50 minutes or until done.

BOSTON BROWN BREAD

Recipe page 60

ANADAMA BREAD

Stories about the origin of Anadama bread abound. One of the more plausible concerns Anna, a fine but temperamental cook. She left her husband and he had to make her bread recipe himself, muttering all the time, "Anna, damn her."

Makes 1 loaf	*1 packet dry yeast*
1/2 cup yellow cornmeal	*3/4 cup boiling water*
3 tablespoons butter	*1/4 cup warm water*
1/4 cup dark molasses	*1 egg, beaten*
2 teaspoons salt	*3 cups flour*

In a large bowl combine cornmeal, butter, molasses, salt and boiling water. Mix well. Let mixture stand at room temperature until lukewarm. ★ Dissolve yeast in 3 tablespoons of lukewarm water in a small bowl. Stir yeast mixture into cornmeal mixture. Stir in egg and 1½ cups flour. Beat well. Stir in remaining 1½ cups flour and mix until dough forms a soft ball. Use your hands to mix dough if easier. ★ Place dough in a greased 9 × 5 × 3-inch loaf pan. Cover with a clean cloth and set in a warm place until dough doubles in bulk, about 1 to 1½ hours. Sprinkle top of loaf with a little cornmeal and salt. Bake in a 350°F oven for 50 to 55 minutes. Cool completely before slicing.

BOSTON BROWN BREAD

The Pilgrims used to say, "Brown bread and Gospel is good fare."

Makes 3 loaves	*1 teaspoon salt*
1 cup rye flour	*3/4 cup dark molasses*
1 cup yellow cornmeal	*2 cups buttermilk*
1 cup whole wheat or graham flour	*1 cup dark seedless raisins*
3/4 teaspoon baking soda	

Sift rye flour, cornmeal, whole wheat flour, baking soda and salt into a large bowl. Add molasses, buttermilk and raisins. Stir well. ★ Divide batter into 3 equal parts. Place each part into a buttered 1-pound coffee can, filling can about three-quarters full (large juice cans also work well). Cover top of each can with buttered wax paper and then aluminum foil. Puff foil and allow approximately 1 inch of space so that bread has room to rise. Tie foil and wax paper in place with string.

★ Place cans on a rack set in a very large pot. Fill pot with enough boiling water to reach three-quarters up the cans. Return water to a boil, cover pot, reduce heat, and steam bread for 2½ hours. Check pot occasionally and add water if necessary to keep water at original level. ★ When bread is done, carefully remove cans from pot. Cool them just enough to remove bread. Serve bread hot with butter.

Picture page 58

PARKER HOUSE ROLLS

The Parker House Hotel was opened in Boston in 1855. Its dining room soon became known as one of the best places in the city to eat.

Makes 24 dinner rolls

½ cup scalded milk
½ cup boiling water
1 teaspoon salt
1 tablespoon butter
1 teaspoon sugar
1 packet active dry yeast dissolved in ¼ cup lukewarm water
3 cups flour
½ cup melted butter

Preheat oven to 400°F. Place milk, water, salt, butter and sugar in a mixing bowl and mix well. Add yeast mixture. Add flour and mix until dough is stiff enough to knead. Cover dough with a clean cloth and let rise until doubled in bulk, about 20 minutes. ★ Shape dough into 24 balls and place on buttered cookie sheets or in muffin pans. Cover with a clean cloth and let rise in a warm place until doubled in bulk, about 15 to 20 minutes. ★ Flour the handle of a wooden spoon and press it against each ball until it is almost in half. Brush one half of each ball with melted butter. Fold over the other half and press halves together. Let dough rise for a further 15 to 20 minutes. ★ Bake for 15 minutes or until golden. Brush tops with butter after baking. Serve warm.

NORTH ATLANTIC SEABOARD

Successful merchants, productive farmlands and a vibrant fishing industry inspired this most European of American culinary traditions. To it we owe the pleasures of hamburgers and ice cream.

It is from the North Atlantic seaboard that America's two dominant culinary traditions emerged: German and English. For, while New England certainly incubated Puritan English cooking, its neighbors to the south provided a less inhibited English cuisine more characteristic of the landed gentry. And a great many German-speaking immigrants settled

In the early days, this was the land of farmers – rich farmers – who settled around the old Dutch colony of New Amsterdam (soon to become New York), Philadelphia and the eastern shore of Maryland and Virginia. Some of these farmers went on to become politicians, others business tycoons and merchants. But, whatever their calling, their banqueting was rarely less than sumptuous.

Soon after New England was settled, a second group of English colonists settled in Maryland and Virginia, known as the Tidewater region, and successfully cultivated all the vegetables and fruits native to England. The early estates along this coast were very English in style. Aristocratic second sons who had not inherited an estate in Britain were attracted here.

Shellfish, terrapin, venison, game and peanut-fed hogs yielding succulent hams were plentiful. The occasional porcupine, hedgehog and swan were also served. Vegetables included cabbages, kale, yams, onions, potatoes, okra, broccoli and carrots. Orchards yielded berries, peaches, pears and apples. The basically English cuisine of the country was complemented by a few French sauces. Some spices, through trade with the West Indies, made their way into the early cooking pots, notably mace, ginger, cinnamon, cloves and pepper. Later, when wealthy families began making the Grand European Tour, they took along their cooks to learn proper European culinary style. Tobacco, rice and indigo were the cash crop for these Tidewater planters.

As the young republic established itself and began making contact with the rest of the world, the influence of the grande cuisine of Europe began to be felt, notably in Virginia. Virginians inhabited the White House in the early years of the nation and official state cooking reflected Virginian tastes. Thomas Jefferson, the third US president, was the first to bring a French chef to the White House. So impressed was he, during his five years as US consul in Paris, by the joys of French haute cuisine that he was prepared to pay up to $28 a month – a munificent sum, almost 50 percent more than the prevailing wage – for a culinary wizard.

To the north, William Penn's Society of Friends – Quakers – settled along the Delaware River and founded the town which was to become Philadelphia. Coming mostly from Wales and England these peaceful dissenting immigrants quickly prospered. Their grand city was the site for the writing and

signing of the Declaration of Independence in 1776, as well as the site of the drafting of the Constitution in 1787.

Perhaps the most significant immigrant group into the area around Philadelphia was the Pennsylvanian Dutch. With no roots at all in Holland, these immigrants were in fact German-speaking religious refugees, mostly from the Rhineland and southern Germany. Amish from Switzerland set up colonies nearby as did Mennonites from southern Germany. It is these two groups who are most identified with Pennsylvania today.

While self denial was an important precept of the Pennsylvanian Dutch, it did not extend to their eating. The kitchen was often the largest room in the house and, as with most farm families, it was often the center of family life. Typical German dishes like smoked sausage, sauerkraut, and apple butter quickly found a place in the American food line-up. Eighteenth-century Philadelphia, by now sophisticated and worldly, was quick to recognize the culinary accomplishments of its country cousins. Scrapple, a loaf made of pork and cornmeal, was soon standard at city breakfasts, as were cinnamon buns. In fact, many quintessentially American dishes are Pennsylvanian Dutch, and thus German, in origin: frankfurters, pretzels, smoked sausages, even hamburgers (named for the northern port city, where chopped beef first became popular).

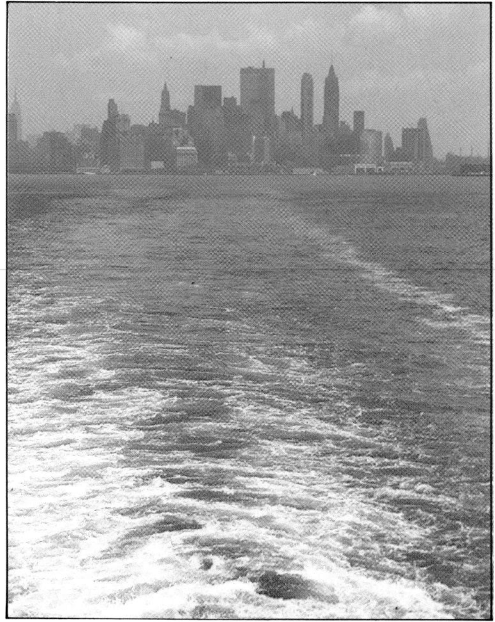

New York, New York...

The idea of the clean plate club also originated in this region – meals took on major proportions, with several courses served at one sitting. Pies were a standard feature of every meal and at least one always accompanied a meat course (of which there could be several). The tradition of "seven sweets and seven sours" was also instigated by the German immigrants: no meal was considered complete unless accompanied by fruits in honey, jams, jellies or spices (sweets) and an equal number of vegetables pickled in vinegars, such as chow chow and pickled beets (sours). The Pennsylvanian Dutch had a seemingly insatiable appetite for cakes, sweet rolls and "koekje" (cookies), all of which have passed into the recipe bag as truly American. While the birthplace of ice cream is a hotly debated topic, most connoisseurs agree that Philadelphia ice cream wrote the book on ice-cream excellence.

To cap off these feasts, the Mennonites in particular served homemade wine (the theory being that water was unsafe for drinking). Usually made from any fermented fruit left over after canning and pickling, blackberry was a typical favorite. Even dandelion wine was bottled. The Mennonites also brewed beers from sarsparilla roots and ginger.

By contrast, the Shakers – a breakaway utopian sect from the Quakers and so named because of the shaking movements they made during their services – practiced thrifty aestheticism. The Shakers also believed in plain, simple food consumed in moderation. They were possibly the first advocates of the high fiber diet and made great use of whole grain flour, vegetables and fruits.

The little Dutch settlement on the banks of the Hudson had been taken over by the English in 1664 and renamed New York. Middle class English farmers continued to settle in the colony and its food was almost purely English until the early part of the nineteenth century. At that time the great restaurants began to appear in response to the increasing wealth and sophistication of the people.

Italian immigrants arriving in the later part of the nineteenth century also left their indelible mark on New York cuisine. Neopolitans and Sicilians arrived first and the mainstays of their food were quickly added to the feast: pasta, shellfish, garlic, mozzarella and Parmesan cheeses, and tomato sauce.

BLACK BEAN SOUP

This is a specialty of the Coach House Restaurant in New York.

Serves 6 as a first course
- *1¼ cups dried black beans*
- *¼ pound smoked bacon, cut into ¼-inch pieces*
- *1 medium-sized onion, finely chopped*
- *1 celery stalk, finely chopped*
- *1 tablespoon chopped fresh parsley*
- *1 bay leaf*
- *½ teaspoon salt*
- *½ teaspoon black pepper*
- *6½ cups water*
- *¼ cup Madeira wine*
- *1 hard-cooked egg, finely chopped*
- *1 lemon, thinly sliced*

Cover beans with cold water and leave to soak overnight. Drain. ★ Put beans into a large pot with bacon, onion, celery, parsley, bay leaf, salt and pepper. Add water and bring to a boil over high heat. Reduce heat, cover pot and simmer beans for about 3 hours, until very tender. ★ Press soup through a fine sieve. Discard residue. Return thick purée to pot, stir in Madeira, and heat soup through over a moderate heat, about 5 minutes. ★ Pour soup into warmed serving bowls and top each with chopped egg and sliced lemon.

SENATE BEAN SOUP

Urged on a reluctant Congress by Senator Henry Cabot Lodge Sr. more than 50 years ago, this soup is still served in the Senate Restaurant.

Serves 6 as a first course
- *2 cups dried pea beans*
- *3 quarts cold water*
- *1 meaty ham bone*
- *3 boiled potatoes, peeled and mashed*
- *3 onions, finely chopped*
- *2 garlic cloves, crushed*
- *1 small head celery, chopped*
- *¼ cup finely chopped parsley*

Cook pea beans in a large, covered pot of boiling salted water until tender. Drain well. ★ Place pea beans, water and ham bone in a large pot. Simmer, covered, for 2 hours, skimming occasionally. ★ Add potatoes, onions, garlic, celery and parsley. Simmer, covered, for 1 hour. ★ Remove ham bone and return any meat on bone to soup. Serve hot.

VICHYSSOISE

Reputed to have got its start in 1910 in the fabled kitchens of New York's Ritz-Carlton, Vichyssoise is named after the elegant French resort.

Serves 6 as a first course

6 cups chicken broth

3 medium potatoes, peeled and cut into 1-inch pieces

3 medium leeks, trimmed, thoroughly washed, and cut into ½-inch slices

1 cup whipping cream

1 teaspoon salt

½ teaspoon white pepper

¼ teaspoon ground allspice

Put broth, potatoes and leeks in a saucepan over a high heat. Bring broth to a boil, reduce heat, and simmer for about 20 minutes, until potatoes are tender. ★ Purée broth and vegetables in a blender or food processor, about 1 minute. Add cream and seasonings. ★ To serve soup hot, return to saucepan and heat through over a moderate heat, 3 to 5 minutes. For cold soup, chill in refrigerator for 2 to 3 hours.

CREAM OF TOMATO SOUP

This can be made ahead and served hot or cold.

Serves 4 as a first course

4 tablespoons butter

1 onion, finely chopped

1 carrot, finely chopped

3 tablespoons flour

4 cups chicken broth

6 large ripe tomatoes, peeled, seeded and coarsely chopped

1 garlic clove, crushed

6 green onions, finely chopped

4 white peppercorns

1 teaspoon salt

1 tablespoon sugar

1 cup whipping cream

toasted croutons

Melt butter in a large pot and add onion and carrot. Sauté until onion begins to brown. Sprinkle with flour and mix well. Slowly add broth, tomatoes, garlic, green onions, peppercorns, salt and sugar. Cover and simmer over a low heat for 1½ hours. ★ Pour soup into a blender or food processor and add cream. Process, in batches if necessary, until smooth. Serve garnished with croutons.

SARATOGA POTATO CHIPS

A demanding guest at the Moon's Lake Lodge in Saratoga, New York – site of an important Colonial victory in the Revolutionary War – insisted on thinner potato slices. Chef George Crum sliced the potatoes as thinly as possible and deep-fried them. They were an instant hit.

Serves 4 as a side dish

4 potatoes, peeled

vegetable oil for frying

salt

Slice potatoes as thinly as possible. Place slices in a large bowl of ice water and let stand for several hours. Drain well and pat dry with paper towels. ★ Fill a large skillet with vegetable oil to a depth of 1 inch. Add potato slices and fry until crisp and golden. Drain on paper towels, sprinkle generously with salt and serve hot or cold.

HASH BROWN POTATOES

Next to hamburgers, there is probably no more typically American food. They are traditionally served at breakfast alongside eggs and bacon.

Serves 6 as a side dish

2¼ pounds boiling potatoes, well scrubbed

1 medium-sized onion, finely chopped

1 teaspoon salt

¾ teaspoon black pepper

3 tablespoons bacon drippings or butter

1½ tablespoons vegetable oil

Cut each potato into a few large pieces. Put in a saucepan of cold water, bring water to a boil over a high heat, then reduce heat to moderate and cook potatoes for 10 minutes. Drain and rinse well under cold running water until potatoes are cool enough to handle. ★ Coarsely grate potatoes into a mixing bowl. Toss with onion, salt and pepper. Melt half bacon drippings or butter with half oil in a heavy skillet over a moderate heat. When fat is hot, add potato mixture, pressing it down to form a thick cake. Fry until underside of cake is brown and crisp, about 5 minutes. Turn cake over with a large spatula (it can be turned in sections), distribute remaining fat and oil around side of skillet, and fry the other side until brown, about 5 minutes more.

WALDORF SALAD

Oscar M. Tschirsky, better known simply as Oscar of the Waldorf, was maître d'hôtel of the famed Waldorf Astoria hotel in New York City from 1893 to 1943. This first-course salad is his invention. The original salad did not call for walnuts, although they are considered indispensable now.

Serves 4 to 6 as a first course

- *3 tart apples, cored and diced but not peeled*
- *2 cups chopped celery*
- *1/2 cup coarsely chopped walnuts*
- *3 tablespoons dark raisins*
- *3 tablespoons lemon juice*
- *3/4 cup mayonnaise*
- *1 teaspoon salt*
- *1/2 teaspoon black pepper*
- *12 romaine lettuce leaves*

Put apples, celery, walnuts and raisins into a large mixing bowl. Add lemon juice, mayonnaise, salt and pepper. Stir until well blended. ★ Line a large salad bowl with lettuce leaves. Add salad to bowl and serve.

Picture page 70

DUTCH CUCUMBER SALAD

The Pennsylvania Dutch trace their stock not to Holland but to Germany and their hearty appetites reflect the Rhineland region they abandoned.

Serves 4 as a first course

- *1 teaspoon salt*
- *1 medium-sized onion, thinly sliced*
- *2 cucumbers, peeled and thinly sliced*
- *2 tablespoons tarragon vinegar*
- *2 cups sour cream*
- *1/2 teaspoon black pepper*

Sprinkle cucumbers and onions with salt and let stand for 30 minutes. ★ Place cucumbers and onion in a cheesecloth and squeeze out liquid. Put cucumbers and onion in a shallow bowl, add vinegar and mix. Pour sour cream over mixture and sprinkle with pepper.

SAUTÉED SOLE
WITH HAZELNUTS

Serves 4 as a main course	*black pepper to taste*
4 6- to 8-ounce sole fillets	*4 thin lemon slices*
plain flour for dredging	*2/3 cup raisins*
3 tablespoons sweet butter	*1/3 cup halved hazelnuts*
3 tablespoons olive oil	*1/4 cup pine nuts* (pignoli)
salt to taste	

Gently pat sole fillets dry. Dredge fillets in flour, shaking off any excess. ★ In a large skillet heat butter and oil together. When hot, add fish fillets. Sauté until golden brown, about 2 to 3 minutes per side. Season with salt and pepper. Using a spatula, transfer fish to a serving platter. Top each fillet with a lemon slice and keep warm. ★ Add raisins, hazelnuts and pine nuts to skillet. Sauté over a low heat until pine nuts are golden brown, about 5 minutes. Stir occasionally. ★ Spoon sauce over fish fillets and serve immediately. *Picture page 71*

LOBSTER NEWBURG

A steady patron of Delmonico's in New York City was a certain Mr Wenburg, who invented this dish. But Mr Wenburg quarreled with Mr Delmonico, who changed the name of the dish to Newburg.

Serves 4 as a main course	*3 tablespoons flour*
4 cups cold boiled lobster meat	*1 cup whipping cream*
1/2 pound butter	*1/2 teaspoon salt*
1/4 cup dry sherry	*1/8 teaspoon cayenne pepper*

Cut lobster meat into chunks. Melt 1/4 pound butter in a skillet, add lobster meat and sauté for 1 minute. Pour sherry over meat. Remove skillet from heat and set aside. ★ Place remaining butter with flour and cream in the top of a double boiler over simmering water. Stir ingredients constantly until sauce thickens and is smooth. Add salt and cayenne pepper and stir to blend. Add lobster meat to cream sauce and continue to cook for 10 to 15 minutes. ★ Remove from heat and cool. Chill in refrigerator for 24 hours and reheat before serving.

MUSTARD SHAD ROE

MANHATTAN-STYLE

The shad is a fish found in New England and along the North Atlantic seaboard. Its roe is considered an especially sophisticated delicacy, and, like soft-shelled crabs, is seasonal.

Serves 4 as a main course
2 large shad roe
4 tablespoons butter
Mustard sauce:
2 teaspoons butter
1 teaspoon dry mustard
6 tablespoons heavy cream
1/2 teaspoon lemon juice
salt to taste
black pepper to taste

Preheat the boiler to high. Parboil roe for 2 to 3 minutes in a saucepan of boiling water. Remove from water, drain well, and place in a broiling pan. ★ Dot roe with 4 tablespoons butter. Broil for 5 minutes on each side, or until browned. ★ To make the mustard sauce, blend mustard and butter together in a small saucepan. Add cream and simmer for 10 minutes. Stir in lemon juice, salt and black pepper. Pour sauce over roe.

MARYLAND CRAB CAKES

This is a traditional English recipe from the Maryland-Virginia area.

Serves 4 to 6 as a main course
3 tablespoons butter
3/4 cup finely chopped onion
1 cup soft breadcrumbs
1 pound crabmeat, flaked and cleaned
3 eggs, beaten
3/4 teaspoon salt
1 teaspoon dry mustard
1 teaspoon Worcestershire sauce
1 to 2 tablespoons light cream
1/2 cup flour
vegetable oil for frying
lemon wedges

In a large skillet melt butter and add onions. Sauté onions until soft but not brown, about 3 minutes. Remove skillet from heat and stir in breadcrumbs and crabmeat. ★ In a large bowl mix together eggs, salt, mustard and Worcestershire sauce. Add crab mixture and enough cream to hold mixture together. Shape mixture into 12 cakes. Dredge cakes in flour. ★ Heat a 1/4-inch layer of oil in a large skillet. When hot add crab cakes. Fry until golden brown, about 3 minutes a side. Serve with lemon wedges and tartar sauce.

WALDORF SALAD

Recipe page 67

SAUTÉED SOLE WITH HAZELNUTS

Recipe page 68

MARYLAND FRIED CHICKEN
WITH GRAVY

Young spring chicken pieces are rolled in seasoned flour and fried in a heavy skillet. The cream gravy, made in the same skillet, is poured over the chicken.

Serves 4 as a main course

- *1 3- to 3½-pound frying chicken, cut into serving pieces*
- *6 slices bacon*
- *vegetable oil for frying*
- *¾ cup flour*
- *1 teaspoon salt*
- *¼ teaspoon black pepper*
- *2 tablespoons flour*
- *1 cup milk*
- *1 cup heavy cream*

In a large skillet, fry bacon until browned. Remove bacon and drain on paper towels. ★ Add enough vegetable oil to bacon drippings to make a 1-inch deep layer in skillet. ★ Place ¾ cup flour, salt and black pepper in a large plastic or paper bag. Shake well to blend. Coat each chicken piece in flour mixture by placing in bag and shaking. ★ Heat fat in skillet. When bubbling hot, add chicken pieces and fry, turning occasionally, until nicely browned on all sides. Cover skillet, reduce heat, and cook over a low heat for about 25 minutes or until tender when tested with a fork. Remove chicken, set aside and keep warm. ★ Drain all but 4 tablespoons of fat from skillet. Stir 2 tablespoons of flour and cook for about 3 minutes. Add milk and cream. Continue cooking, stirring occasionally, until gravy is thick and smooth. Add salt and pepper to taste. Pour gravy over hot chicken and garnish with bacon strips.

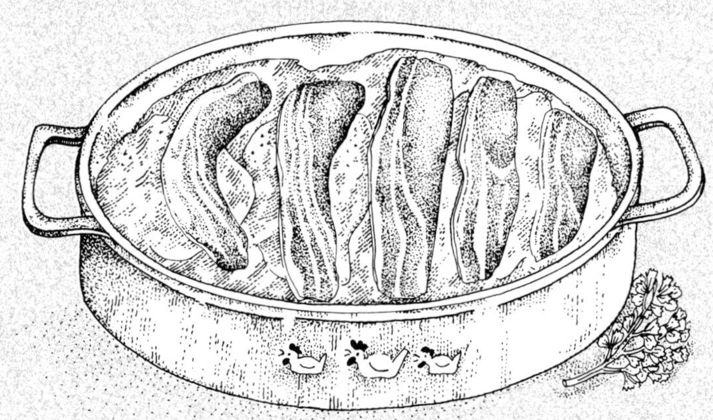

BUFFALO CHICKEN WINGS

In 1964 the owner of a bar in Buffalo, New York, received a large shipment of chicken wings by mistake. She fried them and served them with hot sauce and blue cheese dressing. They were such a success that every 29 July is now Chicken Wing Day in Buffalo.

Serves 4 as an appetizer

20 chicken wings

vegetable oil for frying

Hot sauce:

4 tablespoons butter

4 tablespoons Tabasco sauce

1/8 teaspoon cayenne pepper

salt to taste

black pepper to taste

Blue cheese dressing:

1 cup mayonnaise

2 tablespoons chopped onion

1 teaspoon minced garlic

1/2 cup sour cream

1 tablespoon white vinegar

1/4 cup crumbled blue cheese

Cut tip from each chicken wing. Cut membrane between remaining halves of wing. Fill a deep skillet with vegetable oil to a depth of 2 inches. Heat until very hot and add chicken wings. Deep-fry wings until golden brown, about 10 minutes. Remove from oil and drain on paper towels. ★ To make the hot sauce, melt butter in a small saucepan and add Tabasco sauce. Add cayenne pepper and salt and pepper to taste. Stir well. ★ To make the dressing, combine mayonnaise with onion, garlic, sour cream, vinegar and cheese in a bowl. Mix well. Serve chicken on a platter with bowls of each dressing in center.

CHICKEN À LA KING

Stories about the origins of this dish abound. One popular version is that chef Charles Ranhofer of Delmonico's Restaurant in New York City created it in the 1880s for Foxhall P. Keene, a loyal patron. Another tale claims that chef George Greenwald made it for Mr and Mrs E. Clark King III, the owners of the Brighton Beach Hotel in Brooklyn. Regardless of who invented it, the dish has been a favorite ever since.

Serves 6 as a main course

- *4 tablespoons butter*
- *4 tablespoons flour*
- *1 tablespoon vegetable oil*
- *2 cups chicken broth*
- *2 cups half and half*
- *1 tablespoon chopped onion*
- *1 cup sliced mushrooms*
- *1 green bell pepper, cut into strips*
- *1/2 cup drained chopped pimento*
- *3 cups diced cooked chicken*
- *salt to taste*
- *black pepper to taste*
- *2 egg yolks, beaten*
- *1/2 cup dry sherry*
- *1/2 cup slivered almonds*

Melt butter in a saucepan and stir in flour. Cook, stirring constantly, for 2 minutes. Add chicken broth and half and half; cook, stirring constantly, until thickened. Remove saucepan from heat and set aside. ★ In a skillet sauté onion, mushrooms and green pepper in vegetable oil. Add pimento and chicken. Season to taste with salt and pepper. ★ Add 2 tablespoons of reserved sauce to egg yolks and stir well. Add egg yolks and remaining sauce to skillet, stir well, and cook over low heat for 1 minute. Remove the skillet from heat and stir in sherry and almonds. Serve over rice, on toast or in pastry shells.

SCRAPPLE

Scrapple, a quintessential Pennsylvania Dutch dish, is also called "ponhaws."

Serves 8 as a breakfast dish

- *1 1/2 pounds pork shoulder*
- *1/4 pound pork liver*
- *4 cups water*
- *1 cup yellow cornmeal*
- *1 cup water*
- *1 teaspoon salt*
- *1/4 cup finely chopped onions*
- *1/4 teaspoon dried thyme*
- *1 teaspoon dried marjoram*
- *1/2 teaspoon pepper*
- *4 tablespoons flour*
- *4 tablespoons lard or vegetable oil*

In a saucepan combine pork shoulder and liver with water. Cook over a moderate heat for 1 hour. ★ Drain meat, reserving broth. Discard all bones and chop meat finely. ★ In a saucepan, combine cornmeal, salt, 1 cup water and 2 cups reserved broth. Cook mixture over a moderate heat, stirring constantly, until it thickens. ★ Add meat, onions and spices to cornmeal mixture. Cover pot and simmer for about 1 hour. Place mixture in a 9 × 5 × 3-inch loaf pan and chill until firm. Cut into slices about 1/2 inch thick. Coat slices with flour and fry in lard over a moderate heat until crisp on both sides. Serve at once.

EGGS BENEDICT

Mr and Mrs LeGrand Benedict were regular patrons in the 1920s of the legendary Delmonico's Restaurant in New York City. One day Mrs Benedict complained that there was nothing new on the menu. This dish was the restaurant's response.

Serves 2 as a brunch or supper dish

- *2 English muffins*
- *butter*
- *4 slices baked ham*
- *1 tablespoon vinegar*
- *1 teaspoon salt*
- *8 cups water*
- *4 eggs*

Hollandaise sauce:

- *3 egg yolks*
- *2 tablespoons lemon juice*
- *1/8 teaspoon cayenne pepper*
- *1/4 teaspoon salt*
- *1/2 cup melted butter*

Split and lightly toast muffins. Spread halves with butter. Melt additional butter in a skillet and add ham slices. Sauté until lightly browned on both sides. Arrange a ham slice over each muffin half and set aside in a warm place. ★ Combine vinegar, salt and water in a saucepan and bring to a boil. Break eggs into boiling water and poach for 5 minutes. Remove and drain eggs, then arrange one egg on each muffin half. Top with Hollandaise sauce and serve. ★ To make the Hollandaise sauce, combine egg yolks, lemon juice and cayenne pepper in a blender or food processor. Process for 3 seconds. With motor running, pour in butter in a slow, steady stream. Process 5 seconds longer if butter is not fully incorporated. Serve at once.

SHOOFLY PIE

So sweet that one has to shoo away the flies, this pie comes from the Pennsylvania Dutch.

Makes 1 9-inch dessert pie

- *1/2 recipe Easy Pie Crust (see page 47)*
- *1 1/2 cups flour*
- *1 cup brown sugar*
- *1/8 teaspoon salt*
- *1/4 cup cold butter*
- *1/2 teaspoons baking soda*
- *1/2 cup molasses*

Roll pie crust out and fit it into a 9-inch pie plate. Preheat oven to 350°F. ★ Combine flour, brown sugar and salt in a mixing bowl. With a pastry blender or two knives, work in butter until mixture resembles coarse crumbs. ★ Dissolve baking soda in molasses in a mixing bowl. Add three-quarters of crumb mixture and mix gently. Pour mixture into pie crust. Sprinkle with remaining crumbs and bake for 30 minutes, or until filling is firm.

APPLE FRITTERS

Possibly Italian in origin (frittata), these small pancakes are a favorite fall recipe.

Serves 6 as a snack

- *1/2 cup flour*
- *1/2 cup sugar*
- *1/8 teaspoon salt*
- *2 teaspoons baking powder*
- *2 eggs*
- *1/2 cup milk*
- *1/2 cup whipping cream*
- *2 cups finely chopped tart apples*
- *vegetable oil for frying*
- *superfine sugar*

In a mixing bowl combine flour, sugar, salt and baking powder. Beat in eggs, milk and cream. Continue beating until batter is smooth. Stir in chopped apples. ★ Heat oil in a deep skillet until hot, about 370°F to 375°F on a deep-fat thermometer. Drop batter by teaspoons into oil and fry until lightly golden. Drain on paper towels and sprinkle with superfine sugar. Serve with maple syrup or honey.

LEMONY CHEESECAKE

A rich, calorie-laden dessert, because of its graham cracker crust it resembles a pie more than a cake. For a different effect, a teaspoon or so of your favorite fruit jam or preserve is a good addition.

Makes 1 10-inch cake

4 cups graham cracker crumbs
1 cup sweet butter, melted
1/4 cup cold water
2 tablespoons unflavored gelatin
5 large eggs, separated
dash of salt
1/3 cup milk, scalded
24 ounces cream cheese, softened
1/3 cup lemon juice
1/4 cup orange-flavored liqueur
1/2 teaspoon pure vanilla extract
1/2 cup sugar
finely grated rind of 2 lemons

Preheat oven to 350°F. In a large bowl combine graham cracker crumbs and melted butter. Mix well, remove 1/3 cup crumbs and set aside. Press remaining crumbs into the bottom and up the sides of a buttered 10-inch springform pan. Bake crust for 12 to 15 minutes or until firm. Remove from oven and cool on a wire rack. Turn oven off. ★ In a small cup, soften gelatin in cold water for 4 to 5 minutes. In the top part of a double boiler, combine 3/4 cup sugar, egg yolks and salt. Beat well. Place over slowly simmering water. Add scalded milk, a little at a time, beating constantly until thick and smooth, approximately 5 minutes. Add gelatin mixture and stir until totally dissolved. Remove from heat and cool. ★ In a large bowl beat cream cheese until smooth. Add a small amount of egg yolk mixture and beat well. Fold in remaining egg yolks. Add lemon juice, orange liqueur and vanilla extract. Fold in until well blended. ★ In a large bowl beat egg whites until soft peaks begin to form. Add 1/2 cup sugar, a little at a time, beating until stiff but not dry. Gently fold egg whites in cheese mixture. ★ Turn mixture into prepared pan. Smooth top with a rubber spatula and sprinkle with reserved crumbs and grated lemon rind. Refrigerate for 8 hours or overnight.

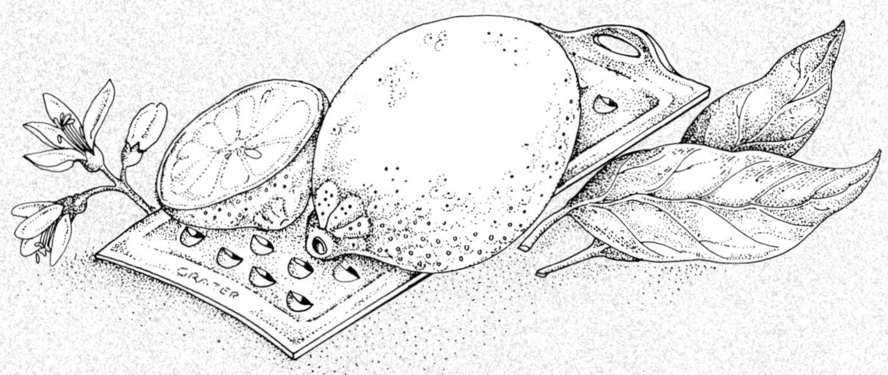

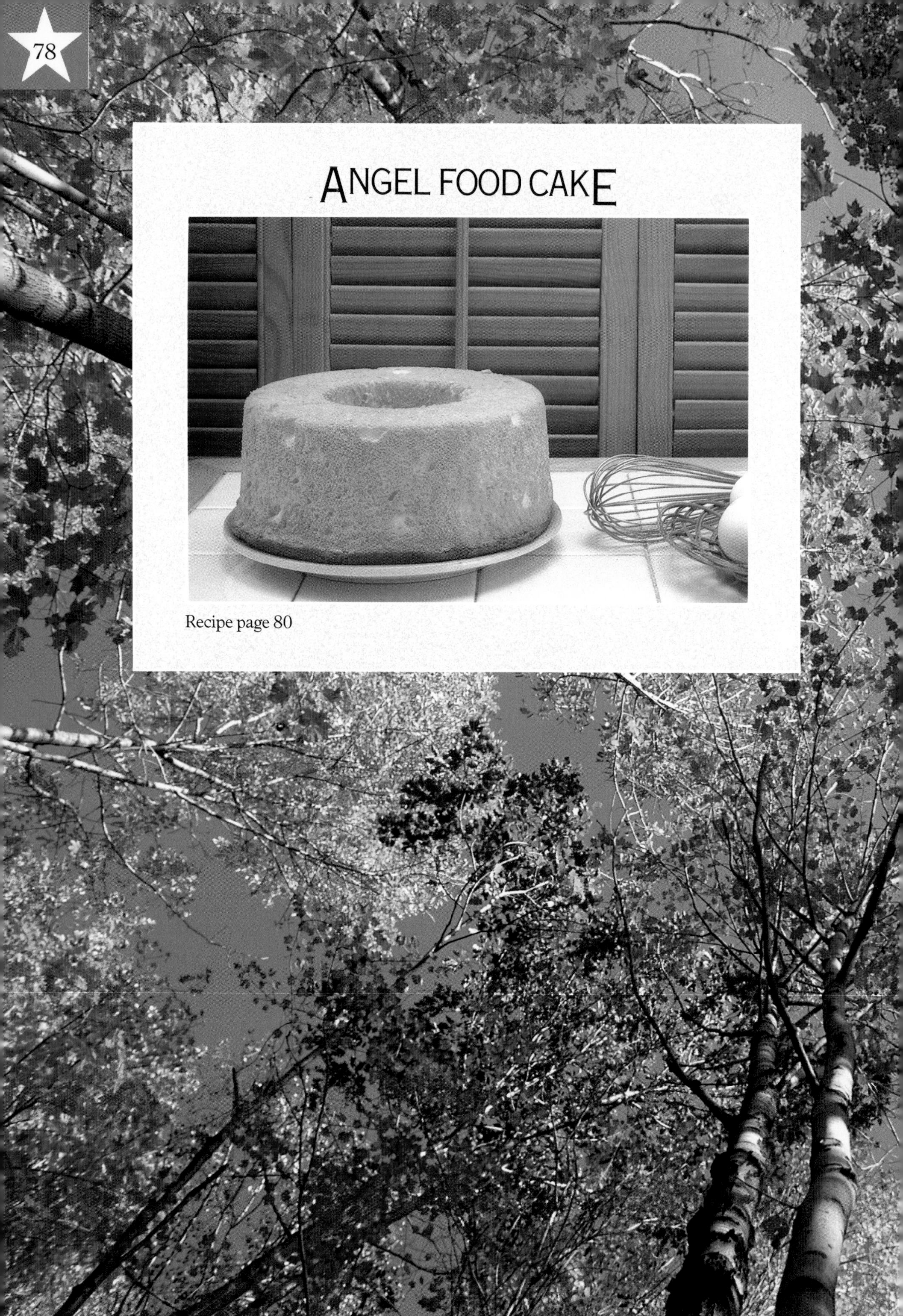

ANGEL FOOD CAKE

Recipe page 80

CHOW CHOW

Recipe page 83

ANGEL FOOD CAKE

This light dessert is often served at weddings.

Makes 1 10-inch cake
1½ cups sugar
6 eggs, separated
¾ teaspoon cream of tartar
1½ cups flour
1 teaspoon salt
½ teaspoon almond extract
½ cup water

Preheat oven to 350°F. Divide sugar into two ¾-cup portions. ★ In a medium-sized bowl beat egg whites until foamy. Add cream of tartar and beat until egg whites hold a soft peak. Add ¾ cup sugar and continue beating until whites are stiff but not dry. ★ In a large bowl beat egg yolks until lemon-yellow in color, approximately 3 minutes. Add remaining sugar and continue beating until yolks have thickened. Add flour, salt and almond extract to egg yolk mixture alternately with water, beating until smooth after each addition. ★ Carefully fold egg whites into egg yolk mixture. Gently pour batter into an unbuttered 10-inch tube pan. Bake for 1 hour or until cake tests done. ★ Remove from oven and place pan on a wire rack. Allow cake to cool completely in pan. Turn cake out on to plate and serve plain or with fresh fruit, ice cream or frost with a favorite frosting. *Picture page 78*

FUNNEL CAKES

Another Pennsylvania Dutch recipe, these cakes melt in the mouth.

Serves 6 as a snack or dessert
2 tablespoons sour cream
2 tablespoons heavy cream
2 eggs
2 cups milk
3-3¼ cups flour
1 tablespoon sugar
½ tablespoon baking powder
vegetable oil or lard for deep frying
superfine sugar

Stir together sour cream and heavy cream, then beat in eggs one at a time. Stir in milk. ★ Gradually stir in just enough flour to make a smooth, thick but easily pourable batter. Stir in sugar and baking powder. ★ Heat oil or lard in a deep fryer or large heavy skillet to a temperature of 375°F. With a funnel or pastry bag, dribble batter into oil in overlapping spirals, 3 to 4 tablespoons at a time. Fry 3 or 4 funnel cakes at one time, about 1 minute per side, until golden. Drain well on paper towels and dust with superfine sugar.

PHILADELPHIA CINNAMON BUNS

The historical city of Philadelphia, founded by Quakers, was the site for the convention held in 1787 to draw up the U.S. Constitution.

Makes 12 breakfast buns
4 cups flour
5 teaspoons baking powder
1½ teaspoons salt
¾ cup butter
⅔ cup whipping cream
2 eggs
1 cup firmly packed brown sugar
1 teaspoon cinnamon
½ cup finely chopped walnuts
½ cup raisins

Preheat oven to 400°F. In a large bowl combine flour, baking powder and salt. Cut in butter, using a pastry blender or two knives, until flour forms coarse crumbs. In a separate bowl beat eggs and add ½ cup cream. Add this to flour mixture and mix well. ★ Roll out dough on to a floured surface. Form it into a square approximately ½ inch thick and 12 × 12 inches square. ★ In a separate bowl mix together brown sugar, cinnamon, chopped walnuts and raisins. Spread this evenly over dough. Roll dough up like a jelly roll and pinch closed. Cut roll with a sharp knife into 12 1-inch slices. Lay slices on a buttered cookie sheet, brush with remaining cream, and bake for 20 minutes or until brown.

DUTCH APPLE BUTTER

For best results use Winesap, Jonathan or other sweetly-tart apples.

Makes 4 pints condiment
8 cups apple cider
3½ pounds cooking apples, cut into eighths
3 cups sugar
½ teaspoon ground cloves
1 tablespoon cinnamon
¼ teaspoon salt

Place apple cider in a large saucepan. Bring to a boil and boil for 15 minutes. Add apples to pot and cook until very tender. ★ When done, force apples through a sieve with the back of a spoon. Put sieved apples back into saucepan; discard peels and seeds in sieve. Add sugar, cloves, cinnamon and salt. Simmer slowly until thick, stirring frequently to prevent burning. Pour into sterilized jars or crocks, seal and store in a cool place.

FISH HOUSE PUNCH

The Fish House, founded in 1732 in Philadelphia, is a men's club. It was originally a fishing club, but it exists today as an exclusive dining society. It is said that the only days George Washington failed to record in his diary are those he spent at the Fish House. The authentic original recipe below explains why.

Serves 30 as a party drink

2 cups lemon juice
½ cup icing sugar
2 75-cl bottles gold rum
1 65-cl bottle brandy
1 cup peach brandy
2 cups cold sparkling water

The day before serving the punch, combine lemon juice and sugar in a mixing bowl. Stir well. Combine mixture with rum, brandy and peach brandy in a large container. Stir well, cover and refrigerate overnight or until well chilled. To serve, place a large ice block in an 8-quart punch bowl and add mixture. Pour in sparkling water and stir gently.

CHOCOLATE EGG CREAM

Chocolate egg cream contains neither eggs nor cream. It gets its name from the foamy, egg-like head that forms when it is properly made. It is a specialty of New York City soda fountains. Ideally, an egg cream is made with pressurized fountain seltzer. If you must use bottled sparkling water, be sure it is very bubbly and pour it from as high as you can.

Serves 1 as a treat

1½ ounces chocolate syrup
1½ ounces very cold milk
cold sparkling water

Put syrup into an 8-ounce glass and add milk. Stir well. Fill glass with sparkling water.

CHOW CHOW

This relish is a relic of New England's China clipper trade.

Makes 7 to 8 quarts relish	*3 tablespoons salt*
8 quarts green tomatoes, stemmed and chopped	*1 quart vinegar*
8 large onions, chopped	*1 tablespoon cinnamon*
10 green peppers, seeded and chopped	*1/4 teaspoon ground cloves*
3 small hot red chili peppers, seeded and chopped	*3 tablespoons dry mustard*
	2 bay leaves
	2 cups sugar
	1/2 cup prepared horseradish

In a large mixing bowl combine tomatoes, onions and peppers. Cover with salt and let stand overnight. Drain mixture well and put into a large pot. ★ Add vinegar to pot. Tie cinnamon, cloves, mustard and bay leaves into a square of cheesecloth and add to pot. Add sugar and horseradish. Bring mixture to a boil and reduce heat. Simmer until ingredients are tender, stirring frequently, about 15 minutes. ★ Place mixture into sterilized glass jars. Seal and cool. *Picture page 79*

MUSTARD-PICKLE BEANS

This recipe was once an efficient "putting-up" garden produce for the winter.

Makes about 4 quarts	*1/3 cup all-purpose flour*
4 quarts fresh green beans or wax beans, trimmed, stringed and cut into 1 1/2-inch pieces	*2 tablespoons whole mustard seeds*
3 cups cider vinegar	*1 teaspoon turmeric*
1/3 cup dry mustard	*1 teaspoon salt*
	2 cups firmly packed brown sugar

Boil beans in salted water for 3 to 5 minutes, until tender-crisp. Drain beans well and reserve. ★ Mix 1/2 cup vinegar with mustard, flour, mustard seeds, turmeric and salt to make a smooth paste. Put remaining vinegar and sugar in saucepan and bring to a boil, stirring occasionally, over a high heat. Reduce heat to a simmer and gradually stir in spice paste. Simmer for 5 minutes, add beans and cook for a further 5 minutes. Transfer beans and sauce to sterilized canning jars.

THE DEEP SOUTH

The South has many immigrant groups: the French, the English – both gentry and debtors – the Scots-Irish, and the black slaves. All have contributed to the rich culinary heritage of the region, retaining their separate identities while producing recipes that are unmistakably Southern.

The South is a romantic land, redolent of contrasts. It can be both mournfully reminiscent of faded glories and splendid with the still-present opulence of plantation life and sophisticated cities. It is a region of extremes, from the violent heat of summer to the soft air of fall (Southerners joke that they have three seasons: February, midsummer and sub-tropical). It is a land steeped in the traditions of gracious living, where youngsters still address adults as "Ma'am" and "Sir." But it is also a land of grinding poverty with the highest illiteracy rate in the nation. Frenetic activity is disdained in the South – Southerners are slow-moving and easy-going, and even their speech is characterized by a slow drawl. The landscape varies from the plantation blooms of rhododendron and magnolia to the decaying, fetid swamps of the bayous.

Southern cooking is a happy marriage of all these contrasts. Techniques and ingredients, both indigenous and imported, have been contributed in almost equal portion by the American Indians, the white settlers and their African slaves. Southern culinary tradition ranges from the plain plebeian fare of the New Orleans dish of red beans and rice (starch, starch and starch) to the Patrician grande cuisine of some of the most elegant tables in America. Southern cuisine can also be basic and hearty, as in the "soul food" staples of fried chicken, mustard greens and grits.

Essentially, the American South can be divided into three regions. The Tidewater region encompasses the area from the eastern shore of Maryland down through Virginia and North Carolina to South Carolina. The Deep South includes the gracious old ladies of Charleston, Savannah and Atlanta, the states of Georgia and Alabama, and parts of Mississippi. The third region is Creole and Acadian country – Louisiana and parts of Mississippi – the bayous, swamps and marshes bounded by the Delta and the Gulf of Mexico.

The Tidewater region was part of the original thirteen colonies and became home to English

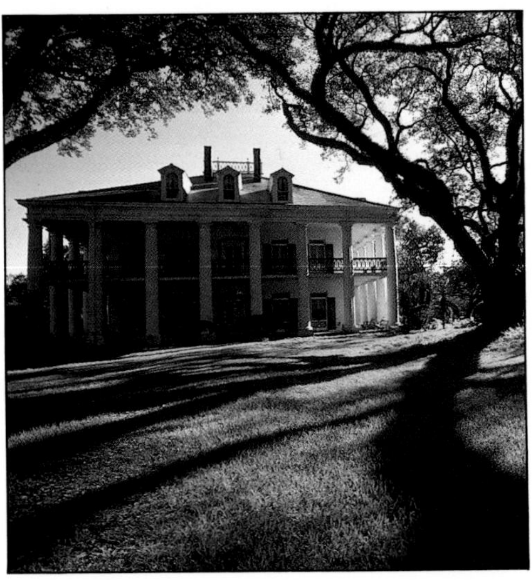

Oak Alley Plantation – the antebellum South

"second sons" – those who did not inherit the family estate often found a new home in the luxuriant countryside of Virginia, Maryland and North Carolina. As with all Britons, settling an alien land meant an opportunity to civilize the barbarians. British country traditions such as fox hunting were imported, along with plain, unadorned English cooking.

The Deep South was similarly settled by displaced Britons, with a large sprinkling of Scots and Irish who would later become the genteel plantation owners living in baronial splendor. Georgia, by contrast, received His Majesty's debtors, as the King cheerfully emptied his prisons of miscreants.

The insect-infested swamps of Louisiana became home to the wandering Acadians, evicted by the conquering British from their original settlement in Canada (once known as Acadia, today as Nova Scotia). These French refugees settled into the isolated bayous and lagoons to fish and farm and became known as "Cajuns," (a corruption of "Acadians" in the same way that "Injuns" is a corruption of "Indians"). To this day, the dialect heard in these wetlands is a curious patois of French, English, with a smattering of Spanish and even African terms.

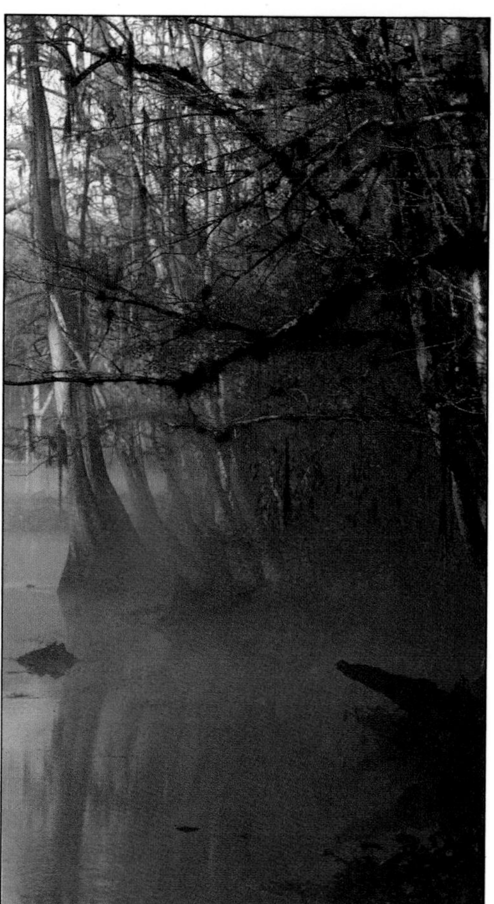

Mysterious Manatree Springs, Florida

Cajun cooking is true country cooking. A mixture of French, Spanish, African and Indian styles, it is hot – if the cooking spices don't bring tears to your eyes, the addition of Tabasco, a Louisiana concoction, will. Cajun food is generally spicier than Creole (city) food. More rice is used and it is often served in one big pot. Cajun kitchens are reputed to be wildly experimental – everything is thrown into the pot, results unknown. Cajun cooking, like Creole cooking, uses the roux – a mixture of fat (or butter) and flour – as the foundation for most recipes.

Creoles, as distinct from their country Cajun cousins, are defined as anyone with Spanish and French blood. The largest Creole concentration is found in New Orleans. This fabled city was founded as a French town by settlers coming up from the Gulf of Mexico, enriched by a Spanish occupation, and then bought from France by Thomas Jefferson as part of the Louisiana Purchase in 1803. Life in New Orleans is lived to the fullest and the city is justifiably proud of its reputation for excellent cooking. Mark Twain once remarked of a typical Creole dish that it was "as delicious as the less criminal forms of sin."

Ingredients in Southern cooking reflect the multi-cultural heritage of the region, enriched by West Indian, Cuban, Mexican and Haitian spices. Rice, corn and beans are the mainstay of most dishes. Rice is especially important: it has been estimated that Southerners eat five times as much rice as the rest of the nation. The mudbugs of the swamps, crayfish (pronounced "crawfish" by those in the know but also known as "crawdads" by some die-hards), are the mainstay of both Creole and Cajun cooking. Shellfish from the sea, lakes and swamps – including river shrimp, lake shrimp, oysters and crab – are important. Freshwater and saltwater fish are also used. To a lesser extent wild turkeys, ducks, frogs, turtles, sausage, pork, tomatoes, okra (originally brought over by African slaves), yams, pecans and oranges are also common in Southern recipes. And, of course, the succulent Virginia hams are world-famous.

SHE-CRAB SOUP

George Washington was served this soup on a visit to Charleston, South Carolina, in 1791. The soup need not be made with female crabs and their roe; any crabmeat will do.

Serves 6 to 8 as a first course

- *6 tablespoons butter*
- *1 tablespoon flour*
- *2 cups milk*
- *2 cups whipping cream*
- *1 teaspoon grated lemon rind*
- *1/4 teaspoon ground mace*
- *1 pound white crabmeat and roe (if possible), picked and flaked*
- *1 teaspoon salt*
- *1/4 teaspoon black pepper*
- *3 tablespoon dry sherry*
- *1 teaspoon finely chopped parsley*

Melt butter in the top of a double boiler over briskly boiling water. When melted, add flour and blend well. Pour in milk and cream. Stir constantly. Add grated lemon rind, mace and crabmeat and roe. Stir well and continue cooking for 20 minutes. Add salt and pepper. ★ Remove mixture from heat and allow to stand over hot water for 15 minutes. Stir in sherry and serve. Garnish each bowl with chopped parsley.

CRAB BISQUE

In the courtly days of antebellum splendor, a true gentleman was measured by how silently he could sip this lip-smacking soup.

Serves 6 as a first course

- *1/2 pound crabmeat, picked and flaked*
- *4 cups fish broth*
- *1 cup unflavored breadcrumbs*
- *1 onion, thinly sliced*
- *2 parsley sprigs*
- *1 bay leaf*
- *1/4 teaspoon dried thyme*
- *2 tablespoons softened butter*
- *1 cup heavy cream*
- *salt to taste*
- *black pepper to taste*
- *1/8 teaspoon cayenne pepper*
- *2 tablespoons chopped cooked shrimp*
- *1 tablespoon sweet butter*

In a large saucepan combine fish broth, crabmeat, breadcrumbs, onion, parsley, bay leaf and thyme. Bring mixture to a boil. Lower heat and simmer gently for 20 minutes. ★ Strain soup through a sieve and return liquid to saucepan. Discard solids in sieve. Add softened butter and heat soup just to boiling point. Add cream and season with salt, pepper, and cayenne. Heat soup through, but do not let it boil. ★ Just before serving, stir in shrimp and sweet butter. Serve hot.

WILLIAMSBURG
CREAM OF PEANUT SOUP

This dish is a specialty of the King's Arms Tavern at the Williamsburg restoration in Virginia. Diners there are served by waiters in authentic eighteenth-century garb.

Serves 8 as a first course

1 medium-sized onion, finely chopped

½ cup finely chopped celery

4 tablespoons butter

2 quarts chicken broth

1 cup smooth peanut butter

2 cups half and half

salt to taste

black pepper to taste

chopped peanuts for garnish

In a large skillet sauté onion and celery in butter until soft but not browned. Add flour and stir well. Pour in 1 cup chicken broth and bring mixture to a boil, stirring frequently. ★ Remove mixture from heat and place ½ cup at a time in a blender or food processor. Blend until smooth. Return blended mixture to skillet and add remaining chicken broth, half and half and peanut butter. Whisk while heating gently. Do not allow mixture to boil. Season to taste with salt and pepper. ★ Serve hot or cold, garnished with chopped peanuts.

BEAN SALAD

This salad is a Southern favorite: two kinds of beans in a spicy mixture of pepper, onions, pimentos and cayenne pepper.

Serves 4 as a side dish

1 cup cooked white beans, well drained
1 cup cooked kidney beans, well drained
1 cup finely chopped green pepper
1 tablespoon chopped onions
1 tablespoon chopped pimento
½ teaspoon salt
¼ teaspoon black pepper
⅛ teaspoon cayenne pepper
¼ cup white wine vinegar
½ cup olive oil

In a large bowl combine beans, green pepper, onions and pimento. Sprinkle salt, pepper and cayenne over salad. ★ In a mixing bowl combine vinegar and olive oil. Whisk until well blended. Pour only enough oil and vinegar over salad to moisten it well. Toss. Chill for 1 hour and serve.

Picture page 92

LOUISIANA CANAPÉS

Garlic, tomato, peppers and cayenne are flavors automatically associated with Creole cooking.

Serves 6 as an appetizer

1 tablespoon butter
1 cup minced boiled ham
2 small onions, minced
1 garlic clove, minced
1 large tomato, peeled and minced
1 large green pepper, minced
⅛ teaspoon cayenne pepper
6 slices toast, buttered and cut into strips
4 tablespoons grated Parmesan cheese
1 teaspoon salt
1 teaspoon freshly ground pepper

Preheat oven to 300°F. Melt butter in a saucepan and add ham, onions and garlic. Stirring constantly, lightly sauté ham, onions and garlic for 3 minutes. Add tomato, green pepper and cayenne. Cook over a medium heat, stirring frequently, until mixture cooks down to an almost dry preparation. ★ Remove almost dry mixture from saucepan and spread evenly on strips of buttered toast. Put toast strips on a heatproof serving dish and evenly sprinkle with Parmesan cheese. Bake for 5 minutes. Serve hot.

CREOLE-STYLE STEWED OKRA

A Creole is any American descendant of early French and Spanish colonists. Creoles settled in New Orleans and the surrounding bayous of Louisiana. Generally Creole cuisine is less spicy than Acadian (Cajun) cooking.

Serves 6 to 8 as a side dish

3 to 4 dozen fresh okra
1 tablespoon butter
3 tomatoes, finely chopped, with their juice
1 onion, minced
1 green pepper, minced
1 garlic clove, chopped
salt to taste
black pepper to taste
cayenne pepper to taste
1 teaspoon chopped parsley

Wash and trim okra. Set aside. ★ In a saucepan melt butter and add onion, garlic and green pepper. Stir well and sauté for 5 to 8 minutes. Add tomatoes and their juice. Season to taste with salt, pepper and cayenne pepper. Add parsley. Add okra and simmer slowly for 20 minutes. Serve hot.

CORN AND OKRA MIX

Okra is a staple of both Creole cooking and Southern Black – or "soul food" – cooking.

Serves 4 to 6 as a side dish

4 strips bacon
4 tablespoons bacon drippings
1 onion, finely chopped
1 cup thinly sliced fresh okra
3 cups fresh corn, cut from the cob
3 large tomatoes, peeled and diced
1 teaspoon sugar
salt to taste
black pepper to taste
1/4 teaspoon Tabasco sauce

In a large skillet, fry bacon until crisp and brown. Drain on paper towels and reserve. Discard all but 4 tablespoons of the bacon drippings. ★ Add corn, okra and onion to hot bacon drippings. Sauté for 10 minutes, stirring constantly. Add tomatoes, sugar, salt, pepper and Tabasco sauce. Cover skillet and simmer over low heat for 25 minutes. Stir occasionally. ★ Remove skillet from heat. Season to taste with additional Tabasco sauce and sprinkle with crumbled bacon.

Picture page 92

HOPPIN' JOHN

How this dish got its name is a mystery. Southern custom holds that, if eaten on New Year's Day, it ensures good luck for the next year.

Serves 6 to 8 as a side dish

1 cup dried black-eyed peas or cowpeas
1 teaspoon salt
1 medium-sized onion, diced
2 ounces salt pork, diced
1/4 teaspoon black pepper
1/8 teaspoon cayenne pepper
1 cup raw long-grain rice
1 tablespoon butter

Rinse black-eyed peas well. Put peas in a bowl with 3 cups of cold water and soak for 8 hours or overnight. Drain well. ★ Place black-eyed peas, salt, onion, and salt pork in a large pot. Add 3 cups cold water. Cover pot and bring to a boil. Lower heat and simmer for 1 1/4 hours, or until peas are tender. There should be very little water left in pot. Season with black pepper and cayenne pepper. ★ Bring 1 1/2 cups water to a boil in a saucepan. Add rice, lower heat, and cook, covered, for 18 minutes or until water is absorbed. Add butter and toss. Add rice to black-eyed peas and cook for 2 to 3 minutes to blend flavors. Serve hot.

HUSH PUPPIES

Deep-fried hush puppies are served with fried fish in the South.

Makes 12 hush puppies

1 1/2 cups white cornmeal
1/2 cup flour
1/8 teaspoon salt
2 tablespoons baking powder
1/2 teaspoon baking soda
1 egg
1 cup buttermilk
1 onion, finely chopped
4 tablespoons bacon drippings, lard or vegetable oil

In a large bowl combine flour, salt, baking powder and baking soda. Mix well. Stir in cornmeal. Add egg and beat mixture with a wooden spoon until smooth. ★ Pour in buttermilk and stir until absorbed. Stir in onion. ★ In a deep skillet heat bacon drippings until very hot – 375°F on a deep-frying thermometer. The fat should be to a depth of 2 to 3 inches in skillet. ★ Drop hush puppies by rounded teaspoons into fat. Fry, turning frequently, until golden, about 3 minutes. Serve warm with butter.

HOMINY GRITS

Hominy grits are hominy ground into a coarse meal. Grits are often served as a side dish with butter or gravy or as a breakfast cereal with butter and cream.

Serves 4 to 6 as a side dish

- *5 cups water*
- *1 teaspoon salt*
- *1 cup regular white hominy grits*
- *1 tablespoon butter*
- *salt to taste*
- *black pepper to taste*

In a heavy saucepan bring water and salt to a boil. Slowly stir in grits. Stir constantly to form a smooth mixture. Lower heat and cover saucepan. Cook 25 to 35 minutes, stirring occasionally. Stir in butter and season with salt and pepper to taste.

FRIED CORN

This popular dish, which is actually stewed, is misleadingly called fried corn throughout the South.

Serves 4 as a side dish

- *1/2 cup boiling water*
- *1/3 cup milk*
- *2 tablespoons bacon drippings*
- *1 teaspoon salt*
- *1/2 teaspoon sugar*
- *1/4 teaspoon black pepper*
- *3 cups fresh corn, cut from the cob*
- *1 tablespoon flour*
- *2 tablespoons cold water*
- *1 teaspoon butter*

In a saucepan combine boiling water, milk, bacon drippings, salt, sugar and pepper. Add corn and stir. Bring mixture to a boil over a low heat. When corn begins to boil, cover and cook for 10 minutes, or until corn is tender. Stir occasionally. ★ In a small bowl combine flour and water. Blend until smooth and add to corn mixture. Stir and cook for a further minute, or until corn begins to thicken. Remove from heat, stir in butter and serve.

BEAN SALAD

Recipe page 88

CORN AND OKRA MIX

Recipe page 89

RED RICE

Rice is the heart and soul of Southern cooking. Southerners consume five times the amount other Americans do.

Serves 4 as a side dish

6 slices bacon
1 cup finely chopped onions
1/2 cup finely chopped sweet red pepper
1 cup raw long-grain rice
1/8 teaspoon Tabasco sauce
1 teaspoon paprika
1 teaspoon sugar
1 teaspoon salt
2 medium-sized ripe tomatoes, peeled, seeded and coarsely chopped
1 1/2 cups cold water

Fry bacon in a heavy skillet until brown and crisp. Drain on paper towels. Crumble and set aside. ★ Discard all but 4 tablespoons of bacon fat. Add onions and red pepper. Sauté, stirring frequently, until onions are soft but not brown, about 5 minutes. Add rice and stir until grains are well coated. Stir in Tabasco sauce, paprika, sugar, salt, tomatoes and water. ★ Bring mixture to a boil over a high heat. Cover skillet, reduce heat, and simmer for 20 minutes or until rice is tender. Remove from heat and let stand, covered, for 5 to 10 minutes. Place rice in a serving bowl, sprinkle with crumbled bacon and serve.

DIRTY RICE

Don't be put off by the name. This dish is unassuming but delicious. It is called dirty rice because of its appearance.

Serves 6 to 8 as a side dish

1 1/2 cups brown rice
3 1/2 cups water
1 1/2 teaspoons salt
2 onions, finely chopped
2 green peppers, finely chopped
4 celery stalks, with leaves, finely chopped
garlic clove, finely chopped
2 tablespoons bacon drippings
1/2 pound chicken giblets, chopped
Tabasco sauce to taste
Worcestershire sauce to taste
salt to taste
cayenne pepper to taste
black pepper to taste

Bring water and salt to a boil in a medium saucepan. Add rice, cover tightly, and lower heat. Cook for 50 minutes or until all the water is absorbed. Set rice aside. Heat bacon drippings in a skillet. Add onions, green peppers, celery and garlic. Sauté for 30 minutes or until most of the liquid is gone. ★ Add chopped chicken giblets (gizzards, livers and hearts) and sauté until browned. Add Tabasco sauce, Worcestershire sauce, salt, cayenne pepper and black pepper. Mix in rice. Combine well and heat thoroughly. Serve hot.

RED BEANS AND RICE

This recipe is to the South what baked beans are to Boston.

Serves 8 to 10 as a side dish

1 pound dried red kidney beans
2 small ham hocks
2 tablespoons vegetable oil
1 tablespoon finely chopped garlic
2 cups finely chopped onion
1 cup finely chopped green pepper
1 cup finely chopped celery
1/4 cup finely chopped parsley
1/4 teaspoon cayenne pepper
1 bay leaf
1/2 teaspoon dried thyme
1 teaspoon Tabasco sauce
1 teaspoon sugar
salt to taste
black pepper to taste
1 cup canned stewed tomatoes
1 pound smoked sausage, cut into thick slices
1 cup finely chopped green onions for garnish

Put beans and ham hocks in a large bowl. Add 8 cups cold water and soak beans and ham hocks overnight. ★ Drain beans and ham hocks and put into a large heavy pot or Dutch oven. Add 8 cups cold water and bring to a boil over a moderate heat. Boil for 10 minutes. ★ Heat oil in a skillet and add garlic, onion, green pepper and celery. Sauté stirring often, for 3 minutes. Add mixture to beans. Add parsley, cayenne pepper, bay leaf, thyme, Tabasco sauce, sugar, salt, black pepper and tomatoes to beans. Stir well. Cook beans, uncovered, over moderate heat for 2 hours. Stir occasionally. After beans have cooked for 1½ hours, add sausage slices. ★ Just before beans are ready to serve, remove 1 cup beans, with cooking liquid, from pot. Puree removed beans in a blender or food processor and return purée to pot. Stir well. ★ Serve beans over rice in deep soup bowls. Garnish each serving with chopped green onions.

CALAS
(DEEP-FRIED RICE BALLS)

This old Creole breakfast dish is still eaten today. Traditionally this New Orleans recipe was served with golden syrup, but nowadays it is often accompanied by fresh seasonal berries and cream cheese.

Serves 6 to 8 as a breakfast dish

- *½ package active dry yeast*
- *½ cup very warm water*
- *1½ cups very soft cooked rice*
- *3 eggs, beaten*
- *1¼ cups flour*
- *¼ cup sugar*
- *½ teaspoon salt*
- *¼ teaspoon grated nutmeg*
- *oil for deep frying*
- *confectioner's sugar*

Pour water into a bowl. Sprinkle on yeast and let stand for a few minutes, then stir until completely dissolved. ★ Place cooked rice in a mixing bowl. Mash and let cool until lukewarm. Stir yeast mixture into rice and mix well. Cover bowl and let rise overnight. ★ Add eggs, flour, sugar, salt and nutmeg to risen mixture and beat until smooth. Let stand in a warm place for 30 minutes (an oven that has been heated and then turned off is ideal). ★ Fill a large deep skillet with oil to a depth of 1 inch. Heat until oil is very hot. Drop rice mixture by tablespoons into oil. Fry until golden, about 3 minutes. Drain on paper towels. Dust with confectioner's sugar and serve hot.

CREOLE BOILED SHRIMP

Shrimp are a keystone of Creole cuisine. Large shrimp dinners are held, with diners attacking huge mounds of boiled shrimp, washed down with bottles of beer.

Serves 6 to 8 as a main course

- *100 uncooked shrimp*
- *3 tablespoons salt*
- *1 large head celery with leaves, coarsely chopped*
- *1 teaspoon whole allspice*
- *½ teaspoon whole mace*
- *6 whole cloves*
- *4 parsley sprigs*
- *4 bay leaves*
- *½ teaspoon dried thyme*
- *1 dried hot red chili pepper*
- *salt to taste*
- *black pepper to taste*
- *cayenne pepper to taste*

Fill a very large pot with water and add 3 tablespoons salt. Add celery, allspice, mace, cloves, thyme, parsley, bay leaves, cayenne pepper and red chili pepper. Bring water to a boil. Allow water to boil for 3 minutes. ★ Drop all shrimp into pot at once. Boil for 10 minutes and then remove pot from heat. Set aside and cool shrimp in the cooking liquid. Drain and serve at room temperature.

SHRIMP GUMBO

Halfway between a stew and a soup, filé powder thickens this dish. Filé was introduced to the white settlers by the Choctaw Indians who inhabited much of modern-day Mississippi, Alabama, Georgia and Louisiana.

Serves 4 to 6 as a main course

- *1/4 cup butter*
- *2 onions, finely chopped*
- *1 garlic clove, finely chopped*
- *3 green peppers, coarsely chopped*
- *1 large can tomatoes*
- *1 bay leaf*
- *2 teaspoons salt*
- *1/4 teaspoon black pepper*
- *1/8 teaspoon cayenne pepper*
- *1 1/2 pounds uncooked shrimp, shelled and deveined*
- *1 teaspoon filé powder*

Melt butter in a large saucepan. Add onions, garlic and green peppers. Stir and cook over a low heat until tender, about 5 to 8 minutes. Add tomatoes with their liquid and bay leaf. Stir and simmer gently for 25 to 30 minutes. Season with salt, black pepper and cayenne pepper. ★ Add shrimp and cook for a further 5 minutes. Add filé powder and stir well. Do not allow mixture to come to a boil after filé has been added or it will become stringy. Serve immediately.

SHRIMP CREOLE

This dish is popular all year round, but is a particular favorite of visitors to the Mardi Gras.

Serves 4 to 6 as a main course
2 tablespoons butter
2 tablespoons flour
1 cup chopped onion
1/3 cup chopped green pepper
2 garlic cloves, chopped
3 cups canned tomatoes, with their liquid
1 pound fresh okra, sliced
2 bay leaves
salt to taste
black pepper to taste
1/2 teaspoon Tabasco sauce
2 pounds uncooked shrimp, shelled and deveined

Melt butter in a large heavy skillet. Stir in flour and cook over a low heat, stirring constantly, until flour is a medium brown color. Add onion, green pepper and garlic. Cook, stirring occasionally, until onion is soft, about 5 to 8 minutes. Stir in tomatoes, okra, bay leaves, salt, pepper and Tabasco sauce. Bring mixture to a boil and then lower heat. Cover skillet and simmer for 30 minutes, stirring frequently. ★ Add shrimp and cook for a further 10 minutes. If mixture is too thick, thin with a little hot water. Serve with rice.

CRAB NORFOLK

Created in 1924 by W.O. Snowden of the Snowden and Mason Restaurant in Norfolk, Virginia.

Serves 4 as a first course
1 pound cooked crabmeat
2 tablespoons vinegar
1/2 teaspoon Tabasco sauce
1/2 teaspoon Worcestershire sauce
salt to taste
black pepper to taste
4 tablespoons melted butter

Preheat oven to 350°F. Combine crabmeat with vinegar, Tabasco sauce, Worcestershire sauce, salt and pepper in a mixing bowl. Divide melted butter among four individual ovenproof serving dishes. Fill each dish with crabmeat mixture and bake until very hot, about 15 minutes.

OYSTERS ROCKEFELLER

In 1899 there was a serious shortage of snails exported from Europe to the United States. Jules Alciatore of the famed Antoine's restaurant in New Orleans, Louisiana, created this dish in response. He named it after one of the wealthiest men in America, John D. Rockefeller, because the green sauce is so rich. At the time oysters were so abundant as to be a poor man's food.

Serves 4 as a first course

24 fresh oysters, in the shell

rock salt

1 green onion, green part only, finely chopped

1 small celery stalk, with leaves, finely chopped

1/2 teaspoon dried chervil

1/2 teaspoon dried tarragon

1/4 cup fine unflavored breadcrumbs

2 teaspoons Tabasco sauce

1/2 cup butter, softened

1 teaspoon Pernod or anisette

1 tablespoon white wine

Scrub oysters well. Remove and discard top shell. Fill a baking pan with rock salt and arrange oysters on the half shell on salt. (This will keep them hot until they are served.) ★ Preheat broiler to high. Combine green onion, celery stalk, chervil, tarragon, breadcrumbs, Tabasco sauce, butter, Pernod and white wine in a blender or food processor. Process until well blended. Force mixture through a sieve with the back of a spoon. Place a spoonful of mixture on each oyster. Broil until brown, about 5 to 8 minutes. Serve at once.

JAMBALAYA

This dish is best when made for a crowd. An amalgam of French and Spanish cooking traditions, jambalaya is a distinctively Cajun dish.

Serves 10 as a main course

3 3-pound chickens, cut into serving pieces
flour for dredging
4 tablespoons lard or bacon drippings
3 cups chopped onion
2 cups chopped sweet red pepper
1 green onion, thinly sliced
2 garlic cloves, chopped
½ pound lean baked ham, cut into ½-inch squares
1½ pounds lean pork, trimmed of fat and cut into ½-inch cubes
6 hot sausages, thinly sliced
½ pound cooked shrimp, shelled and deveined
3 teaspoons salt
1 teaspoon black pepper
½ teaspoon Tabasco sauce
4 bay leaves
1½ cups raw long-grain rice
2 cups hot chicken broth
1 cup hot water

Wash chicken pieces and remove all fat and skin. If breasts are very large, cut in half. Dredge chicken in flour and shake off any excess. ★ In a large deep casserole, heat lard or bacon drippings. Add chicken and quickly brown pieces on all sides over high heat. Remove browned chicken pieces to a warm place. ★ Add onion, red pepper, green onions, garlic, ham and pork to casserole. Reduce heat to medium and cook, stirring constantly, for 15 to 20 minutes, or until both vegetables and ham are browned. Add sausage slices to casserole. Stir in salt, pepper and bay leaves. Cook, stirring constantly, for 4 minutes. ★ Return chicken pieces to pot. Stir in shrimp, rice, chicken broth and hot water. Mix well. Raise heat and bring mixture to a boil. Immediately reduce heat to very low. Cover pot and cook for 20 minutes, stirring occasionally. Uncover casserole, raise heat to medium, and cook, stirring often, for 10 minutes longer, or until rice is fluffy and dry. Serve immediately.

SOUTHERN FRIED CHICKEN

Southern fried chicken is synonymous with the South.

Serves 4 as a main course

- *1 3-pound frying chicken, cut into serving pieces*
- *2½ cups vegetable oil*
- *1 cup flour*
- *1 teaspoon salt*
- *1 teaspoon freshly ground black pepper*

Put flour into a strong, small brown paper bag. Drop 2 pieces of chicken into bag at a time and shake until well-coated. Put coated pieces on a flat surface and sprinkle with salt and pepper. ★ Heat oil in a large, heavy skillet until hot. Carefully place chicken in hot oil, using kitchen tongs. Cover and cook, turning pieces over 4 to 5 times, for 25 to 30 minutes, or until golden brown. Remove chicken and drain on paper towels. To keep chicken crisp, loosely wrap each piece in waxed paper.

BOUDIN BLANC

Literally "white pudding," these sausages are still made at large hog-butchering parties in Cajun country.

Makes 3 pounds dinner sausages

- *1 pound white chicken meat, ground*
- *1 pound pork shoulder, ground*
- *1 pound pork fat, ground*
- *salt to taste*
- *black pepper to taste*
- *cayenne pepper to taste*
- *1 onion, finely chopped*
- *1 garlic clove, finely chopped*
- *¼ cup unflavored breadcrumbs*
- *2¼ cups whipping cream*
- *2 egg yolks, beaten*
- *sausage casings*

Combine ground chicken, pork and pork fat in a large bowl. Season liberally with salt, black pepper and cayenne pepper. Add onion, garlic, breadcrumbs and ¼ cup cream. Mix well. ★ Put remaining cream into a saucepan and add sausage mixture. Cook over a moderate heat for 15 minutes. Add egg yolks, stir well and remove from heat. Let cool. ★ Fill sausage casings with mixture, making sausages about 3 to 4 inches long. ★ Boil sausages for 20 minutes in a large pot filled half with water and half with milk. Drain, prick sausages gently with a fork and broil until browned.

GUMBO FILÉ

A true gumbo must be made with filé powder, which gives it a slightly astringent flavor. This Cajun specialty from the bayous of Louisiana is made from sassafras leaves. Most well-stocked gourmet shops carry the powder.

Serves 6 as a main course

1 5-pound chicken, cut into serving pieces
2 teaspoons salt
1 teaspoon black pepper
1 garlic clove, chopped
3 tablespoons butter
2 medium-sized onions, chopped
1/2 pound boiled ham, cut into strips
3 quarts water
1/2 teaspoon dried thyme
1/2 teaspoon dried rosemary
1/4 teaspoon chili powder
1 cup canned stewed tomatoes
1 cup sliced fresh okra
24 oysters, shelled
1 tablespoon filé powder

Rub salt, pepper and garlic pieces into chicken. ★ In a large saucepan, melt butter. Add onions and chicken and cook until chicken pieces are lightly browned, about 8 minutes. Add ham, water, thyme, rosemary, chili powder and tomatoes. Cover and simmer for 2 hours. Add okra and cook for 1 hour longer. ★ Add oysters. Bring mixture to a boil and cook for 3 minutes. Remove saucepan from heat and stir in filé powder. Mix well. Do not allow gumbo to boil. Do not reheat gumbo after filé powder has been added or gumbo will become stringy. Serve hot in soup bowls.

BRUNSWICK STEW

The original recipe for Brunswick stew called for squirrel instead of chicken. Brunswick County, North Carolina, and Brunswick County, Virginia, still argue about where this stew originally came from.

Serves 12 as a main course

2 3-pound chickens, cut into serving pieces
2 pounds boneless veal shoulder, in 1 piece
1 ham bone
3 quarts water
1/2 cup sugar
1 bay leaf
1 teaspoon dried basil
1 tablespoon chopped fresh parsley
2 onions, sliced
4 cups tomatoes, peeled and chopped
4 cups celery sticks with leaves, chopped
2 cups fresh lima beans
4 cups fresh corn, cut from the cob
1/2 cup butter
1 teaspoon hot red pepper flakes
4 medium-sized potatoes, peeled, boiled and mashed

In a very large pot combine chicken, veal, ham bone, water, sugar, bay leaf, basil and parsley. Cook over a low heat until veal and chicken are very tender, about 50 minutes. Remove veal and chicken pieces from broth and set aside. ★ Add onions, tomatoes, celery and lima beans to broth. Cook over a low heat until beans are tender, about 15 minutes. Stir often. ★ Cut veal into small pieces. Remove chicken from bones and cut into small pieces. Discard bones and skin. ★ Return veal and chicken meat to pot. Add corn and simmer stew for 10 minutes. ★ Stir in butter, red pepper flakes and black pepper. Season with salt. Stir mashed potatoes into stew. Cook, stirring constantly, for 15 minutes or until stew thickens and potatoes are absorbed. Serve hot.

Pecan Pie

Recipe page 108

KENTUCKY BURGOO

Although burgoo originated as a sort of thick porridge on board sailing vessels in the mid-1800s, it came to mean a thick meat stew as made in Kentucky. Burgoo is made in huge quantities for large events like fourth of July picnics and Kentucky Derby Day.

Serves 10 as a main course

- *2½ tablespoons lard or olive oil*
- *1 pound lean beef shank*
- *1 pound beef bones*
- *½ pound boneless veal shoulder*
- *1 3-pound chicken, quartered*
- *2 quarts water*
- *1½ teaspoons salt*
- *2 cups chopped onion*
- *1 garlic clove, chopped*
- *1 large potato, peeled and diced*
- *4 celery stalks with leaves, diced*
- *1 large can tomatoes*
- *3 carrots, diced*
- *1 large green pepper, chopped*
- *1 cup fresh butter beans or waxed beans*
- *½ teaspoon hot red pepper flakes*
- *1 small onion*
- *1 bay leaf*
- *3 tablespoons dark brown sugar*
- *¼ teaspoon black pepper*
- *1 cup sliced fresh okra*
- *1½ cups fresh corn, cut from the cob*
- *¼ cup butter*
- *½ cup flour*
- *½ cup finely chopped parsley*

In a large pot, heat 1¼ tablespoons lard or oil. Add beef shank, beef bones and veal. Brown well for about 8 minutes. Add chicken, water and salt. Cover and cook over a low heat until very tender, about 30 to 40 minutes. ★ Remove meat and chicken to a plate. When cool enough to handle, remove meat and chicken from bones. Cut into small pieces and return to pot. Discard bones and chicken skin. ★ In a skillet, sauté onions in remaining lard or oil until soft but not brown, about 5 minutes. Add to meat in pot. Stir in garlic, potato, celery, tomatoes, carrots, green pepper, beans, hot red pepper, whole onion, bay leaf, brown sugar and black pepper. Cook over a low heat for 2 hours, stirring occasionally. ★ After 2 hours, add okra and corn. Cook for a further 15 minutes. ★ In a small bowl, blend together butter and flour. Add to burgoo and cook, stirring constantly, until mixture thickens. Season to taste and sprinkle with chopped parsley before serving.

HAM WITH REDEYE GRAVY

This traditional Southern gravy takes its name from the "red eye" that appears when it is reduced. Serve it over ham, biscuits or grits.

Serves 4 as a main course
2 teaspoons butter
2 large ham steaks
½ cup strong black coffee

Melt butter in a large heavy skillet and add ham steaks. Fry until browned on both sides, about 10 minutes. Remove ham and set aside. ★ Add coffee to drippings in skillet and cook for 3 minutes, stirring constantly to scrape up and dissolve pan deposits. Pour gravy over ham.

"SHUSHED" EGGS

This is the Mississippi version of scrambled eggs.

Serves 4 as a breakfast dish
8 eggs
4 teaspoons butter
salt to taste
black pepper to taste

In a heavy skillet, melt butter and let it brown slightly. Break eggs into a bowl and season to taste with salt and black pepper. Beat only until yolks and whites are barely mixed. Do not overmix. ★ Pour eggs into brown butter. Stir, cooking only until eggs are set, about 3 minutes. Serve hot.

PECAN PIE

This is probably the single most classic dessert of the Southern repertoire. The filling should be meltingly chewy.

Makes 1 9-inch dessert pie	*2 tablespoons butter, melted and cooled*
1/2 recipe Easy Pie Crust (see page 47)	*1 teaspoon pure vanilla extract*
4 eggs	*1 1/2 cups pecan halves*
2 cups dark corn syrup	

Preheat oven to 400°F. Roll out pie crust and fit into a 9-inch pie plate. Line pie-crust with a buttered sheet of aluminum foil. Bake for 10 minutes. Remove foil and bake for a further 2 minutes. Remove from oven and cool. ★ In a large bowl whisk eggs for about 30 seconds or until smooth. Continue whisking and pour in corn syrup in a slow continuous stream. Add vanilla extract and melted butter. Continue to whisk until ingredients are well blended. ★ Pour mixture into cooled pie shell and top with pecan halves. Bake on middle shelf of oven for 35 to 40 minutes or until firm. Serve warm with whipped cream.

Picture page 105

OSGOOD PIE

This "spice islands" pie recalls the early explorers.

Makes 1 9-inch dessert pie	*1/2 cup chopped pecans*
1/2 recipe Easy Pie Crust (see page 47)	*1/2 cup raisins*
1/2 cup butter	*1/2 teaspoon ground cloves*
1 cup sugar	*1/2 teaspoon cinnamon*
2 eggs, separated	*2 teaspoons cocoa*
	1 teaspoon vinegar

Preheat oven to 375°F. Roll pastry out on to a lightly floured surface. Fit into a 9-inch pie plate and set aside. ★ In a large bowl cream butter and sugar together until light and fluffy. Beat egg yolks and add to creamed mixture. Blend well. ★ Stir in pecans, raisins, cloves, cinnamon, cocoa and vinegar. Mix well. ★ In a small bowl, beat egg whites until stiff but not dry. Fold egg whites into sugar mixture. Turn mixture into pie shell and bake for 10 minutes. Reduce heat to 325°F and bake for a further 30 minutes. Cool before serving.

KEY LIME PIE

This luscious, cool green pie is named after the islands off the tip of Florida. It is just the thing for a sultry summer day.

Makes 1 9-inch dessert pie

- *1/2 recipe Easy Pie Crust (see page 47)*
- *1 cup plus 2 tablespoons sugar*
- *1/3 cup cornstarch*
- *1/4 cup cold water*
- *1/2 teaspoon salt*
- *1 1/2 cups hot water*
- *6 tablespoons lime juice*
- *3 eggs, separated*
- *3 tablespoons butter*
- *1 tablespoon grated lime rind*
- *6 tablespoons sugar*
- *1/8 teaspoon salt*
- *1 sliced lime, for garnish*

Preheat oven to 450°F. Roll out pie crust and fit into a 9-inch pie plate. Prick shell all over with a fork and bake for 12 to 15 minutes. Cool completely. Reduce oven temperature to 300°F. ★ In a saucepan combine 1 cup plus 2 tablespoons sugar, cornstarch, 1/2 teaspoon salt, and cold water. Mix well. Add hot water and cook over a very low heat, stirring constantly, until mixture is very thick. Remove saucepan from heat and stir in lime juice. Return saucepan to low heat and cook until mixture as thickened. ★ In a small bowl lightly beat egg yolks. Add 1 teaspoon sugar mixture from saucepan and beat in. Remove saucepan from heat and slowly stir in egg yolks. Return saucepan to heat and cook for 2 minutes, stirring constantly. Add butter and grated lime rind. Stir well. Remove saucepan from heat and cool. ★ Pour cooled filling into pie shell. In a small bowl beat egg whites until stiff but not dry. Gradually beat in 6 tablespoons sugar and 1/8 teaspoon salt. Beat until well blended. Spread meringue over top of pie and bake for 20 minutes. Cool before serving.

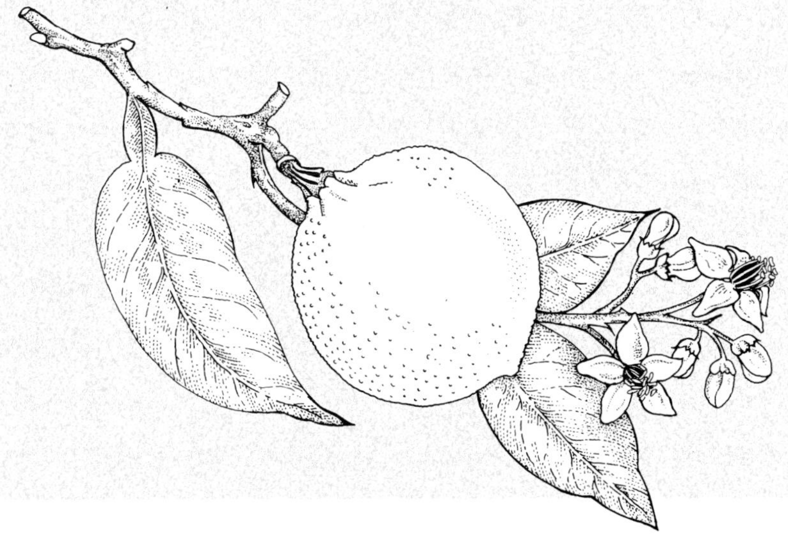

CHARLESTON TORTE

Charleston is the gracious old lady of South Carolina. The architecture and ambience of this seaport town typify the Old South.

Makes 1 dessert torte

- *3 eggs*
- *1½ cups sugar*
- *¼ cup flour*
- *1 teaspoon baking powder*
- *¼ teaspoon salt*
- *1 cup finely chopped apples*
- *1 cup finely chopped pecans*
- *1 teaspoon pure vanilla extract*
- *1 cup chilled heavy cream*
- *2 tablespoons chopped pecans*

Preheat oven to 400°F. Generously butter a 12 × 8 × 2-inch baking pan. Set aside. Sift together flour, baking powder and salt. Set aside. ★ Beat eggs briefly. Add sugar and vanilla to eggs and beat until mixture is thick, about 4 to 5 minutes. ★ Beat in flour mixture until well blended. Add chopped apples and finely chopped pecans. Mix gently but thoroughly into batter with a rubber spatula. Turn batter into pan and bake for 30 to 35 minutes, or until a cake tester inserted into the center comes out clean. Remove cake from oven and cool slightly. ★ Whip cream in a chilled mixing bowl until stiff. Transfer cream to a serving bowl and sprinkle with 2 tablespoons chopped pecans. Serve cake directly from baking pan while still warm. Serve whipped cream on side.

AMBROSIA

This nineteenth-century dessert is still popular today.

Serves 8 as a dessert

- *4 cups seeded grapefruit sections*
- *3 cups seeded orange sections*
- *1½ cups grated unsweetened coconut*
- *½ cup confectioner's sugar*
- *1 cup sliced strawberries*

Arrange a layer of grapefruit sections in a serving dish. Sprinkle with some of the coconut and confectioner's sugar. Top with a layer of orange sections. Sprinkle with some of the coconut and confectioner's sugar. Repeat until grapefruit, oranges, coconut and sugar are used up. Cover and refrigerate until well chilled. Garnish with strawberries before serving.

PRALINES

Pralines originated in New Orleans during the Spanish and French colonial period.

Makes 1 dozen candies	2 tablespoons butter
2 cups firmly packed brown sugar	2 cups coarsely chopped pecans
1/4 cup water	

Put sugar and water in a heavy saucepan and bring to a boil over a moderate heat. Cook for 2 to 3 minutes, stirring constantly, or until a small amount dropped in ice water forms a soft ball. Remove mixture from heat and stir in butter and pecans. Beat mixture for 30 seconds, but do not let mixture crystallize. Drop mixture by heaped tablespoons on to a sheet of waxed paper. Let stand until firm.

BENNE COOKIES

Benne, or sesame seeds, came to America with slaves from Africa. Dishes made with benne are particularly associated with South Carolina and Charleston.

Serves 6 as an appetizer	3/4 cup butter
2 cups flour	1/4 cup ice water
1 teaspoon salt	1 cup sesame seeds
1/8 teaspoon cayenne pepper	salt

Preheat oven to 350°F. In a large bowl mix flour, 1 teaspoon salt and cayenne pepper. With a pastry blender or two knives, cut in butter. Add enough ice water to make a dough with consistency of pie crust. ★ Spread sesame seeds in a shallow baking dish. Roast in oven for 20 minutes, or until seeds are well browned. Shake pan during roasting to turn seeds. Remove sesame seeds and lower oven temperature to 300°F. ★ Add sesame seeds to dough mixture and stir well. On a lightly floured surface, roll dough out to 1/4-inch thickness. Cut circles from dough with a small round cookie cutter. Place rounds in muffin pans and bake for 20 to 30 minutes, or until browned. Before removing cookies from pans, sprinkle with salt. Cool completely. ★ Store cookies in cans. To crisp, heat them in a 300°F oven before serving.

PICKLED WATERMELON RINDS

Recipe page 115

LIME RELISH

Recipe page 115

SPOON BREAD

To lessen their dependence on imported white flour, early colonists adapted many Indian recipes employing cornmeal. This bread is like a soufflé because of its soft center.

Serves 6 as a breakfast or dinner bread

- *2 cups milk*
- *1/4 cup butter*
- *1 cup white cornmeal*
- *1/2 teaspoon salt*
- *1 tablespoon sugar*
- *2 egg yolks, beaten*
- *2 egg whites, beaten*

Preheat oven to 350°F. Melt butter in a large saucepan. Add milk and bring just to boiling point. Stir in cornmeal, salt and sugar. Cook over a moderate heat for 5 minutes, stirring constantly. Remove saucepan from heat and let mixture cool. ★ Stir in egg yolks and fold in egg whites. Pour mixture into a well-greased 9-inch cake pan. Bake spoon bread for 45 minutes. Serve immediately.

CORN BREAD

Although this bread can be made in a baking dish, for true authenticity it should be made in a cast-iron skillet.

Makes 1 corn bread

- *2 tablespoons bacon drippings or butter*
- *1 1/2 cups yellow cornmeal*
- *1 1/2 teaspoons baking powder*
- *3 tablespoons flour*
- *1/2 teaspoon salt*
- *1 1/2 cups milk*
- *1 egg*

Preheat oven to 450°F. Melt bacon drippings or butter in a heavy 9-inch cast-iron skillet. ★ In a mixing bowl, combine cornmeal, flour, salt and baking powder. Add milk and egg. Mix well. Add melted butter and stir to blend. Pour batter into hot skillet. ★ Place skillet in oven and bake for 20 to 25 minutes or until golden brown. Serve warm with butter.

PICKLED WATERMELON RINDS

This sweet, pastel-colored condiment is reminiscent of summer picnics.

Makes about 2 pints pickles

8 cups pared watermelon rinds, white part only, cut into 1/4 × 1-inch pieces
2 tablespoons salt
6 cups sugar
3 cups water
3 cups cider vinegar
3 tablespoons lemon juice
4 cinnamon sticks, broken into 1-inch pieces
2 tablespoons whole cloves
2 tablespoons whole allspice
1 tablespoon whole white peppercorns
2 teaspoons whole mustard seeds

Toss watermelon rinds together with salt. Cover with cold water and leave to soak overnight. Drain and rinse well. Put rinds in a saucepan with enough cold water to cover and bring to a boil over a high heat. Reduce heat and simmer for about 10 minutes. Drain well. ★ Bring remaining ingredients to a boil in a large saucepan and simmer, stirring constantly, for about 10 minutes, until sugar is completely dissolved. Add watermelon rinds and simmer for about 45 minutes, until rinds are transparent. ★ Transfer rinds and syrup to sterilized canning jars and seal. Store pickles for 3 to 4 weeks before using.

Picture page 113

LIME RELISH

Spanish colonists from Georgia to Florida are thought to have planted limes for use as condiments.

Makes 2 pints relish

12 limes, washed
cold water
1 1/2 cups sugar
1 cup vinegar
1/2 cup water

Place limes in a large pot and add enough cold water to cover. Soak limes for 24 hours. Drain limes and return to pot. Add enough cold water to cover and cook for 15 to 20 minutes, or until limes can be easily pierced with a fork. Drain well and set aside to cool. ★ When limes are cool, cut into eighths. Remove seeds. Set limes aside. Place sugar, vinegar and water in a saucepan. Cook over a medium-low heat until syrupy, about 15 minutes. ★ Place lime pieces into hot sterilized canning jars. Cover with syrup. Seal, cool, and store. *Picture page 113*

TEXAS
AND THE
SOUTHWEST

This is a region of huge ranches and green mesas, interrupted by arid deserts of sagebrush. The realm of the cowboy and the vaqũero, their legacy is the food of the campfire and the hacienda.

Like the rest of the nation, the history of Texas and the Southwest begins with Indians. But unlike tribes elsewhere in the US, these Indians were for the most part settled in small communal pueblos – small villages – where they lived comfortably and grew their own crops. The second most influential group were the Spaniards, who arrived in the sixteenth century in search of seven legendary cities with streets paved with gold and silver.

What they found instead were the lush green valleys of the upper Rio Grande River (now New Mexico). Fierce Indian tribes repelled the Spanish advance into Texas and the endless sand and sage brush of most of the other states in the Southwest caused them to look elsewhere for a place to settle. Soon American settlers from the eastern colonies began moving into the area, encroaching on Spanish territory.

Texas and its denizens are some of the more colorful in the nation's folklore. Everything is bigger and better in Texas, they boast, and indeed it quite often is. The world according to Texans is one of wry humor and down-home stories told with flamboyant imagination.

Texas was for many years populated primarily by cattle, cowboys and ranchers. Much of the state was vast range country, where huge herds of longhorn cattle grazed before beginning the long trek north to the stockyards of Chicago, guided over the prairies by leather-skinned cowboys. Oil barons set up operation along the Gulf and Southern farmers brought their slaves and settled along the eastern edge of the state.

Chow time in Texas means sumptuous repasts of amazing proportions. Barbecues are gargantuan feasts of delectable beef and chicken. Rice, okra and crayfish dishes are popular in east Texas but the rest of the state enjoys cuisine heavily influenced by Mexico. Because Texan cooks have adapted Mexican dishes to their own tastes, the resulting recipes are classified as "Tex-Mex" and indeed many connoisseurs prefer Tex-Mex to pure Mexican. As a generalization, Tex-Mex differs from Mexican in the use of more expensive ingredients, such as meat. Chilies are found in nearly every dish, from corn bread to green salads, and from stews to German potato salad.

Chili con carne, which purists call "bowl of red," is practically the national dish of Texas. Possibly invented in a San Antonio kitchen, chili con carne is a perfect example of Tex-Mex food. Beans do not intrude in real chili con carne but are served on the side, along with rice. The use of chilies is, of course, fundamental and often their hotness is enough to make strong men weep. In this "macho man" state, real men eat chilies right off the bush without flinching.

Corn is still the basis of much Texan cooking, together with red pinto beans, squash, tomatoes and, you guessed it, chilies. Chicken-fired steak is a uniquely Texan method of preparation, designed to make tough steak edible. Both beef and chicken are popular meats, and to a lesser extent pork.

New Mexico, Arizona, Utah and Nevada are the majestic soul of what has been called the Great American Desert. Fewer than ten million people live in this enormous area, and most of these are clustered around the major cities of Albuquerque, Sante Fe, Phoenix, Salt Lake City and Las Vegas. Some of the nation's most impressive landscapes are found here, including the grand Canyon in Arizona. These states are characterized by flat, arid deserts and high, grassy plateaus.

New Mexico and southern Arizona were home to the Pueblo Indians long before the Spaniards arrived in the sixteenth century to establish their outposts along the Rio Grande. Arizona was fairly ignored by white settlers until the discovery of copper in the last half of the nineteenth century. Cattlemen followed close on the heels of the prospectors. Consequently, the cuisine of both of these desert states is heavily influenced by Mexico, Spain and its earliest Indian inhabitants. Both prospectors and cowboys imported their eastern eating habits. The recipes of southern Arizona show the strong Sonoran influence. In the state of Sonora, just across the Mexican border, more wheat than corn is grown, and it plays a concomitantly larger role in cooking. Tortillas, or Mexican bread, are most often made out of wheat instead of corn. Sonoran, and thereby Arizonan, cuisine is also less spicy than other types of Mexican food. Beef, lamb and goat are the predominant meats in these two states.

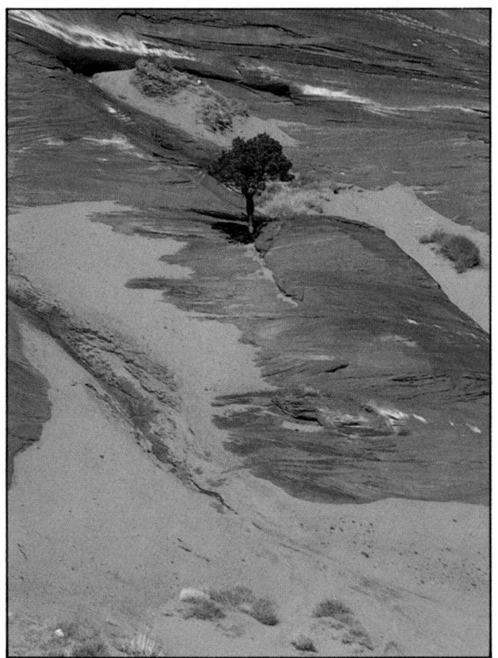

The ever-eroding desert – New Mexico

Utah was settled by the industrious Mormons, members of the Church of Jesus Christ of Latter-day Saints, seeking refuge from the persecution that they suffered in the east and Midwest. Led by Brigham Young, originally from Vermont, they found their paradise in a seemingly barren land dominated by the Great Salt Lake and bordered by the formidable Wasatch mountain range.

Today, three-quarters of the population are Mormons and their religious beliefs color everything in Utah, including eating habits. There are, for example, few restaurants in Utah because Mormons prefer eating with their generally large families in the comfort and familiarity of their own homes.

Utah cuisine is generally that found on most Eastern tables,with the addition of German and Scandinavian dishes – people of these nationalities were converted to Mormonism by the ardent evangelicism of the sect. Spanish recipes have been Anglicized and very few chilies are found anywhere near a Mormon table.

Discovery of the Comstock Lode in the Sierras in 1859 caused a huge migration of prospectors to Nevada, seeking their fortunes in gold and silver. Rambunctious mining towns mushroomed everywhere, of which Virginia City was by far the most bawdy and certainly the most famous. The prospectors brought with them their Eastern tastes and recipes. With the depletion of the Comstock Lode, most of these towns crumbled into forlorn relics, including Virginia City. Others disappeared entirely, their remains now dubbed "ghost towns."

Las Vegas today has a multi-ethnic population. The cuisine ranges from mundane to international. There isn't an indigenous recipe bag for this glittering city built on false dreams, although it does show Mexican influence in its name, which means incongruously "the meadows." Owing to a strong connection with New York City, whose citizens came out to gamble until Atlantic City was legalized as a gambling center, many restaurants feature excellent New York cuisine.

GUACAMOLE

This dip is almost a party requisite and even those who disdain the blandness of avocado will become converts. Spices and ingredients can vary but the lemon juice is a must – it keeps the avocado from discoloring.

Serves 6 as an appetizer

- *1 avocado, peeled, stoned and coarsely chopped*
- *1 tablespoon minced onion*
- *2 teaspoons lemon juice*
- *½ garlic clove*
- *4 tablespoons softened cream cheese*
- *2 teaspoons mayonnaise*
- *4 tablespoons chopped celery*
- *½ teaspoon chili powder*
- *½ teaspoon salt*

Put avocado, onion, garlic and lemon juice in a blender or food processor and blend until smooth. In a mixing bowl, beat mayonnaise and cream cheese until fluffy. Combine cream cheese mixture and avocado mixture in a blender or food processor. Add celery, chili powder and salt and blend until well mixed. Serve with tortillas or corn chips.

Picture page 124

SOPA DE ARROZ

(SHRIMP AND RICE SOUP)

This dish, adapted from Mexico by Texans, is really more of a stew than a soup, but it is traditionally served as a first course in the Southwest.

Serves 4 as a first course

- *2 tablespoons olive oil*
- *1 cup long-grain rice*
- *1 cup chopped tomatoes*
- *1 cup cooked shrimp, shelled and deveined*
- *3 cups hot water*
- *1 teaspoon salt*
- *1 teaspoon Tabasco sauce*

Heat olive oil in a heavy skillet until very hot. Add rice and cook, stirring constantly, until it turns a deep golden brown. Add tomatoes, shrimp, hot water, salt and Tabasco sauce. Cover and cook until rice is tender and has absorbed almost all the liquid, approximately 15 to 20 minutes.

FRIJOLES REFRITOS

(REFRIED BEANS)

These beans form the basis for most Mexican dishes and often help to bind the other toppings piled on a tortilla (as in tostadas). Home cooked frijoles refritos are much more delicious than canned. Incidentally, don't take refritos ("refried") literally to mean "fried again." The prefix "re" in Spanish means "thoroughly" in this case.

Serves 4 to 6 as a side dish

2 cups dried pinto or kidney beans

6 cups water

1 cup coarsely chopped onions

1 medium-sized tomato, peeled, seeded and coarsely chopped

3 garlic cloves, chopped

8 tablespoons lard or bacon drippings

1 teaspoon salt

Rinse beans under cold running water. In a heavy saucepan, combine beans, water, ½ cup onions, ¼ tomato, garlic and 1 tablespoon lard. Bring to a boil over a high heat, boil for 10 minutes; reduce heat and simmer mixture, partially covered for 1½ hours. Stir in salt and continue to simmer, partially covered, for 30 to 40 minutes longer, or until a bean can be easily mashed against the side of the saucepan. Stir occasionally as beans cook and add water, ¼ cup at a time, as necessary. Drain beans and reserve liquid. ★ Melt 2 tablespoons lard in a heavy skillet. When hot, add remaining onions and cook, stirring frequently, for 5 minutes or until onions are soft but not brown. Add remaining chopped tomatoes, stir, and cook for 2 to 3 minutes. Reduce heat to low. ★ Add ½ cup beans to skillet. Mash with a fork and stir in 1 tablespoon lard. Repeat, alternating 1 cup beans with 1 tablespoon lard, until all beans and lard are mashed together. The mixture should be creamy yet slightly crisp. If beans seem too dry, add some reserved bean liquid, 1 tablespoon at a time. Serve hot.

SPICY GARBANZO SALAD

Garbanzos came to the New World via Spain, hence the American adoption of the Spanish term "garbanzo" instead of the French "chickpea." Garbanzos must be soaked before being boiled, preferably overnight, otherwise it is nearly impossible to digest the beans.

Serves 4 as a side dish

- *2 medium-sized carrots*
- *2 cups cooked garbanzos*
- *1 small onion, finely chopped*
- *1 tablespoon finely chopped parsley*
- *1/4 cup olive oil*
- *2 tablespoons cider vinegar*
- *1 teaspoon salt*
- *1/2 teaspoon black pepper*
- *1 1/2 teaspoons hot red pepper flakes*
- *1/8 teaspoon cayenne pepper*
- *lettuce leaves*

Dice carrots and cook in a large pot of boiling water for 5 to 7 minutes. Drain well. In a large bowl, mix together garbanzos, onion, parsley, carrots, oil, vinegar and red pepper flakes. Add salt, black pepper and cayenne pepper. ★ Chill in refrigerator for 1 to 2 hours. To serve, line a large serving bowl with lettuce leaves and spoon in salad.

SOUTHWESTERN CABBAGE SALAD

Many of the earliest Mormon converts were recent immigrants. This recipe was contributed by Germans, with a nod to local ingredients such as chilies.

Serves 6 as a side dish

- *1 large head cabbage, shredded*
- *1 green pepper, coarsely chopped*
- *1/4 cup mayonnaise*
- *1/4 cup sour cream*
- *3 tablespoons white wine vinegar*
- *3 tablespoons sugar*
- *1/2 teaspoon chili powder*
- *1/2 teaspoon salt*
- *1/4 teaspoon black pepper*
- *1/8 teaspoon cayenne pepper*

Place shredded cabbage in a large bowl and add green pepper. Mix well and chill. ★ In a mixing bowl combine mayonnaise, sour cream, vinegar, sugar, chili powder, salt, pepper and cayenne pepper. Blend well and chill for 2 hours. Pour dressing over cabbage mixture and toss thoroughly.

HUEVOS RANCHEROS

(RANCH-STYLE EGGS)

This simple recipe is sometimes called "huevos en purgatorio" – eggs in purgatory – depending on how many red chili peppers are added.

Serves 4 as a breakfast dish

- *3 tablespoons butter*
- *1 garlic clove, finely chopped*
- *2 large onions, chopped*
- *1½ teaspoons hot red pepper flakes*
- *1 large can whole tomatoes*
- *salt to taste*
- *black pepper to taste*
- *8 eggs*

Melt 2 tablespoons butter in a skillet. Add garlic and onions and sauté until lightly browned, about 5 to 7 minutes. Add hot pepper flakes and tomatoes. Simmer, covered, for 45 minutes or until sauce is thick. Season to taste with salt and pepper. Break eggs into a bowl and beat well. ★ In another skillet, melt remaining butter. Pour in eggs and cook until bottom of omelet is lightly browned. Turn eggs over and cook until the other side is lightly browned. Slide omelet on to a serving plate and pour over sauce. Cut omelet into quarters and serve hot.

CHILIES RELLENOS

Serve this Mexican-American favorite with guacamole (see page 118) and chopped onions.

Serves 4 as a main course

12 large green chili peppers

½ pound Cheddar cheese, cut into thin strips

1 cup flour

1 teaspoon baking powder

½ teaspoon salt

¾ cup yellow cornmeal

1 cup milk

2 eggs

vegetable oil for frying

Preheat the broiler to high. Place chili peppers in a broiling pan and broil, turning often, until charred all over. Remove peppers from broiler and place in a paper bag. Fold bag closed and let stand for 5 minutes. Remove peppers from bag and peel off skin. Slit peppers down the side and remove seeds; do not remove stems. Stuff peppers with cheese strips. Set aside. ★ Combine flour, baking powder, salt and cornmeal in a bowl. Add milk and eggs and beat well to form a batter. Dip stuffed peppers into batter and coat well. Fill a deep skillet with oil to a depth of ½ inch. Add peppers and fry until golden all over. Drain on paper towels.

PORK TOSTADAS

DOUBLE DECK

Tostadas are really the Mexican version of open-faced sandwiches with crisply fried corn tortillas as their base.

Serves 4 as a main course

1 pound ground pork

1 medium-sized onion, chopped

1½ teaspoons chili powder

1 teaspoon salt

¼ teaspoon ground cumin

1 garlic clove, finely chopped

2 cups cooked kidney beans, mashed

¼ cup bean cooking liquid

½ cup water

8 tortillas (see page 28)

1 cup shredded lettuce

½ cup shredded mild cheese

1 tomato chopped

Brown pork and onion together in a large skillet. Pour off fat. Add chili powder, salt, cumin and garlic. Add mashed beans to pork. Stir in bean liquid and water. Cook slowly for 15 minutes, stirring occasionally. ★ Spread about 1/3 cup pork mixture on each of 4 tortillas. Place 1/4 cup of lettuce over each. Top each with a second tortilla. Spread each with an equal portion of remaining pork mixture. Top with shredded cheese and chopped tomato.

COWBOY BEANS

More than anything else, cowboys symbolize Texas and the Southwest. The life of these taciturn, hard-bitten loners has been romanticized in song and poem. The truth is probably somewhat less glamorous: eating trail dust for days on end as they followed the cattle, enduring in the open both extremes of freezing winters and broiling desert summers. Cowpoking may have had its attractions, but comfort wasn't one of them.

Serves 6 as a side dish

- *4 cups cooked pinto or kidney beans*
- *1 meaty ham bone*
- *1 red hot chili pepper*
- *1 1/2 teaspoons salt*
- *2 cups water*
- *1/4 pound salt pork, coarsely chopped*
- *1 large onion, chopped*
- *1 garlic clove, chopped*
- *4 tomatoes, seeded and coarsely chopped*
- *1/2 teaspoon ground cumin*
- *1 1/2 tablespoons chili powder*

Combine beans with ham bone, red chili pepper, salt and water in a large saucepan. Cover and bring to a boil. Reduce heat and simmer gently for 30 minutes. Drain and reserve 1 cup of liquid. ★ While beans cook, heat salt pork in a large skillet. Stir in onion and garlic and cook for 5 minutes. Add tomatoes, reserved bean liquid, cumin and chili powder. Mix well. Cook over a low heat, stirring frequently, for 45 minutes. Mix in beans and simmer for a further 5 minutes.

GUACAMOLE

Recipe page 118

CHILI CON CARNE

Recipe page 129

CHIMICHANGOS

Serve these deep-fried stuffed tortillas with shredded lettuce, sour cream, guacamole (see page 118) and chili sauce.

Serves 6 as a main course
- *2 pounds boneless beef, coarsely chopped*
- *2 potatoes, peeled and diced*
- *6 small green chilli peppers, seeded and chopped*
- *1 onion, chopped*
- *3 garlic cloves, chopped*
- *1 teaspoon oregano*
- *salt to taste*
- *black pepper to taste*
- *12 tortillas (see page 28)*
- *vegetable oil for frying*

Combine beef, potatoes, chili peppers, onion, garlic, oregano and salt and pepper in a saucepan. Add enough cold water to cover and simmer until meat is tender, about 1 hour. ★ Place a spoonful of meat mixture in the center of each tortilla and fold tortilla into a packet. Fill a deep skillet to a depth of 1 inch with vegetable oil. Heat until very hot and add chimichangos. Fry until golden brown all over.

PICADILLO

This meat stew takes its name from the Spanish word for hash.

Serves 4 as a main course
- *2 tablespoons olive oil*
- *1 large onion, thinly sliced*
- *3 garlic cloves, finely chopped*
- *1/2 pound ground lean beef*
- *1/2 pound ground pork*
- *salt to taste*
- *black pepper to taste*
- *1/4 teaspoon ground cumin*
- *1 bay leaf*
- *1/2 cup red wine*
- *2 large tomatoes, peeled and chopped*
- *1/4 cup dark raisins*
- *1 sweet red pepper, cut into strips*

Heat olive oil in a large deep skillet. Add onion and garlic. Cook, stirring constantly, until soft and golden, about 5 to 7 minutes. Add beef, pork, salt, pepper and cumin. Mix well. Cook over a low heat, stirring constantly, until meat is well browned. Drain off fat. Add bay leaf, wine, tomatoes and raisins. Mix well and cover skillet. Simmer mixture over a low heat for 15 minutes, stirring frequently. If mixture is too wet, remove cover and continue cooking. Stir in red pepper strips and cook for a further 2 minutes. Serve over rice or fill tacos.

ENCHILADAS

Enchilada means "filled with chili," although these baked stuffed tortillas are often served filled with chorizo sausage, cheese and/or other ingredients.

Serves 6 as a main course

4 cups canned tomatoes

2 hot red chili peppers, seeded

½ teaspoon salt

¼ teaspoon black pepper

1 cup sour cream

2 cups diced cooked chicken

1 cup grated Cheddar cheese

12 tortillas (see page 28)

1 tablespoon vegetable oil

Purée tomatoes with chili peppers, salt and black pepper in a blender or food processor. Stir in sour cream and set aside. ★ Combine chicken and ½ cup cheese in a bowl. Set aside. ★ Preheat oven to 350°F. Grease a baking dish. Heat vegetable oil in a large skillet. Add tortillas, one at a time, and sauté briefly until golden on both sides. Drain on paper towels. Spread each tortilla with some chicken and cheese and roll up. Arrange tortillas in baking dish and pour over tomato sauce. Cover with aluminum foil and bake for 30 minutes. Remove foil, sprinkle with remaining cheese, and broil until browned.

BASQUE BARBECUED LAMB

Many of the sheepmen of the Southwest are of Basque descent. A Basque barbecue always means lamb.

Serves 6 as a main course

1 7-pound leg of lamb, boned

1 strip pork tenderloin, cut to fit into bone cavity of leg of lamb

1 teaspoon dried rosemary

6 garlic cloves, minced

salt to taste

black pepper to taste

¾ cup lemon juice

Have your butcher bone the leg of lamb and cut the pork tenderloin so that it is the same length as the leg and is just enclosed by the cavity left by the bone. ★ Rub inside of lamb with rosemary, 3 minced garlic cloves, salt and pepper. Place pork tenderloin on inside surface of lamb. Roll up and tie securely with string. Rub outside of lamb with lemon juice and remaining garlic. ★ Place lamb on a rack or spit and roast 4 inches above hot coals. If lamb is on a rack, turn it every 30 minutes. Barbecue for approximately 2 hours.

CHUCKWAGON STEW

A recipe from cattle-driving days. Serve with plenty of mashed potatoes.

Serves 6 as a main course	*3 tablespoons all-purpose flour*
2 tablespoons lard or vegetable oil	*2 cups beer (preferably dark beer)*
2½ pounds stewing beef, trimmed and cut into 1-inch cubes	*2 cups canned tomatoes*
salt to taste	*1 tablespoon molasses or honey*
black pepper to taste	*2 teaspoons chili powder*
3 large onions, cut into large chunks	*2 bay leaves*

Heat lard or oil in a heatproof casserole or Dutch oven over a moderate heat. Season beef cubes liberally with salt and pepper. Add with onions to casserole and brown evenly, about 10 minutes. Sprinkle flour over beef and onions and let brown slightly, less than a minute. Pour in beer and stir and scrape to dissolve all brown deposits on the bottom and sides of the casserole. ★ Add remaining ingredients and stir well. Raise heat to high and bring stew to a boil. Then reduce heat to very low, cover casserole tightly, and cook for 2 to 3 hours, or until beef is tender. Alternatively, cook casserole for same length of time in a preheated 300°F oven.

OVEN-CURED BEEF JERKY

Once a staple of Western diets because it traveled well without the benefit of refrigeration, beef jerky is still found on grocery market shelves throughout the Southwest. It is hard, dry and smoky tasting.

Makes about 1 pound for appetizers and snacks	*3 tablespoons brown sugar*
5 pounds lean beef steak, cut into 1-inch wide strips	*½ tablespoon oregano*
6 tablespoons coarse salt	*1 large onion, finely chopped*
	1 garlic clove, finely chopped

Chill beef strips in freezer for 1 to 2 hours, until firm enough to cut easily into thin slices. Remove from freezer and, with a very sharp knife, carefully cut each strip lengthwise into ⅛-inch thick slices. ★ Place a single layer of slices in the bottom of a glass or ceramic dish.

Sprinkle with some remaining ingredients, then continue layering beef slices and seasonings, ending with a layer of seasonings. Pour in enough water just to submerge meat. Cover dish and leave meat in refrigerator to marinate overnight. ★ Set oven at lowest setting. Remove oven racks. Take meat from brine and place pieces directly on rack without overlapping. Leave beef in oven for 7 to 11 hours, depending on temperature and thickness of slices, until strips are dry and brittle enough to snap. Refrigerate in an airtight container.

CHILI CON CARNE

The arguments about what constitutes the ingredients for real *chili rage passionately. Some claim that venison is the correct meat; others say only jackrabbit should be used. Aficionados divide into armed camps over whether the mixture should contain tomatoes or not. Even the onion question is hotly debated. This recipe is not definitive; not even the annual World Championship Chili Cookoff, held in Terlingua, Texas, since 1967, has come up with that.*

Serves 6 as a main course

- *3 tablespoons olive oil*
- *2 garlic cloves, minced*
- *2 medium-sized onions, chopped*
- *2 pounds lean ground beef*
- *2 cups beer*
- *1 cup water*
- *2½ cups canned stewed tomatoes*
- *2 teaspoons salt*
- *1 teaspoon black pepper*
- *⅛ teaspoon dried sage*
- *½ teaspoon dried oregano*
- *¼ teaspoon cayenne pepper*
- *1 teaspoon ground cumin*
- *2 tablespoons chili powder*
- *2 large cans red kidney beans (drain 1 can)*

Heat oil in a large saucepan and add garlic and onions. Sauté onions until golden brown. Add ground beef and cook until brown. Add beer and cook over a moderate heat for 10 minutes. Stir in water, tomatoes, salt, pepper, sage, oregano, cayenne pepper, cumin and chili powder. Cook over low heat, uncovered, for 2½ hours. Add kidney beans and cook for a further 10 minutes. *Picture page 125*

BAKED CUSTARD
OR FLAN

Baked custard is a light, creamy dessert typical of Mexican, and therefore Southwestern, cooking.

Serves 4

3/4 cup sugar
3 eggs
3 cups milk
1/2 teaspoon pure vanilla extract

Preheat oven to 350°F. In a saucepan heat 1/4 cup sugar until it becomes a light brown syrup. Coat sides and bottom of a custard dish or medium soufflé dish with syrup. Set aside to cool. ★ In a mixing bowl beat eggs and remaining sugar. Add milk and vanilla. Beat well. Pour mixture into coated custard dish. ★ Set dish into a pan of hot water and bake for 30 minutes, or until a knife inserted into center comes out clean.

EMPANADAS

In Spanish, "empanar," means "to bake in pastry." These dessert turnovers can be filled with anything, although mincemeat or fruit preserves are recommended. Serve dusted with cinnamon or sugar.

Serves 4 as a snack or dessert

1 package active dry yeast
1/2 cup lukewarm water
4 tablespoons butter
4 cups flour
1 teaspoon salt
1 tablespoon sugar
vegetable oil for frying

Dissolve yeast in water in a small bowl. Using a pastry blender or two knives, blend butter with flour in a mixing bowl until mixture resembles coarse crumbs. Add salt, sugar and yeast mixture. Mix well to form a smooth dough and leave to rise until double in size. ★ Roll dough out into a thin sheet on a floured surface. Cut circles 3 inches in diameter. Place a spoonful of filling in the center of each round. Moisten edges and top with another round, pressing to seal. ★ Fill a deep skillet with vegetable oil to a depth of 1 inch. Heat until very hot. Add empanadas and fry until golden brown on all sides. Drain on paper towels.

BUÑUELOS

Hot chocolate and buñuelos are traditionally served by Mexican-Americans on Christmas Eve. Serve them sprinkled with cinnamon and sugar.

Serves 6 as a snack or dessert

4 eggs
½ cup milk
¼ cup melted butter
3 cups flour
1 tablespoon sugar
1 teaspoon salt
vegetable oil for frying

Beat eggs in a mixing bowl and add milk, butter, flour, sugar and salt. Stir well. Roll dough into balls with a diameter of about 1 inch. Flour a surface and rolling pin and roll balls out into rounds about 6 to 8 inches in diameter. ★ Fill a deep skillet with vegetable oil to a depth of ½ inch. Heat until very hot and add buñuelos, one at a time. Fry until golden on both sides. Drain on paper towels.

FRY BREAD

One of the few American Indian breads that uses wheat, this is a specialty of the Hopi and Navajo tribes. The recipe below is Hopi-style. For Navajo bread, punch a hole in the center of each dough disc before frying – the Navajos used to lower their bread into the oil with a stick pushed through the dough. Serve with honey, cinnamon or icing sugar.

Serves 6 as a snack or for breakfast

2 cups all-purpose flour
2 tablespoons baking powder
1 teaspoon salt
½ cup warm water
vegetable oil for frying

Combine flour, baking powder and salt in a mixing bowl. Add warm water and stir to form an elastic dough, adding more water if necessary. Divide dough into 2-inch balls. On a floured surface roll balls out with a floured rolling pin to a thickness of ¼-inch. ★ Fill a deep skillet with vegetable oil to a depth of ½ inch. Heat until very hot and add bread discs, one or two at a time. Fry until lightly golden on each side. Drain on paper towels.

SUPPER BREAD

Also known as "onion and cheese bread" in the Midwest, this recipe probably arrived in the Southwest with the homesteaders.

Serves 12 as a side dish
- *1 cup yellow cornmeal*
- *2 tablespoons flour*
- *2 teaspoons baking powder*
- *2 tablespoons sugar*
- *1/2 teaspoon salt*
- *1 egg, beaten*
- *1 tablespoon melted butter*
- *1/2 cup milk*
- *1/2 cup canned green chili peppers, chopped*
- *2 tablespoons butter*
- *1 medium-sized onion, chopped*
- *1/2 cup grated sharp Cheddar cheese*
- *1/2 cup sour cream*

Preheat oven to 375°F. Combine cornmeal, flour, baking powder, sugar and salt in a large mixing bowl. Add egg, butter and milk. Mix until well combined and stir in chili peppers. ★ Heat butter in a small skillet. Add onions and sauté until onions are golden brown. Pour batter into an 8-inch loaf pan. Spread sautéed onions on top of batter. ★ In a small mixing bowl, combine sour cream and grated cheese. Pour mixture on top of onion layer. Bake for 30 minutes. Remove from pan and let cool for 5 minutes before serving.

NACHOS

These tortilla chips, dipped in melted cheese and sprinkled with blistering hot jalapeño peppers, are a calorie-laden snack.

Serves 6 as an appetizer
- *6 tortillas (see page 28)*
- *bacon drippings or vegetable oil*
- *6 tablespoons refried beans (see page 119)*
- *6 tablespoons shredded Cheddar cheese*
- *3 canned jalapeño peppers, coarsely chopped*

Cut each tortilla into quarters. Heat drippings or oil in a skillet and fry tortilla pieces until crisp. Drain on paper towels. ★ Preheat broiler. Spread each tortilla piece with refried beans and arrange in one layer in a broiling pan. Sprinkle with cheese and chopped peppers. Broil until cheese melts, about 5 minutes. Serve hot.

SOPAPILLAS

Sopapillas, or "sofa pillows," are a Southwestern specialty. Only Yankees butter them. For a sweet bread, roll the sopapillas in brown sugar and cinnamon after frying.

Makes 36 sopapillas

4 cups flour
2 teaspoons salt
4 teaspoons baking powder
1/4 cup lard or solid vegetable shortening
1-1 1/4 cups warm water
vegetable oil for frying

Sift flour, salt and baking powder together in a large bowl. Add lard or shortening and work with fingers until mixture resembles a coarse meal. Add just enough warm water to hold dough together. Place dough in refrigerator for 10 minutes. ★ Roll dough out on to a lightly floured surface to 1/8-inch thickness. With a pastry wheel or sharp knife cut dough into 3-inch squares. Heat vegetable oil in a deep skillet to a depth of 3 inches. When oil is very hot (400°F on a deep-frying thermometer) add sopapillas, as many as will fit at one time, and fry for 2 to 3 minutes per side. When they are puffed and crisp on both sides remove and drain on paper towels. Serve hot.

GREEN CHILI SALSA

This mild relish is used on a variety of dishes, from topopo (the Mexican version of chef's salad) to enchiladas.

Makes about 2 cups of salsa

3 fresh or canned green chili peppers, with seeds, chopped
4 medium-sized green tomatoes, chopped
2 medium-sized onions, chopped
1 cup boiling water
1 garlic clove, finely chopped
1 teaspoon dried oregano
salt to taste

Place chili peppers in a saucepan. Add enough water to cover and bring to a boil. Cook peppers for 10 minutes. Remove from heat and drain well. ★ Return peppers to saucepan and add tomatoes, onions and boiling water. Simmer over a medium heat for 20 minutes. ★ Remove from heat and press mixture through a sieve. Discard any solids remaining in sieve. Add garlic, oregano and salt. Stir well. The mixture should be very thick. Refrigerate tightly covered.

CALIFORNIA AND HAWAII

Nearly every race, nationality and religion is represented in these two states, the nation's melting pot. Their food reflects the contradiction between their easy lifestyle and hard health-consciousness.

Agriculture is one of California's primary revenue producers. The tidy farms of the Central Valley, stretching nearly half the length of the state, contrast sharply with the cosmopolitan coastal areas. Apart from Palm Springs, just a few hours' drive east of Los Angeles, the forbidding deserts of the state are empty but for an occasional fly-blown village of a ghost town. Enthusiastically dubbed "the golden state," California has vast ranch land, populated only by live oak and cattle. Yet it is a populous state: one out of eight Americans lives in California.

Long before the Puritans landed at Cape Cod, Spaniards were plying the coast in their pitifully small ships, searching for the legendary City of Gold. Franciscan friars accompanied these early expeditions, setting up missions a day's march apart, to "civilize" the Indians.

Close on their heels came the Spanish dons, who established themselves in elaborate adobe haciendas on vast ranches of range land and orchards. Their sumptuous tables groaned with Western plenty and left their indelible mark on California cuisine. Long after California joined the young republic, Spanish ways and cuisine predominated – and today the influence of Mexican-American food is unmistakable.

At the beginning of the nineteenth century, explorers from the eastern states began to arrive, with trappers not far behind the first scouts. In 1849 all hell broke loose – literally – when gold was was discovered at Sutter's Mill near what is today the state capital, Sacramento. Gold-fever gripped the state as California galloped into the twentieth century on its newfound wealth.

There is strong ethnic representation in Californian with the hispanic population leading the way. Both Asians and blacks lend the state their strong cultural heritage. Asian immigration began in 1850 when gold fever gripped the world. The Chinese in particular came to seek their fortunes in a land purportedly paved with gold. Their industriousness was legendary and they were quickly drafted into laboring on the railroads.

Today's immigrants to California are primarily from Indochina – and most of these are Vietnamese. Attracted by established communities of their own people in a country still often hostile to their culture, and comforted by the temperate climate of California, large concentrations of Thais, Laotians, Cambodians and Vietnamese are found throughout the state.

The food of California today is a blend of Mexican and immigrant cuisine. At times sophisticated and sublime, at others earthy and robust, it epitomizes the values of healthy good living.

What is today called the new American cuisine, or "new wave cuisine," originated, as do many trend-setting fashions, in California. Undoubtedly this culinary style has been influenced by France's nouvelle cuisine, but its strongest influence must be the cornucopia of abundance provided by the golden state. Like the Pacific Northwest, Californian cuisine is predicated on freshness, together with a ferocious zeal for organic, natural ingredients.

The list of foods grown in California is endless and impressive: almonds, artichokes, asparagus, avocados and garlic are but a few. Less well known, but no less important, are melons, persimmons, figs and olives. Vegetables abound – from brussel sprouts to spinach. California is the leading strawberry and lima bean producer in the world and citrus is synonymous with the state.

When you wake up in Hawaii you could be forgiven for thinking you've died and the gone to heaven. Even with the commercialism and the development evils of tourism, Hawaii is still an earthly paradise. Made up of eight islands situated in the north Pacific, Hawaii is full of contradictions. Alternately tropical and desert, most of the islands are a lush landscape of verdant growth punctuated by sharp-edged lava rock and mountains, all fringed by the blue Pacific. Largest in the group is the island of Hawaii, covering 4,000 square miles.

God's Country – open hills in California

Hawaii was originally settled by Polynesians who set sail in their long canoes from the Indo-malayan region and navigated by the stars and the ocean currents. These early Hawaiians lived peacefully and apparently joyously in thoroughly Polynesian style until the nineteenth century, when Yankee clipper ships hove into view. The wooden ships bore New England missionaries, intent on clothing the barbaric Hawaiians, and getting them into the neat, white, New England-style churches that the zealous missionaries built in short order. Gone forever was the easy-going, carefree Polynesian lifestyle.

When the first missionaries arrived they found sensuously beautiful people living on a diet of fish and fruit. Except for an inedible species of bat there were no native animals. The sea, however, offered a vast choice – there were no poisonous fish in the coral atolls surrounding the islands. The cornucopia included shellfish, octopus, porpoise, whale, even turtle. Salmon was so common in the Pacific waters that the Hawaiians referred to it as "the pig of the sea." The indigenous Hawaiians also consumed large quantities of seaweed and tree ferns.

The Yankees had survived the long trip in their clipper ships on a steady diet of dried meat and salted fish, both of which were promptly adapted for use by the Hawaiians. Pipikaula, for example, is a popular dish made of small pieces of broiled beef jerky served in a sweet and sour sauce. Lomi lomi – a standard item at luaus – comprises thin fillets of salted salmon. Today, many New England recipes participate in Hawaii's culinary melting pot, including fish chowders.

Within a generation, the missionary families had branched out into commerce. Vast plantations of pineapples, sugar cane and kona coffee were set up and Chinese, Japanese and Korean workers were brought in. Soon, through intermarriage, few true Polynesians remained and today full-blooded Hawaiians are a minority in their own state. But the seeds of Hawaii's international cuisine were sown and today's Hawaiian cuisine is a delightful pot-pourri of European, American and Oriental cuisine.

BONGO BONGO SOUP

Vic Bergeron, owner of Trader Vic's restaurants in San Francisco and several other cities, created this soup.

Serves 8 as a first course	*1 small garlic clove, crushed*
1 cup cooked spinach	*salt to taste*
10 ounces shucked oysters	*black pepper to taste*
2½ cups whipping cream	*cayenne pepper to taste*
2 tablespoons butter	*2 teaspoons cornstarch*
1 teaspoon Worcestershire sauce	*2 tablespoons water*

Purée spinach in a blender or food processor. Poach oysters in a saucepan of boiling water until their edges curl, about 5 to 8 minutes. Drain well and chop oysters finely. ★ Heat cream in a saucepan until just below boiling point. Add spinach purée, chopped oysters, butter, Worcestershire sauce, garlic, and salt, black pepper and cayenne pepper to taste. Stir gently and simmer. Do not let boil. ★ In a small bowl dissolve cornstarch in water. Add to soup and stir well. Simmer until soup thickens. Serve at once.

GAZPACHO

This dish is Andalusian in origin, but the name is derived from the Arabic term for "soaked bread," here represented by croutons.

Makes 2 quarts for a first course	*2 tablespoons red wine vinegar*
3 pounds ripe tomatoes, seeded and coarsely chopped	*2 cups chicken broth*
1 onion, quartered	*1 teaspoon salt*
1 green pepper, coarsely chopped	*½ teaspoon black pepper*
1 garlic clove, crushed	*chopped green onions for garnish*
	chopped cucumbers for garnish
	croutons for garnish

Combine tomatoes, onion, green pepper, cucumber and garlic in a blender or food processor. Blend, in batches if necessary, until puréed. Pour mixture into a large bowl and stir in vinegar, chicken broth, salt and pepper. Cover and chill overnight. ★ Strain into a large pitcher. Thin with more chicken broth, if desired. Serve very cold, garnished with chopped green onions, cucumbers and croutons.

Picture page 139

GRAPEFRUIT AVOCADO SOUP

Two unlikely companions in a dish, the citrus perks up the blandness of the avocado in this tasty soup.

Serves 6 as a first course

2½ cups grapefruit juice
2 ripe avocados, peeled and chopped (reserve pits)
1 cup plain yogurt
½ teaspoon salt
1 teaspoon ground coriander
1 lemon, thinly sliced

Place 1 cup grapefruit juice, chopped avocados, yogurt, salt and coriander in a blender or food processor. Blend until smooth. ★ Pour mixture into a large bowl. Stir in remaining grapefruit juice. Place reserved avocado pits into bowl and chill mixture for 5 hours or overnight. The pits will keep the mixture from darkening as it chills.

GOAT CHEESE SOUFFLE

Goat cheeses, commonly referred to as "chèvres," have found their way from organic health-food stores to mainstream groceries.

Serves 4 to 6 as a main course or supper dish

2 tablespoons butter
2 tablespoons flour
¾ cup half-and-half
3 eggs, separated
1⅓ cups crumbled goat cheese
4 teaspoons chopped chives
1 teaspoon dried oregano
salt to taste
black pepper to taste
grated nutmeg to taste

Preheat oven to 400°F. In a saucepan melt butter. Add flour and stir until well blended. Gradually stir in half-and-half. Cook, stirring constantly, until mixture is smooth and thick. Remove from heat. ★ In a small bowl beat egg yolks. Gradually stir yolks into half-and-half mixture. Return saucepan to a low heat and stir in goat cheese, oregano, salt, pepper and nutmeg. Cook, stirring constantly, until mixture is smooth and creamy. Do not allow mixture to boil. Remove from heat and cool to room temperature. ★ In a bowl beat egg whites until stiff but not dry. Fold into goat cheese mixture. Fold in chopped chives. ★ Turn mixture into a lightly buttered 1½-quart soufflé dish. Place dish in pan of hot water and place in oven. Bake for 25 to 30 minutes or until top is browned. Serve *immediately*.

BROCCOLI AND RED PEPPER WITH GARLIC

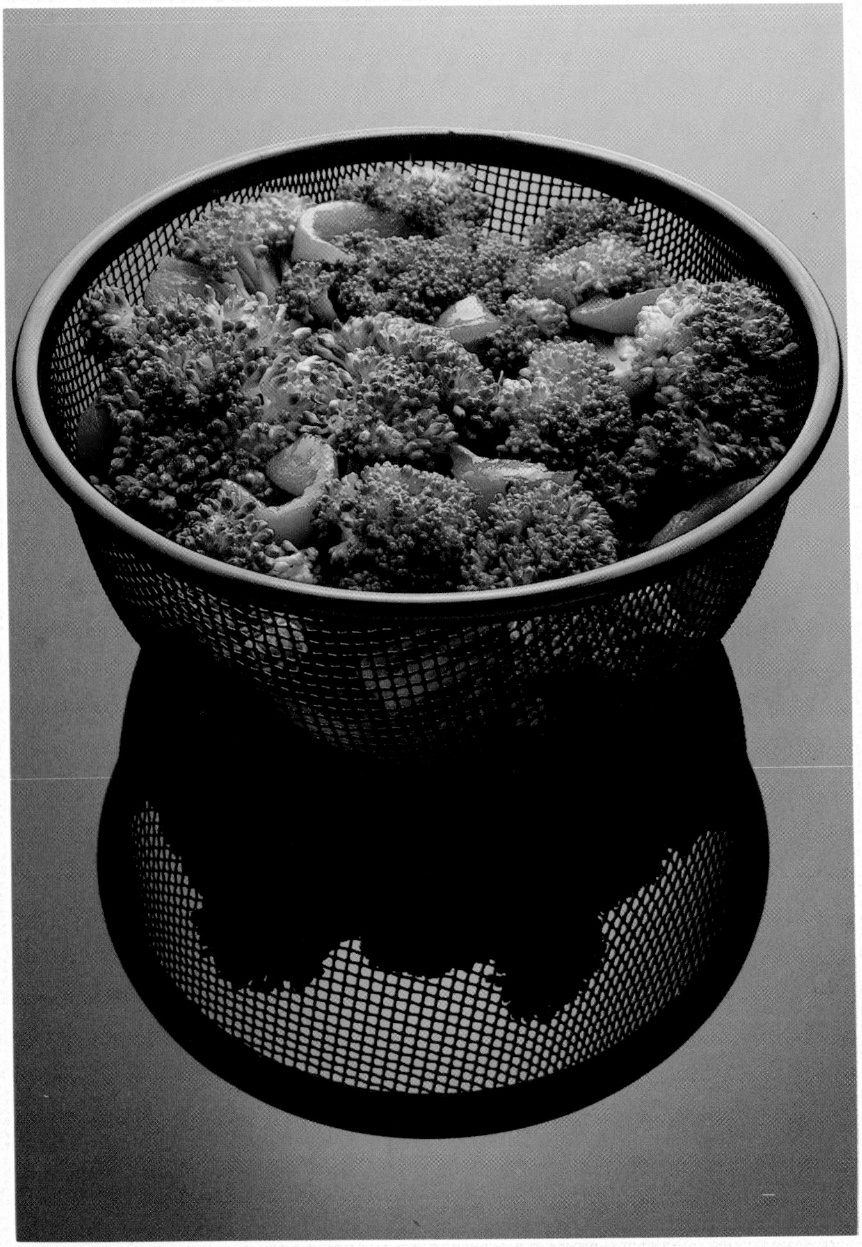

Recipe page 140

GAZPACHO

Recipe page 136

BAKED WHOLE GARLIC

Recipe page 141

BROCCOLI AND RED PEPPER
WITH GARLIC

The broccoli spears should be boiled until they are just tender but still crisp.

Serves 6 as a side dish or first course

1 large sweet red pepper
2½ pounds fresh broccoli, trimmed into spears
salt to taste
3 garlic cloves, crushed
¼ cup olive oil
1 small dried red chili pepper

Put sweet red pepper on to a broiling pan and broil, turning frequently, until blackened all over. Put pepper into a paper bag and fold bag closed. Let stand for 5 minutes, then remove from bag. Peel and seed pepper and cut into ¼-inch strips. Set aside. ★ Cook broccoli in a large pot of boiling water until just tender, about 5 to 7 minutes. Drain well and rinse under cold running water. Drain well again and gently pat dry. Set aside. ★ Heat oil, garlic and chili pepper together in a skillet over a high heat until bubbles form around garlic. Lower heat to moderately low and cook, stirring constantly, until garlic and chili pepper are light brown. Strain mixture through a fine sieve into a bowl. Discard garlic remaining in sieve and chili pepper. Let strained oil cool slightly and season with salt. ★ Generously brush broccoli spears and roasted red pepper strips with garlic-flavored oil. Arrange on a serving platter and serve. *Picture page 138*

CELERY VICTOR

Victor Hirtzler was chef at the famed St. Francis Hotel in San Francisco. This dish, at one time extremely fashionable, is his creation.

Serves 6 as a side dish or first course

3 heads celery
1 to 2 cups chicken broth
3 parsley sprigs
1 bay leaf
1 teaspoon dried thyme
1 medium-sized onion, sliced
1 carrot, cut into 1-inch pieces
1½ cups olive oil
½ cup white wine vinegar
salt to taste
black pepper to taste
6 anchovy fillets, drained
6 strips pimento

Rinse celery and trim off tough outer stalks. Cut off tops and bottoms, leaving stalks about 7 inches long. Cut each stalk in half lengthwise. ★ Place parsley, bay leaf and thyme in a square of cheesecloth. Tie square closed with string. In a large saucepan arrange celery in a single layer. Pour in just enough chicken broth to cover celery. Add cheesecloth bag, onion and carrot. Quickly bring mixture to a boil. Lower heat and simmer for 10 minutes, until celery is tender but still firm. Drain well and remove onion and carrot pieces. ★ Cool celery. Using your hands, gently squeeze celery to press out excess liquid. Arrange celery in a layer in a serving dish. In a small bowl whisk together oil, vinegar, salt and pepper. Pour mixture over celery and marinate in refrigerator for 2 to 3 hours. To serve, garnish each serving with an anchovy fillet and strip of pimento.

BAKED WHOLE GARLIC

Don't even think of socializing with anyone who hasn't just shared this meal with you. Although garlic is believed to help thin the blood, peeling large quantities of it can cause blistering on the skin. To prevent this happening, let the garlic cloves sit out in the sun for a few hours before you peel them.

Serves 8 as an appetizer

8 large whole garlic heads

1 cup sweet butter

2 sprigs fresh or 1 teaspoon dried rosemary

2 sprigs fresh or 1 teaspoon dried oregano

Preheat oven to 375°F. Remove paper outer layers from garlic heads, leaving cloves and heads intact. ★ Place whole heads on a large sheet of heavy aluminum foil. Top each head with equal amounts of butter and herbs. Fold up foil around heads and fold it sealed. ★ Place packet of garlic on a baking sheet and bake for 1 hour, or until heads are soft. Remove packet from oven and open foil. When just cool enough to handle, squeeze baked garlic cloves from skin. Spread cooked cloves on to thinly sliced pieces of crusty bread or pumpernickel and serve hot.

Picture page 139

IRVIN COBB'S BROWN DERBY SALAD

This is a version of the popular salad served at the Brown Derby restaurant in Hollywood during the 1930s and 1940s. It was invented and consumed in large quantities by the noted American humorist, writer and actor, Irvin Cobb. There are many variations on the original recipe, but they all have one thing in common: the ingredients are cut into incredibly tiny pieces. Add the dressing in front of your guests with a flourish and toss dramatically. Nostalgia reigns supreme with this salad – serve it to your favorite movie stars.

Serves 6 to 8 as a light supper or luncheon dish

1/2 head iceberg lettuce, torn into tiny pieces

1 head Belgian endive, torn into tiny pieces

2/3 bunch chicory, torn into tiny pieces

1/3 head romaine lettuce, torn into tiny pieces

2/3 bunch watercress, torn into tiny pieces

2 medium-sized tomatoes, finely diced

3 cups minced boiled chicken

1 green pepper, seeded and minced

1 sweet red pepper, seeded and minced

1/4 cup crisply cooked bacon, crumbled into tiny pieces

1 avocado, finely chopped

3 tablespoons minced green onion

3 hard-cooked eggs, finely chopped

1/4 cup grated Romano cheese

1 1/3 cups Balsamic Vinaigrette (see page 161)

Put iceberg lettuce, Belgian endive, chicory, lettuce and watercress in a large salad bowl. All ingredients should rest at the bottom of the bowl. ★ Add remaining ingredients except vinaigrette dressing in distinct layers, in any order. Chill for 30 minutes. Add dressing and toss.

SPINACH AND MUSHROOM SALAD

The incredible California climate allows anything to grow in profusion. To use anything but fresh spinach and mushrooms in this or any other salad would be sacrilege.

Serves 4 as a first course	*1/4 teaspoon dried basil*
1 pound fresh spinach	*1/4 teaspoon ground cumin*
8 large mushrooms	*1/4 teaspoon dried oregano*
Dressing:	*salt to taste*
2 tablespoons water	*3/4 cup olive oil*
1 garlic clove, crushed	*7 teaspoons white wine vinegar*
1 green onion, finely chopped	

Carefully wash spinach to remove all grit. Discard any tough stems and blemished leaves. ★ Wipe mushrooms clean with a damp paper towel. Remove stems and discard. Cut caps into thin slices. Put mushroom slices into a large salad bowl. Tear spinach into bite-sized pieces and put on top of mushroom in salad bowl. ★ In a small mixing bowl, combine water, garlic, green onion, basil, cumin, oregano and salt. Whisk until well blended. ★ Pour dressing over spinach and mushrooms. Let dressing collect in bottom of bowl. Wait 3 minutes while mushrooms marinate briefly in dressing. Toss gently and serve.

FENNEL SALAD

Fennel, also known in California markets by its Spanish name "hinojo," has tough outer ribs which must be peeled away. It should be prepared in the same manner as celery.

Serves 4 as a first course	***Dressing:***
1 medium-sized fennel	*6 tablespoons olive oil*
4 radishes, thinly sliced	*3 tablespoons cider vinegar*
2 seedless oranges, peeled and sectioned	*1 teaspoon Pernod or other anise-flavored liqueur*
4 black olives, pitted and halved	*salt to taste*
4 tablespoons minced onion	*cayenne pepper to taste*
several torn feathers from fennel	

Slice bulb and stalk of fennel into rings and put into a salad bowl. Arrange radish slices, orange sections, olives, onion and torn fennel feathers over fennel rings. ★ In a small mixing bowl combine olive oil, vinegar, Pernod, salt and cayenne pepper. Whisk until well blended. Pour over salad and serve.

Picture page 146

FRESH MOZZARELLA
WITH TOMATOES AND BASIL

Basil is popping up everywhere in contemporary California cuisine. For this salad to be especially delicious try to find garden-fresh tomatoes – store-bought (hot house) tomatoes have comparatively little flavor.

Serves 6 as a first course

- *½ pound fresh mozzarella cheese, thinly sliced*
- *4 large ripe tomatoes, peeled and thinly sliced*
- *¼ cup coarsely chopped fresh basil leaves*
- *2 tablespoons Balsamic Vinaigrette (see page 161)*

Arrange mozzarella and tomato slices in overlapping circles on a serving platter. Sprinkle cheese and tomatoes with chopped basil. ★ Pour balsamic vinaigrette over cheese and tomatoes and serve.

HAWAIIAN RICE

This dish is excellent served alongside lamb, pork or curried dishes. Vary the amount of raisins and coconut to suit your taste. Avoid substituting sweetened coconut in this recipe.

Serves 4 as a side dish

- *¾ cup chopped onion*
- *4 tablespoons butter*
- *1¼ cups long-grain rice*
- *½ teaspoon curry powder*
- *½ cup seedless golden raisins*
- *1¼ teaspoons salt*
- *2½ cups water*
- *½ cup shredded unsweetened coconut*

Preheat oven to 400°F. Melt butter in a skillet. Add onion and sauté until soft, about 5 minutes. Remove skillet from heat. ★ Place rice, curry powder, raisins, salt and water into a buttered 1½-quart casserole or baking dish. Add onions and butter and stir until well combined. Cover dish and bake for 5 minutes. Lower temperature to 350°F and bake for a further 40 minutes. ★ Remove from oven and cool slightly. Sprinkle coconut over top and serve directly from dish.

LEMON RICE WITH CAPERS

The importance of rice in Hawaii and California is directly related to the presence of large populations of Orientals. San Francisco has the largest Chinatown outside of mainland China.

Serves 6 as a side dish

- *1 cup long grain rice*
- *3 tablespoons sweet butter*
- *salt to taste*
- *black pepper to taste*
- *2 tablespoons lemon juice*
- *1 tablespoon capers, rinsed and drained*
- *1 teaspoon grated lemon rind*

Bring 4 cups water to a boil in a large saucepan. Add rice and cook over a high heat, stirring often, until rice is just tender, about 15 minutes. Remove rice from heat and drain in a colander. Rinse with cold running water and drain well. ★ Melt 1 tablespoon butter in a large skillet over a low heat. Add rice, salt and pepper. Heat rice, fluffing it with a fork. When rice is hot, add lemon juice, capers and lemon rind. Stir gently for 5 seconds, then remove skillet from heat. Add remaining butter and stir gently. Transfer to a serving dish and serve at once.

Picture page 146

BAKED TUNA STEAK

Fresh tuna is a rich, meat-like fish, and goes best with a light salad and boiled potatoes.

Serves 4 to 6 as a main course

- *6 fresh tuna steaks*
- *salt to taste*
- *black pepper to taste*
- *grated nutmeg to taste*
- *$1^1/_2$ cups fish stock*
- *4 tablespoons tomato paste*
- *3 tablespoons lemon juice*

Preheat oven to 350°F. Sprinkle tuna steaks with salt, black pepper and nutmeg to taste. ★ Place steaks in a buttered baking dish and add fish stock. Cover with aluminum foil and bake for 30 minutes. Remove foil and bake 5 minutes longer. Remove dish from oven and place tuna steaks on a hot serving platter. ★ Pour liquid in the baking pan into a saucepan and bring to a boil over a high heat. Cook until liquid is reduced by about one-third. Add butter and tomato paste. Season to taste with salt and black pepper and add lemon juice. Pour sauce over fish.

FENNEL SALAD

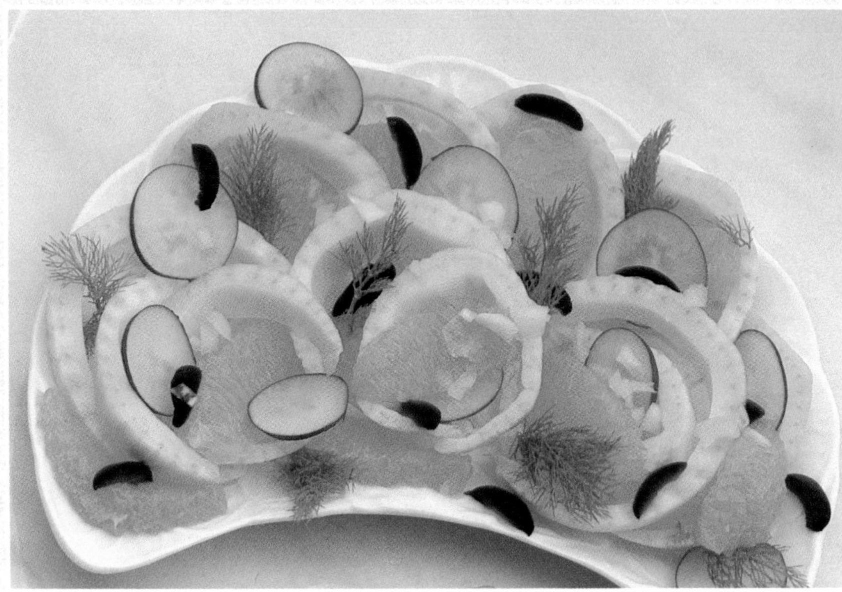

Recipe page 143

LEMON RICE WITH CAPERS

Recipe page 145

RED SNAPPER HAWAIIAN

This dish should properly be made with the opakapaka fish, which is found in Hawaiian waters. It is traditionally an important feature of a luau. Red snapper is a very close substitute.

Serves 4 to 6 as a main course

1 4- to 5-pound whole red snapper, cleaned
coarse salt
meat of 1 fresh coconut, broken into small pieces
1 cup water
2 tablespoons sherry
1 orange, peeled and sectioned
1 fresh pineapple, cut into chunks
1 papaya, sliced

Season fish well, inside and out, with coarse salt. Place fish in a shallow buttered baking dish. ★ In a blender or food processor, combine coconut meat and water. Process at high speed for 30 seconds. Strain coconut through a sieve into a bowl, pressing with back of a spoon to extract all liquid. Let stand for 1 hour or until coconut cream has risen to top. Skim off cream and pour over fish. (Canned coconut milk may be used instead, but the results are not as good.) ★ Preheat oven to 350°F. Bake fish for 20 minutes. Pour sherry into pan and bake for a further 15 minutes. Surround fish with the orange, pineapple and papaya pieces and bake for a further 10 minutes or until fish flakes easily.

SHRIMP WITH ZUCCHINI

An unpretentious way to blend two of the west coast's finest fresh ingredients.

Serves 4 as a main course

1 pound shrimp, shelled and deveined
3 tablespoons olive oil
1 large onion, chopped
2 garlic cloves, finely chopped
1 green pepper
2 cups fresh tomatoes, chopped
2 small zucchini, sliced
½ teaspoon black pepper

Heat oil in a skillet. Add onion, garlic and green pepper. Cook over a moderate heat for 3 minutes, stirring occasionally. Add tomatoes, zucchini, salt and pepper. Cover and simmer for 5 minutes. ★ Add shrimp and simmer for another 5 minutes or until shrimp turn pink. Serve at once.

Picture page 154

SEA BASS
WITH GOAT CHEESE TOPPING

Fish has never been considered "famine food" on the western edge of America. A lot of both Californian and Hawaiian cuisine is based on seafood. The goat cheese topping adds a distinctive taste to this recipe.

Serves 4 as a main course

- *2 tablespoons sweet butter, melted*
- *4 6- to 8-ounce sea bass or red snapper fillets*
- *coarse salt to taste*
- *black pepper to taste*
- *1/3 cup dry vermouth*
- *1/3 cup chicken broth*
- *2 teaspoons lemon juice*

Goat cheese topping:

- *3 ounces Montrachet or other goat cheese, at room temperature*
- *6 tablespoons heavy cream*
- *1/2 cup coarsely chopped walnuts*
- *3 tablespoons sliced whole green onions*
- *2 tablespoons finely chopped parsley*
- *2 tablespoons finely chopped fresh or 1 teaspoon dried marjoram*
- *coarse salt to taste*
- *black pepper to taste*

In a small bowl blend softened goat cheese and cream with a spoon until smooth. Add walnuts, green onions, parsley, marjoram, salt and pepper. Blend well and set aside. ★ Preheat oven to broil. Brush a broiling pan with 1 tablespoon melted butter. ★ Brush fillets with remaining butter. Season fish on both sides with salt and pepper. ★ Broil fillets 4 inches from heat until fish is not quite opaque in center, about 9 to 10 minutes per inch of thickness. ★ Remove pan and spread topping evenly over fish fillets. Return pan and cook until cheese begins to melt and fish is opaque in center, about 1 to 2 minutes longer. Remove fillets from pan and keep warm on a plate. ★ Put broiling pan over a moderate heat and stir in vermouth and chicken broth. Bring mixture to a boil, stirring constantly to loosen any brown bits on bottom of pan. When liquid comes to a boil, pour into a small saucepan. Bring to a boil again. Continue to boil until liquid is reduced to 1/3 cup. Stir in lemon juice and season to taste with salt. Spoon sauce over fish and serve.

Picture page 155

HANGTOWN FRY

Legend has it that Hangtown Fry was created during the California Gold Rush of 1849. A miner who had struck it rich swaggered into Hangtown (now called Placerville) and demanded the most expensive meal the hotel could offer. When informed that oysters and eggs were the most costly items on the menu, he told the chef to combine the two. The result is a genuine Californian dish. For true authenticity, small Pacific Coast Olympia oysters should be used.

Serves 4 as a main course

12 oysters, shucked
2 tablespoons flour
salt to taste
black pepper to taste
9 eggs
fine breadcrumbs
3 tablespoons butter

Drain oysters thoroughly on paper towels. Beat 1 egg in a small bowl. Place breadcrumbs in another small bowl. ★ Combine flour, salt and pepper in a bowl. Dip each oyster into flour mixture, then into beaten egg, and then into the breadcrumbs. ★ Heat butter in a large skillet. Add oysters and fry until golden brown on both sides, about 3 minutes. ★ Beat remaining 8 eggs with salt and pepper. Pour over oysters in skillet. Cook over a moderate heat until eggs are firm on bottom. Turn eggs with a large spatula and continue to cook on the other side for 1 to 2 minutes.

LOMI-LOMI SALMON

A favorite dish at Hawaiian luaus.

Serves 6 as a main course

1 pound salted salmon
5 large ripe tomatoes, peeled, seeded and chopped
1 onion, finely chopped
2 green onions, finely chopped

Soak salmon overnight in enough cold water to cover. Drain well, remove skin and cut salmon into small pieces. Put pieces into a large bowl and add tomatoes, onion and green onions. Mix well. Cover and refrigerate until thoroughly chilled.

CIOPPINO

Cioppino is a San Francisco fish stew with Italian origins.

Serves 6 as a main course	*1 green pepper, coarsely chopped*
1 1/2 pounds firm white fish fillets	*4 ripe tomatoes, peeled and chopped*
1 pound shrimp, shelled and deveined	*1/2 cup canned tomato paste*
1 lobster	*2 cups red wine*
1 quart mussels	*1/2 cup chopped parsley*
1/2 cup olive oil	*1 teaspoon salt*
1 large onion, coarsely chopped	*1/2 teaspoon black pepper*
2 garlic cloves, chopped	

Cut fish into large chunks. Insert a knife into lobster where tail and body meet. Sever spinal cord and cut lobster in pieces. Scrub and debeard mussels. ★ Place fish, shrimp and lobster in layers in a large kettle. ★ Heat oil in a saucepan. Add onion, garlic and green pepper. Cook for 5 minutes. Add tomatoes, tomato paste, wine, 1/4 cup parsley, salt and pepper. Cover and cook over low heat for 15 minutes. ★ Pour sauce over layers of fish, shrimp and lobster. Cover and simmer gently for 30 minutes or until fish flakes easily when tested with a fork. Add mussels and continue cooking until they open, about 5 minutes. ★ Transfer cioppino to a large serving dish and sprinkle with remaining parsley. Serve hot.

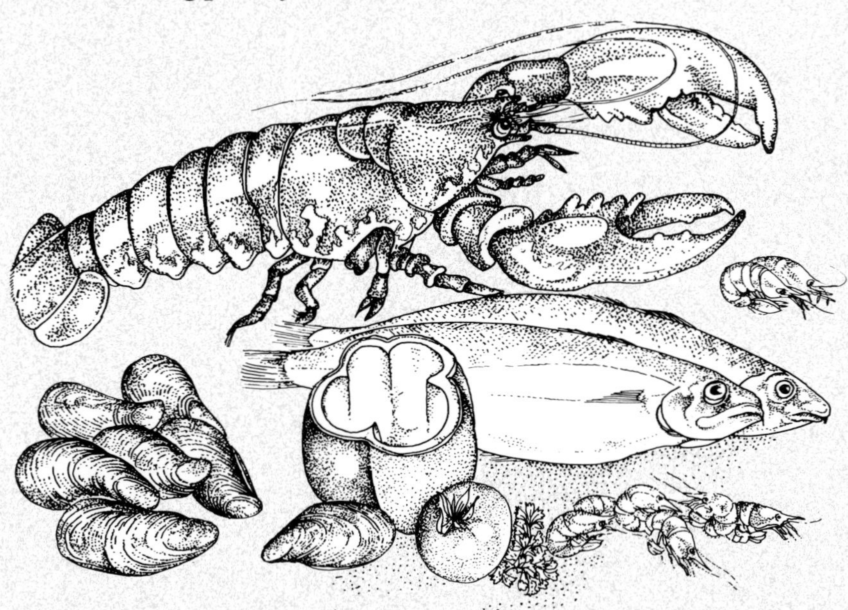

VEAL MEDALLIONS
WITH AVOCADO

This variation on a standard recipe uses one of California's most prized fruits. California is also the largest commercial producer of avocados in the nation.

Serves 6 as a main course

1½ cups chicken broth
1 cup half and half
2 ripe avocados
¼ cup lemon juice
12 3-ounce veal cutlets
1 teaspoon salt
1 teaspoon white pepper
6 tablespoons flour
4 tablespoons butter
2 tablespoons vegetable oil

Bring chicken broth and half and half to a boil in a saucepan over a moderate heat. Reduce heat and simmer briskly until liquid is reduced to 1½ cups, about 20 minutes. ★ While sauce is reduced, halve, pit and peel avocados and cut into 6 wedges each. Put wedges in a shallow bowl and very gently toss with lemon juice to keep from oxidizing. ★ Season cutlets with salt and pepper and dust with flour. Melt butter in oil in a large skillet over a moderate to high heat. When butter is sizzling, add cutlets in batches without crowding and sauté for about 3 minutes per side, until nicely browned. Keep warm. ★ Pour off excess fat from skillet. Pour lemon juice from avocados into skillet and stir and scrape to dissolve pan deposits. After a minute or so, when juice has reduced almost to a syrup, add broth and cream mixture and simmer for about 2 minutes to heat sauce through. ★ Spoon sauce on to 6 heated serving plates. Place 2 cutlets on top of sauce on each plate. Top each cutlet with a slice of avocado.

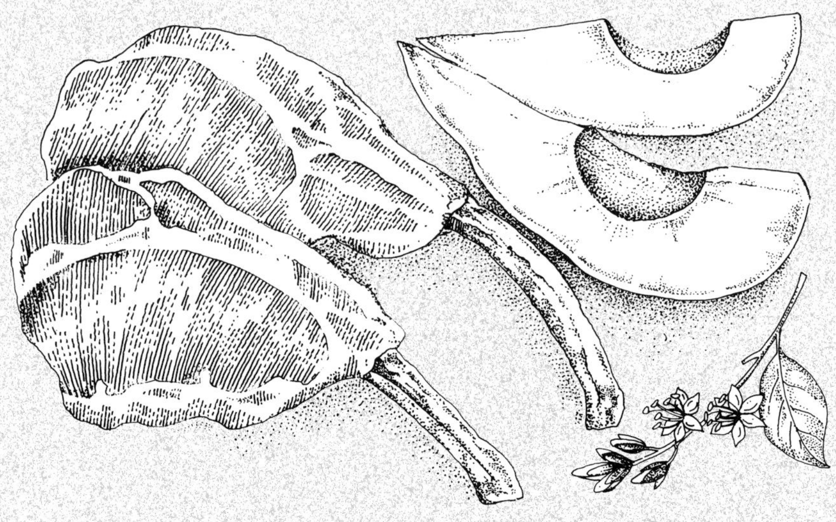

OAHU POT ROAST

Hawaii's version of the standard Yankee pot roast (there are as many variations of pot roast as there are states). It is a delicious way to tenderize meat – and has the added advantage of utilizing a cheap cut of beef.

Serves 8 as a main course

- *1 3½- to 4-pound chuck or rump roast*
- *1 large onion, sliced and separated into rings*
- *1 cup apple cider*
- *3 tablespoons soy sauce*
- *1½ teaspoons chopped fresh ginger*
- *½ teaspoon salt*
- *3 celery stalks, thinly sliced*
- *4 carrots, thinly sliced*
- *1 small sweet potato, peeled and thinly sliced*
- *½ pound fresh spinach*
- *6 mushrooms, sliced*
- *1 tablespoon cornstarch*
- *2 tablespoons cold water*

Place meat in a large shallow dish. In a small bowl combine onion rings, apple cider, soy sauce, ginger and salt. Combine thoroughly and pour over meat. Marinate overnight, turning frequently. ★ Place meat and marinade in a large heavy pot. Quickly bring to a boil, reduce heat and cover. Simmer for 2 hours or until meat is tender. Add celery, carrots and sweet potato. Simmer, covered, for a further 15 minutes. Place spinach and mushrooms on top of meat and other vegetables. Cover and cook only until spinach wilts, about 5 minutes. ★ Remove meat and vegetables to a serving platter. Skim any fat from liquid in pot. ★ In a small bowl combine cold water and cornstarch, stirring until smooth. Stir into broth and cook, stirring constantly, until gravy is thickened. Serve with meat.

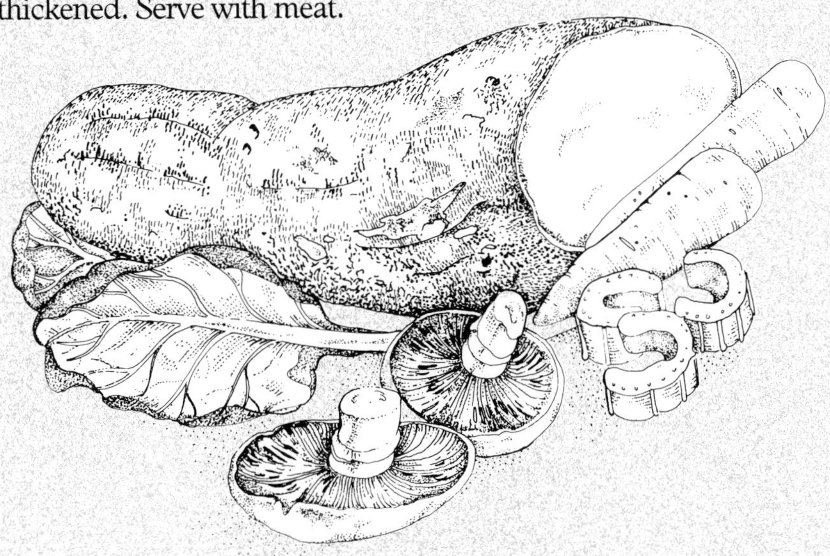

SHRIMP WITH ZUCCHINI

Recipe page 148

SEA BASS WITH GOAT CHEESE TOPPING

Recipe page 149

PINEAPPLE SNOW

Indigenous to South America, pineapples were being cultivated in the West Indies when the first Europeans hoved into view. It is believed that Captain James Cook introduced pineapples to Hawaii, but other theories argue that the Spanish were the first to introduce the sweet fruit to the islands.

Serves 4 to 6 as a dessert
2 cups whipping cream
1 fresh pineapple
4 egg whites
1/2 cup superfine sugar
1 tablespoon sherry

Fill a large bowl with cracked ice and place a smaller bowl inside it. Put cream in smaller bowl. Refrigerate until needed. ★ Trim, peel and grate pineapple. Reserve all juice and pulp. ★ In a bowl, beat egg whites until foamy. Add sugar gradually and continue beating. Gently stir in sherry. Stir in very cold cream. Add pineapple pulp and juice and continue beating. Add only as much pineapple as mixture will hold without becoming too soft. ★ Transfer to a serving bowl and chill for 3 to 4 hours before serving.

MACADAMIA NUT CAKE

Dr John MacAdam is the man who first listened to the aborigines extolling the virtues of this nut over 100 years ago. Consequently it bears his name. Australia has belatedly caught on and now grows macadamias commercially.

Makes 1 9-inch cake
2 1/3 cups unsalted macadamia nuts
3/4 cup plus 2 tablespoons sugar
1/4 cup flour
5 large eggs, separated
3/4 teaspoon pure vanilla extract
1/4 teaspoon cream of tartar

Filling:
6 tablespoons sweet butter, softened
5 tablespoons sifted superfine sugar
1 egg yolk
1 tablespoon nut-flavored or almond liqueur
1/2 cup unsalted macadamia nuts

Topping:
1 cup very cold heavy cream
1 tablespoon sugar
2 teaspoons pure vanilla extract
chopped toasted, unsalted macadamia nuts

Preheat oven to 325°F. Butter a 9-inch springform pan. Line bottom of pan with foil. Butter foil and flour entire pan. Set aside. ★ To make the cake, grind half the quantity of macadamia nuts with 3 tablespoons sugar in a blender or food processor. Process until very fine. Empty nut mixture into a bowl and reserve. Process the remaining nuts with 3 tablespoons sugar until very fine and add to other nut mixture. Sift flour over nut mixture. Stir until blended. ★ In a medium-sized bowl beat egg yolks with 1/4 cup sugar for 5 minutes or until very light in color. Add vanilla and beat to blend. ★ In a small bowl beat egg whites with cream of tartar until they form soft peaks. Add remaining 1/4 cup sugar, a little at a time, beating until whites are stiff but not dry. Alternately fold nut mixture and egg whites into egg yolks. ★ Gently turn batter into prepared pan. Bake for 50 minutes or until a cake tester inserted into center of cake comes out clean. ★ Remove from oven. Cool in pan on a wire rack for 10 minutes. Carefully run a knife around cake and remove springform pan sides. Invert cake on to another wire rack. Remove bottom of pan and foil. Invert again so that cake is right-side up. Cool completely. ★ To make the filling, beat together butter and 1/4 cup superfine sugar in a small bowl until smooth. Add egg yolk and beat. Blend in liqueur. ★ In a blender or food processor grind nuts with remaining 1 tablespoon superfine sugar. Process until fine. Add to butter mixture and stir. ★ Carefully cut cooled cake in half, forming two layers. Spread filling evenly on bottom layer. Place second layer on top. Refrigerate for 1 to 1 1/2 hours. ★ To make the topping, beat cream with sugar until soft peaks begin to form in a well-chilled mixing bowl. Add vanilla extract and continue beating until firm peaks form. ★ Remove cake from refrigerator. Spread topping on sides and top of cake. Sprinkle chopped macadamia nuts in center of cake. ★ Refrigerate but serve at room temperature.

MACADAMIA NUT AND CHOCOLATE MUFFINS

Native to the coastal forests of New South Wales and Queensland in Australia, macadamias are actually associated with Hawaii, which today is the largest grower of these sweet, oily nuts.

Makes 12 breakfast muffins

- *2 cups sifted flour*
- *1/3 cup sugar*
- *1 tablespoon baking powder*
- *1 teaspoon salt*
- *1/2 cup cold vegetable shortening, cut into small pieces*
- *1/2 cup semisweet chocolate bits*
- *3/4 cup coarsely chopped unsalted macadamia nuts*
- *1 large egg, lightly beaten*
- *1 cup milk*
- *1 teaspoon dark rum*

Preheat oven to 400°F. Sift flour together with sugar, baking powder and salt into a large bowl. Add shortening pieces, cutting them in with a pastry blender or two knives until mixture resembles a coarse meal. Add chocolate pieces and stir. Add 1/2 cup of macadamia nuts and stir again. ★ Combine egg, milk and rum in a bowl. Beat lightly until blended. Add to flour mixture and stir only until mixtures are just combined – muffin batter should be lumpy. ★ Divide batter among 12 buttered muffin pans. Sprinkle tops of muffins with remaining macadamia nuts. Bake muffins until a cake tester inserted into center of a muffin comes out clean, about 25 minutes. ★ Remove muffins from oven and cool in pan on a wire rack for 5 minutes. Turn muffins out of pan on to a wire rack and cool completely before serving.

CARROT CAKE

This Californian recipe first gained popularity in the 1960s and quickly made the leap from hippie health-food counters to ordinary restaurants and grocery stores.

Makes 1 cake
1 cup sugar
1/2 cup butter, softened
1 1/2 cups flour
2 teaspoons baking powder
1/2 teaspoon baking soda
1/2 teaspoon salt
1/4 teaspoon grated nutmeg
1 teaspoon cinnamon
1/8 teaspoon allspice
1 cup grated carrots
2 eggs
1 cup chopped walnuts

Frosting:
1/4 cup cream cheese, softened
1 1/4 cups confectioner's sugar
1/2 teaspoon pure vanilla extract
1 egg white

Preheat oven to 350°F. Butter a medium-sized baking pan. ★ Combine sugar, butter, flour, baking powder, baking soda, salt, nutmeg, cinnamon and allspice in a mixing bowl. Add carrots and eggs and beat well. Add walnuts and mix again. Pour into prepared baking pan and bake for 1 hour. ★ To make the frosting, beat cream cheese with confectioner's sugar, vanilla and egg white until smooth. Spread over cooled cake.

AVOCADO SPREAD

This dish is sometimes called poor man's butter, perhaps from the buttery taste of a ripe avocado and the relative cheapness of both avocados and tomatoes in fertile Southern California. It makes an excellent filling for tacos.

Makes about 2 cups as an appetizer spread

2 large ripe avocados
2 tablespoons lemon juice
2 large firm ripe tomatoes, peeled, seeded and cubed
boiling water
1 canned green chili pepper, seeded and chopped
3 tablespoons red wine vinegar
1 tablespoon vegetable oil
salt to taste

Halve avocados and remove pits and any brown fibers around pits. Carefully peel the avocados, using fingers or a small knife. Cut avocados into small cubes and place in a bowl. Add lemon juice and toss gently to coat avocado. Add tomatoes, chili, vinegar and oil. Toss together until well mixed. Season with salt and let stand for 30 to 45 minutes before serving.

CALFORNIA RELISH

Californians love this relish together with mild, creamy cheese and crackers.

Makes approximately 3 cups of relish

1 tablespoon French-style mustard
1 cup sugar
1/3 cup cider vinegar
2/3 cup water
2 cinnamon sticks
1 large piece fresh ginger root
4 medium apples, peeled, cored, and cut into eighths
1/2 cup seedless raisins
1/4 cup chopped walnuts

Combine mustard and sugar in a saucepan. Add vinegar, water, cinnamon sticks, and ginger root. Bring mixture to a boil. Reduce heat and simmer for 10 minutes. ★ Cut each eighth of an apple into 4 equal pieces. ★ Remove cinnamon sticks and ginger root from the hot mixture. Add apples, raisins, and nuts. Bring mixture to a boil. Reduce heat and simmer for 10 minutes. ★ Remove mixture from heat and cool. Store in the refrigerator in a tightly covered bowl or jar.

BALSAMIC VINAIGRETTE

Tossed green salads are consumed in such variety and such quantities that it's a good idea to have an equal number of dressings available. This one is French in origin.

Makes ½ cup salad dressing	*2 teaspoons balsamic vinegar*
1 shallot, finely chopped	*6 tablespoons olive oil*
1 teaspoon Dijon-style mustard	*salt to taste*
1½ tablespoons red wine vinegar	*black pepper to taste*

In a small bowl, combine shallot, mustard, red wine vinegar and balsamic vinegar. Whisk together until well blended. ★ In a slow, steady stream, whisk in olive oil. Continue to whisk until vinaigrette is smooth and well blended. Season to taste with salt and pepper and whisk gently.

GREEN GODDESS DRESSING

The matinee idol George Arliss (1868-1946) played the leading role in William Archer's play The Green Goddess *both on stage and in the two movie versions (1923 and 1930). This dressing was created for him in the mid-1920s at the Palace Hotel in San Francisco. Serve it over a green salad or use instead of mayonnaise.*

Makes 4 cups	*1 teaspoon dried tarragon*
8 anchovy fillets, finely chopped	*3 cups mayonnaise*
1 green onion, finely chopped	*¼ cup tarragon vinegar*
¼ cup chopped parsley	*½ cup chopped chives*

Combine all ingredients in a mixing bowl and blend well.

PACIFIC NORTHWEST
AND
ALASKA

These magnificent states are still wild in many areas. It is an area of rugged coastline, huge irrigated plains and snow-clad mountains. The food shares in this majestic simplicity.

This region offers the delightful combination of spectacular natural scenery and delicious natural foods. Few other areas can offer the variety or quality of foods which are native to this region: the seafood cornucopia from hundreds of miles of Pacific coastline; the products of lush coastal dairylands; crops from the farmlands and orchards of inland valleys fed by hundreds of streams and enriched by glacial and volcanic soil; the harvest from vast stretches of irrigated, sun-drenched croplands along the rivers east of the Cascades; and choice meats from the huge cattle and sheep ranges across the semi-arid eastern sections of Oregon and Washington. Much of the cooking is based on fresh ingredients.

Dungeness crab, another specialty in this area, is famous for its tender, sweet flesh. Oregon shrimp have become a major industry since their discovery off the coast only a decade ago. Olympic oysters are farmed in several coastal bays and mussels still die of old age, their quantity on coastal rocks easily defying the demand. Clams are there for the digging. There's also ling cod, snapper, sole, giant halibut, rock bass, squid and whiting to tantalize the fish connoisseur.

The specialties of the coast are legion but salmon is the headliner. When the salmon run begins, fishermen get so tired of eating the fine, red flesh that they resort to Indian methods of keeping the fish edible by smoking, pickling or salting the flesh. Salmon roasts are one of this region's mouth-watering traditions. The fish are "planked" – attached to pieces of hardwood – and smoked the Indian way. Salmon, steelhead, bass, perch, sturgeon and trout inhabit the sparkling rivers.

When a diet of fresh fish pales, the coastal pastures of this region produce some of the nation's best-fed and most contented bovines, who turn out the raw material for

Snow-capped Mount Baker rises above the flatlands

gourmet cheeses and other dairy products.

The central part of this region is orchard and berry country. Luscious pears, apples, plums, peaches and berries of all descriptions supply a worldwide distribution system. The Indians of the area used native berries as a diet staple. Today, growers have developed perfect strains of strawberries, raspberries, blueberries and cranberries (the latter imported from the bogs of New England). These have encouraged local production of premium jams and preserves.

Pasturelands at the foot of the several mountain ranges along the far eastern borders of Oregon and Washington support one of the nation's most important meat and wheat production areas. Beef here is enjoyed in the traditional Western style – grilled or barbecued over open charcoal or wood fires. In the southeastern part of Oregon, populated by Basque sheepherders, lamb is a delicacy.

Game is abundant, particularly in Alaska, where the human population is still relatively small. Hunters in Alaska can bag brown or grizzly bears, mountain sheep, black and glacier bears, caribou, deer, elk, goat, moose, wolf and wolverine. Deer, elk, moose, bear and mountain goat still roam freely in Alaska and in the more remote mountainous areas of Washington. Grouse, pheasants and migrating Canadian geese can be taken, as well as smaller game such as rabbits, muskrats, opossum and raccoons.

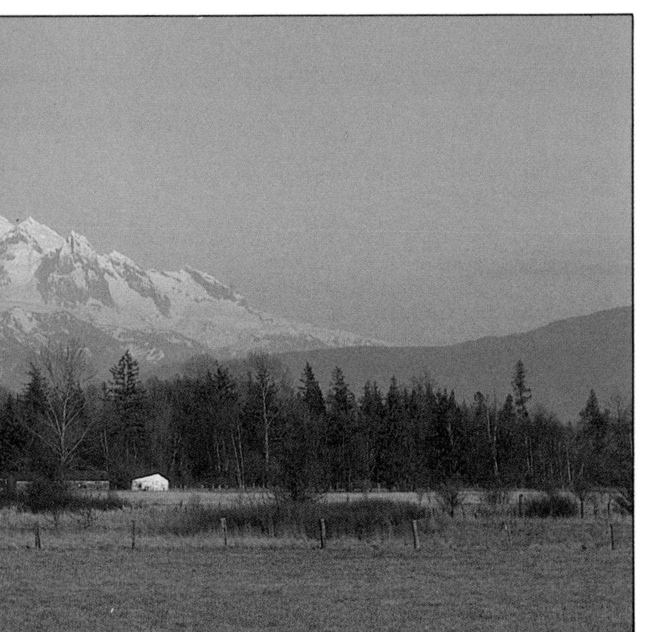

American missionaries and trappers began moving into Oregon and Washington as early as 1806 – pushing Russian trappers north into the wilds of Alaska. Gold discoveries in Washington in 1855 and in Alaska in 1880 brought a rush of prospectors. (Alaska had been bought by Secretary of State William Seward from the Russians in 1867 for about a cent an acre. His purchase was disparaged at the time as "Seward's Folly.") It is to the Yukon traders, following in the wake of the prospectors, that we owe the secret of sourdough – one of the more quintessentially American ingredients now used in everything from bread to cakes and pizzas. Close on the heels of the prospectors came the white settlers, lured by tales of lush valleys and free land grants. Most of these pioneers were of Dutch, German and Scandinavian origin. Each brought their own distinct culinary traditions, linked by a commitment to simple, unadorned cooking.

Local food was not always an appetizing prospect as one woman, quoted in Fred Lockley's *Oregon Journal*, recalls: "One of the men of the party killed a skunk, which they cooked. Dr White started to ask the blessing over the skunk, but Orris Brown said, 'I won't stand for any blessing being asked over a skunk. It would be too much like sacrilege. You'd better save your blessings until we get some deer meat or something fit to eat.'" And, in spite of all the wild berries and fruits available, it wasn't long before apples, pears, peaches, grapes and melons of all kinds were being cultivated. Fresh apple pie became as routine on the daily menu as in any proper New England household.

As purely American as the regional cuisine of this region is, the European influences are unmistakable. Most of the immigrants toiling over the Oregon Trail and north to Alaska were not many generations removed from their European antecedents. They added fresh American ingredients to recipes handed down from mother to daughter in the old country. Oriental culinary traditions were added to this European melting pot when hundreds of Chinese were brought into the gold and silver fields as cheap labor. These early pioneers stayed on, adding their exotic spices and recipes to the already rich cuisine of the region.

LIMA BEAN SOUP

Early goldminers and pioneers, faced with primitive cooking conditions, relied heavily on dried beans and salt pork as the staple of their diet. Drying legumes and salting meat were two methods for safely storing food for long periods of time.

Serves 6 as a first course	*1 garlic clove, finely chopped*
2 cups dried lima beans	*1 bay leaf*
1 pound lean salt pork, cut into ½-inch dice	*1 tablespoon chopped fresh parsley*
2 large carrots, finely chopped	*1 tablespoon savory*
2 celery stalks, finely chopped	*1 teaspoon thyme*
2 medium-sized onions, finely chopped	*1 teaspoon salt*
	1 teaspoon black pepper
	3 quarts water

Soak lima beans overnight in enough cold water to cover. ★ Drain beans and put in a large pot with remaining ingredients. Bring liquid to a boil over a high heat, skimming occasionally. Reduce heat, cover pot and simmer soup for about 3 hours, until beans are tender.

CRABMEAT AND APPLE SALAD

The Pacific Northwest coast offers seafood second to none, hence many recipes are based on fresh seafood. Dungeness crab is rated the finest crab in all of North America by some fans.

Serves 6 as a first course	*2 tablespoons lemon juice*
1½ pounds cooked crabmeat	*½ tablespoon dried tarragon*
2 crisp apples, cored and coarsely chopped	*½ teaspoon sugar*
	½ teaspoon white pepper
2 celery stalks, finely chopped	*6 large lettuce leaves*
½ cup slivered almonds	*6 watercress sprigs*
¾ cup mayonnaise	*1 lemon, cut into 6 wedges*

Toss together crabmeat, apples, celery and almonds. Stir together mayonnaise, lemon juice and seasonings and mix crabmeat mixture with dressing. Chill well in refrigerator for at least 1 hour. ★ To serve the salad, place a scoop on top of a lettuce leaf on a chilled plate. Garnish with watercress and wedge of lemon.

ANGELS ON HORSEBACK

It's anyone's guess as to the origin of this recipe's name. Most Pacific oysters are farmed in commercial beds and most of these are found along the southern coast of Washington.

Serves 6 as a first course

- *2 dozen oysters, shucked*
- *24 thin slices lean bacon*
- *1 lemon*
- *Tabasco sauce*
- *salt to taste*
- *black pepper to taste*

Preheat broiler. Place each oyster in the middle of a strip of bacon and season with a few drops of lemon juice, a dash of Tabasco and a light sprinkling of salt and pepper. Wrap each oyster in its bacon strip and secure with a toothpick. ★ Broil "angels" about 4 inches from heat for 5 to 7 minutes, turning once, just until bacon is crisp. Carefully remove toothpicks and serve at once.

BARBECUED SALMON

Compared to the dysentery-ridden white immigrants who stumbled into their paradise, the Indians of this region were healthy, thanks to their rich diet of salmon. Indians believed the salmon were ancestors who returned to their birthplace to bring food to the tribe – their family.

Serves 6 to 8 as a main course

- *1 5- to 6-pound salmon, cleaned*
- *salt to taste*
- *black pepper to taste*
- *2 tablespoons butter, softened and cut into pieces*
- *½ medium onion, thinly sliced*
- *½ lemon, sliced*
- *2 parsley sprigs*
- *vegetable oil*
- *lemon wedges*

Sprinkle salmon inside and out with salt and pepper. Dot with butter. Arrange overlapping slices of onion and lemon with parsley sprigs in the cavity. Brush fish with oil. ★ Wrap salmon in heavy aluminum foil. Seal edges with double folds to make a leakproof package. Place package on wire grill over medium-hot barbecue coals. Carefully turn package every 10 minutes. Test for doneness after 45 minutes. The fish is done when it flakes easily when fork-tested at thickest part. ★ To serve, transfer salmon to a serving platter and fold back foil. Lift off each serving. Serve with lemon wedges.

BAKED TROUT
WITH SOUR CREAM

Game fishing is a popular pastime in the Pacific Northwest and Alaska. Trout is the prize of rivers.

Serves 6 as a main course	*1 teaspoon savory*
6 trout, 8 to 10 ounces each	*½ teaspoon tarragon*
1 teaspoon salt	*3 tablespoons white wine*
½ teaspoon white pepper	*½ tablespoon lemon juice*
2 tablespoons butter	*⅓ cup sour cream*
1 small onion, finely chopped	*¼ cup fine breadcrumbs*
1 tablespoon chopped parsley	*¼ cup grated Parmesan cheese*
1 teaspoon chopped fresh dill	

Season trout inside and out with salt and pepper. Set aside. ★ Melt 1 tablespoon butter in a small skillet over a moderate heat. Sauté onion until transparent, about 3 minutes. Add the herbs, sauté 1 minute more and stir in wine and lemon juice. ★ Preheat oven to 425°F. Grease a shallow baking dish with remaining butter. Place trout side-by-side in dish and stuff with onion and herb mixture. Pour any excess liquid from skillet over fish. Cover dish tightly with a lid or aluminum foil and bake trout for about 15 minutes, until firm and flaky. ★ Preheat broiler. Spread sour cream evenly over trout, then top with breadcrumbs and Parmesan. Broil for 3 to 5 minutes, until lightly browned.

CHILLED POACHED SALMON STEAKS

In many areas the Indians' entire economy depended on salmon. What they didn't immediately consume was dried into a food called "pemmican," edible even years later. Pemmican was used as a trading item with other tribes.

Serves 6 as a main course	*½ cup sour cream*
6 salmon steaks	*¼ cup mayonnaise*
4 cups water	*1 tablespoon chopped parsley*
5 whole black peppercorns	*1 tablespoon finely chopped onion*
1 tablespoon lemon juice	*2 teaspoons vinegar*
1 tablespoon lime juice	*salt to taste*
1 cup finely grated cucumber	*black pepper to taste*

In a large pot combine salt, peppercorns, lemon juice and lime juice and bring to a boil. Add 3 salmon steaks and poach for 10 minutes. Remove and repeat with remaining steaks. Chill. ★ To make the sauce, combine cucumber, sour cream, mayonnaise, parsley, onion, vinegar, salt and pepper in a mixing bowl. Mix well and chill. Serve separately in a sauce boat.

SALMON

WITH LIME AND WALNUT OIL

The annual migration of the salmon up the rivers of the Pacific Northwest and Alaska – and the promise of some as big as 30 pounds – lures sport fishermen the world over.

Serves 4 as a main course	*rind of 1 lime*
4 salmon steaks	*7 tablespoons chilled sweet butter*
salt to taste	*2 tablespoons lime juice*
black pepper to taste	*3 tablespoons walnut oil*

Season salmon steaks with salt and pepper. Preheat oven to 250°F. ★ Cut lime rind into julienne strips. Blanch strips in boiling water for 1 minute. Drain well. ★ Heat 2 tablespoons of butter in a large skillet. Add salmon and sauté over a medium-high heat until lightly browned, about 4 minutes per side. Transfer salmon to a plate, cover, and keep warm in oven. ★ Add lime juice, lime rind and walnut oil to skillet. Stir well and cook over a low heat until mixture is just heated through. Whisk in remaining butter 1 tablespoon at a time. Be careful not to let sauce get too hot. Remove skillet from heat and let cool slightly if necessary. The sauce should be slightly thick, the same consistency as hollandaise sauce. Season with salt and pepper and remove from heat. ★ Remove salmon from oven. Spoon sauce over steaks and serve.

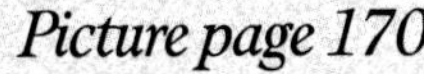
Picture page 170

MARINATED FRESH SALMON

In Washington state alone almost 850,000 pounds of salmon are caught each year by sport fishermen – not to mention the amount caught by commercial fishermen. However, salmon spawning is increasingly threatened by river pollution. This is a Scandinavian recipe popular in the Pacific Northwest.

Serves 6 as a first course

- *2 salmon fillets, about 1 pound each*
- *½ cup chopped fresh dill*
- *¼ cup brown sugar*
- *1 tablespoon ground white pepper*
- *½ tablespoon crushed juniper berries*

Place one salmon fillet in a shallow glass or ceramic dish, skin side down. Combine dill, sugar, salt and pepper and spread mixture on top of the fillet. Place the other fillet on top, skin side up. ★ Cover fillets with a piece of plastic wrap or aluminum foil. Place a small cutting board or a plate smaller than the dish on top of fish and weight down with kitchen weights or heavy cans. ★ Refrigerate fish for 3 to 5 days. Twice a day, uncover salmon, separate fillets and baste them with juices that have collected in the dish, reassemble them, reversing their positions, and return them to refrigerator. ★ To serve, scrape off seasonings from salmon fillets and slice fish thinly, on the bias. Serve salmon with onions, capers and toast.

VENISON STEW

Venison stew was a staple of the backwoodsmen, who lived and cooked on the trail. Venison is a particularly healthy red meat, since it is very low in fat.

Serves 6 as a main course

- *2½ pounds venison, cut into 1-inch cubes*
- *2 cups red wine*
- *4 medium onions, each cut into 8 pieces*
- *4 large carrots, cut into ½-inch pieces*
- *2 garlic cloves, unpeeled and crushed*
- *1 bay leaf*
- *¼ teaspoon whole cloves*
- *¼ teaspoon juniper berries*
- *¼ teaspoon whole black peppercorns*
- *¼ teaspoon salt*
- *¼ cup flour*
- *3 tablespoons lard*

Put venison in a large bowl and combine with wine, vegetables and seasonings. Cover and refrigerate for 2 to 3 days, to marinate meat. ★ Remove venison cubes from marinade and coat with flour. Melt lard in a large saucepan over a moderate heat. Add venison cubes and sauté for 5 to 7 minutes until lightly browned. Add all marinade ingredients, bring liquid to a boil over a high heat, then reduce heat, cover and simmer for about 2½ hours until meat is tender.

CHICKEN BRAISED IN CIDER

Apple cider is making something of a comeback, after many years of neglect. It was a staple of nineteenth-century farm "cabinets."

Serves 6 as a main course

- *3½ pounds chicken parts*
- *1 teaspoon salt*
- *1 teaspoon freshly ground black pepper*
- *2 tablespoons unsalted butter*
- *1 tablespoon vegetable oil*
- *2 cups dry apple cider*
- *1 cup chicken broth*
- *1 teaspoon dried thyme*
- *1 teaspoon dried rosemary*
- *2 large baking apples, peeled, cored and cut into ¼-inch slices*

Season chicken pieces with salt and pepper. Heat butter and oil in a Dutch oven or large ovenproof casserole over a moderate to high heat and sauté chicken in 2 or 3 batches until evenly browned, 4 to 5 minutes per side. Set chicken aside. ★ Preheat oven to 375°F. ★ Pour off all but about 1 tablespoon fat from the casserole, return to the heat and sprinkle in flour. Sauté for 2 to 3 minutes, then add cider and stock, raise the heat to high, and stir and scrape the bottom of the casserole to dissolve pan deposits. ★ When liquid comes to a boil, stir in herbs and return chicken pieces to the casserole. Cover the casserole and bake for about 45 minutes, until chicken is tender; add sliced apples for the last 15 minutes. *Picture page 171*

SALMON
WITH LIME AND WALNUT OIL

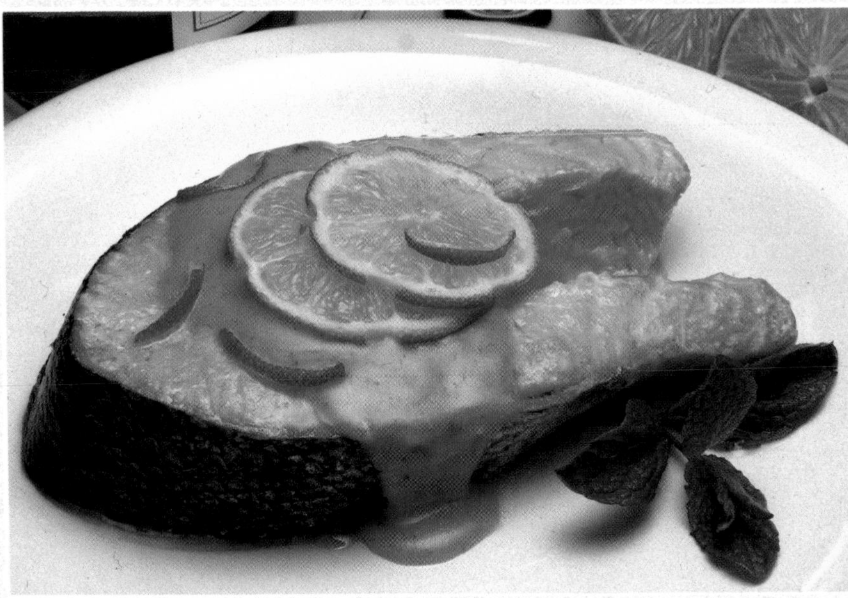

Recipe page 167

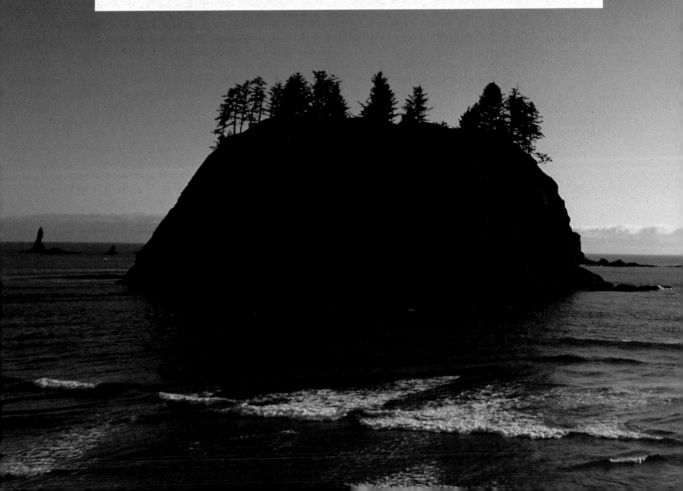

CHICKEN BRAISED IN CIDER

Recipe page 169

BLUEBERRY MUFFINS

Most blueberry recipes originated in Maine on the extreme northeastern tip of the U.S. Alaska also has an abundance of the dark blue-purple fruit growing wild. It's not unusual to come across a black bear munching rapturously on blueberries alongside a road.

Makes about 3 dozen breakfast muffins

- *2 cups blueberries, washed and thoroughly dried*
- *2 cups all-purpose flour*
- *1/4 cup butter, softened*
- *1/2 cup sugar*
- *2 eggs, beaten*
- *1 cup milk*
- *2 teaspoons grated lemon rind*
- *2 teaspoons baking powder*
- *1 teaspoon salt*

Preheat oven to 400°F. Put berries into a sieve and add a few spoonfuls of flour. Shake sieve to dust berries lightly. ★ Cream together butter and sugar. Stir in eggs, then milk and lemon rind. Sift together flour, baking powder and salt and gradually stir into moist ingredients to make a lumpy batter (do not overstir). Gently stir in berries. ★ Fill greased muffin cups two-thirds full with batter. Bake muffins for about 25 minutes, until firm and golden. *Picture page 174*

FRESH PEACH AND WHISKEY PIE

Pomology – the science of fruit cultivation – is a difficult occupation. Huge orchards of fruit drape the central portion of the Pacific Northwest in color and fragrance every spring.

Makes 1 9-inch dessert pie

- *1/2 recipe Easy Pie Crust (see page 47)*
- *8 large peaches, peeled, halved, pitted and sliced*
- *3/4 cup brown sugar*
- *2 tablespoons cornstarch*
- *1 teaspoon ground cinnamon*
- *3 tablespoons orange juice*
- *3 tablespoons whiskey*
- *1 cup whipping cream, whipped*
- *1 tablespoon superfine sugar*
- *1/2 teaspoon vanilla extract*

Preheat oven to 400°F. Roll out pie crust dough to a circle large enough to line a 9-inch pie plate. Press dough into plate. Line dough with parchment paper, waxed paper or foil, and fill it with pie weights, dried beans or peas. ★ Bake crust for about 10 minutes, just until dough has hardened. Remove weights and paper; lightly prick dough

all over with a fork, and bake for about 15 minutes longer, until golden. Let shell cool. ★ Purée half the peach slices in a food processor or blender. Combine sugar, cornstarch and cinnamon and stir into purée in a saucepan over a moderate heat. Add orange juice and cook, stirring constantly, until mixture is thick enough to stand a spoon in, about 15 minutes. Remove pan from the heat and stir in whiskey. ★ Spread purée evenly into baked pie shell. Top with remaining peach slices in a concentric design. Refrigerate pie. ★ Before serving, whip cream with superfine sugar and vanilla. Serve whipped cream alongside sliced pie.

BLUEBERRY GRUNT

The sound of this homespun dessert thickly bubbling away in the saucepan is the source of its unusual name.

Serves 6 as a dessert	*2 cups flour*
1 quart fresh blueberries	*1 tablespoon baking powder*
1/2 cup sugar	*2 teaspoons brown sugar*
1/2 cup water	*1/2 teaspoon salt*
1/2 teaspoon cinnamon	*1 1/2 tablespoons butter*
1/8 teaspoon nutmeg	*1/2 cup milk*

Put blueberries, sugar, water, cinnamon and nutmeg in a large saucepan. Bring to a boil over a moderate heat, cover pan and simmer gently for about 30 minutes, until berries are swimming in a rich juicy sauce. ★ While berries are simmering, stir together flour, baking powder, sugar and salt. Rub butter into mixture with fingertips. Stir in milk to make a soft dough. ★ Drop spoonfuls of batter into simmering berries. Cover pan and continue cooking, without uncovering pan, for 15 minutes, until dumplings are cooked through. Serve immediately.

BLUEBERRY MUFFINS

Recipe page 172

LATTICE-TOPPED SOUR CHERRY PIE

Many immigrants to this region hailed originally from the New England states. They brought with them their Yankee cooking habits – and a love of pie. Sour cherry pie ranks high on the list.

Makes 1 9-inch dessert pie

1 recipe Easy Pie Crust (see page 47)
1 cup brown sugar
2 tablespoons all-purpose flour
1 teaspoons grated lemon rind
1/8 teaspoon salt
3 cups pitted cherries, preferably sour
2 tablespoons butter

Roll out pie crust dough into 2 circles large enough to fit a 9-inch pie plate. Line plate with one circle, pressing it into bottom and sides. ★ Preheat oven to 400°F. Stir together sugar, flour, lemon rind and salt. Toss cherries with mixture and pour into pie plate. Cut remaining circle of dough into strips about 1/2 inch wide. Decorate top of pie with crisscrossing strips of dough woven into a lattice pattern, pressing ends of the strips to secure them to rim of crust. Bake pie for about 40 minutes, until golden.

DRIED APPLE CRUMBLE

A simple version of a pie, without all the bother of pastry-making, this dessert can be served hot or cold. Vanilla ice cream is a delicious alternative to cream.

Serves 6 as a dessert

2 cups dried apples
1/4 cup sugar
1 tablespoon lemon juice
1/2 cup butter
1/2 cup raisins
1/2 cup chopped walnuts
3/4 cup brown sugar
3/4 cup rolled oats
1/2 cup wholewheat flour
1 teaspoon cinnamon
1/2 teaspoon baking powder
1/2 teaspoon salt
1/4 teaspoon nutmeg
1 cup heavy cream

Cover apples with cold water and leave to soak overnight. Then bring to a boil in soaking water with 1/4 cup sugar and lemon juice and simmer for about 10 minutes, until tender but still slightly chewy. Drain well. ★ Preheat oven to 350°F. Grease a casserole with 1 tablespoon butter. Place apples in the bottom of a casserole and sprinkle with raisins and walnuts. ★ Stir together brown sugar, oats, flour, cinnamon, baking powder, salt and nutmeg. With your fingertips, rub remaining butter into mixture until it resembles coarse crumbs. Sprinkle crumbs evenly over apples. ★ Bake crumble for about 30 minutes, until nicely browned and bubbly. Serve with heavy cream.

McGINTY PIE

This recipe dates back to Oregon in the 1870s when drying was a common way of preserving the state's abundant apple harvest. The name probably derives from a surname common to the many loggers, miners and trappers found in the Northwest Territories in those days.

Makes 1 9-inch dessert pie

1 pound dried apples

about 2 cups firmly packed dark brown sugar

1½ tablespoons cinnamon

1 recipe Easy Pie Crust (see page 47)

Place dried apples in a large bowl and add enough cold water to cover. Soak overnight. Drain well and place apples in a large saucepan. Add enough cold water to cover and simmer until apples are very soft. ★ Push apples through a sieve into another bowl. Add brown sugar and cinnamon and stir well until a thick purée is formed. (Add more brown sugar if needed.) ★ Preheat oven to 400°F. Roll out half pie crust and fit it into a 9-inch pie plate. Fill pie shell with apple purée. Roll out remaining pie crust and fit over pie shell. Press edges together. Cut 3 small gashes in top crust with a sharp knife. Bake for 15 minutes. Reduce oven temperature to 325°F and bake for a further 15 minutes. Serve hot with cream.

SOURDOUGH STARTER

Make this starter at least 3 days in advance of first using it, to allow time for its flavor to develop. The tang of sourdough develops as wild yeasts present in the air cause the flour-and-water starter to ferment. Since relying on such yeasts alone is a hit-or-miss affair, this sourdough starter gets a boost from commercial yeast. For even more flavor, use the cooking water from potatoes – an extra source of starchy food – for the yeast.

Makes about 4 cups starter

1 packet granulated yeast
1 teaspoon sugar
3 cups lukewarm water
3 cups all-purpose flour

In a large glass, ceramic or plastic bowl, dissolve yeast and sugar in water. Let stand for about 15 minutes, until yeast begins to foam. ★ A little at a time, stir flour into yeast mixture to make a thick batter. Cover bowl with plastic wrap. Leave starter at warm room temperature. Within 24 hours, its surface should be covered with a rich froth of bubbles. ★ To keep the starter alive, replenish with equal parts of flour and lukewarm water after each use. On days you don't use it, ladle out a little and replace with fresh flour and water. The starter may also be refrigerated to slow fermentation; feed it every seven days or so, and let it stand at room temperature overnight before use.

SOURDOUGH HOTCAKES

Mix the batter the night before, to let the sourdough flavor develop.

Serves 4 to 6 for breakfast

2 cups milk
1 cup Sourdough Starter (above)
3 tablespoons butter, melted
2 tablespoons honey
2 eggs
2 cups all-purpose flour
1 teaspoon baking soda
1 teaspoon salt

In a large glass, ceramic or plastic mixing bowl, beat together milk, starter, 2 tablespoons butter, honey and eggs. ★ Sift together remaining ingredients, and gradually beat into liquid mixture to make a smooth batter. Cover with plastic wrap and leave overnight at room temperature. ★ Heat a large skillet or griddle over a medium heat. Grease lightly with some of remaining butter before every batch of

hotcakes. Pour about 2 tablespoons of batter on to skillet for each hotcake, making only as many as can comfortably fit at one time. When the surface of a hotcake is covered with bubbles, after about 3 minutes, turn it over. Cook 1 to 2 minutes more, just until underside is golden. Remove finished pancakes to a heated plate. Serve with more melted butter and maple syrup.

SOURDOUGH RYE BREAD

Sourdough was the bread of the California gold rush of 1849 and half a century later in the Klondike. This bread has a distinctive tangy taste.

Makes 2 10-inch round loaves

- *1½ cups Sourdough Starter (see page 178)*
- *1 cup lukewarm water*
- *2 cups all-purpose flour*
- *2 cups whole wheat flour*
- *½ cup brown sugar*
- *2 cups rye flour*
- *1 teaspoon salt*

Stir together starter and lukewarm water. Sift together all-purpose and whole wheat flours and stir about half of the mixture along with sugar into starter mixture. Cover and leave to rise at warm room temperature for about 1½ hours, until doubled in bulk. ★ Stir rye flour and salt into mixture, then work in enough of remaining all-purpose and wholewheat flour to make a soft, firm dough. Turn dough out on to a floured surface and knead for about 10 minutes. Place in a bowl, cover and let rise at warm room temperature for about 2 hours, until doubled in bulk. ★ Divide dough in half and knead each portion briefly, shaping into a round loaf. Place loaves on a lightly greased baking sheet and let rise for a further 45 minutes. ★ Preheat oven to 375°F. Cut 2 or 3 shallow slashes in top of each loaf with a sharp knife. Bake loaves for 45 minutes to 1 hour, until they are deeply browned and sound hollow when their bottoms are rapped with a knuckle.

MIDWEST
AND
MOUNTAIN STATES

The heartland is sometimes characterized as dull in scenery. The food too suffers dismissal. But where would we be without Midwestern corn-fed beef, bumper grain and thirst-quenching beer?

The center of the continental United States is indeed a flat, treeless, grass-covered prairie. While the far north consists of woodlands – stands of willows, oaks and other hardwoods adorn the river banks – most of this region is made up of vast, rolling plains, interrupted only occasionally by undulating hills, until the great spiky ridges of the Rocky Mountains rear their heads on the western fringe.

It is a wide, open land with few people. It can be lonesome or peaceful, depending on your disposition. The clear air and endless sky will gladden your soul but the persistent wind may also drive you mad. In winter, temperatures drop well below zero and blizzards can close down entire cities. In the furnace-hot summer months temperatures soar over 100 degrees and the humidity wipes away any vestiges of human energy.

The movement of ancient glaciers sculpted the land and deposited the rich black soil which is the foundation for modern American prosperity. The broad Mississippi and Missouri rivers allowed trade and communication to flourish. Today, the Midwest is America's heartland. Its bounty is the breadbasket of the world.

In the middle of the sixteenth century, the Spanish explorer, Francisco Coronado, traveled into the Great Plains region from the Southwest and claimed it for the Spanish crown. While no lasting settlements were established, important trade links were set up with various Indian tribes – links that drastically altered the way of life of the Plains Indians. The nomadic, war-like Apache and Sioux began using Spanish horses to broaden their range, and soon horses were introduced to Kiowa and even the semi-nomadic Pawnee, who farmed for part of the year and followed the buffalo herds in the summer.

Almost a hundred years later, the French began exploring the Midwest under the leadership of Father Marquette. Place names like Dubuque and Des Moines are testimony to this exploration. Simultaneously the French were staking claims to the Midwest from the South as an extension of their French-held Louisiana region.

In 1803, President Andrew Jackson signed the Indian Removal Act – the beginning of the bloody stain of American history. Over 70,000 eastern tribes, including the Cherokee and Seminole, were forcibly moved into the then unwanted lands west of the Mississippi. A series of army forts were established along the supposedly permanent Indian frontier to protect the trade routes along the Missouri River and the Sante Fe and Oregon Trails.

By 1845 St Louis had become the gateway to the Plains and by 1850 the great tide had swelled to 50,000 a year. Easterners, together with Scots and Irish, settled along the great rivers of Iowa, Missouri and Arkansas and along the eastern fringe of Kansas. Germans, Scandinavians and Russians, driven out of northern Europe by disastrous harvests and a system of almost feudal autocracy, moved into Minnesota.

Then President Lincoln signed two important pieces of legislation which changed the course of American history – and effectively doomed the Indian nation. The Homestead Act of 1862 allowed American citizens to file claims on 160 acres for a fee of $10 – provided that they lived on or cultivated their land for five years, after which time title was granted. The second crucial act signed by Lincoln granted a charter to the Pacific Railroad to cross the Plains and extend the railway all the way to the Pacific Ocean.

The Homestead Act brought a great tidal wave of northern European immigration, as well as discontented easterners, to the hitherto undesirable lands of Nebraska, western Kansas, and the Dakotas. The legendary mountain men and trappers were replaced by cattle ranchers in Colorado, Wyoming and Montana. Southerners and Texans claimed cattle range rights to much of the area being settled and fenced by farmers, and the stage was set for the bloody range wars between farmers and ranchers.

Generally, Midwesterners are ultra-conservative politically – what Richard Nixon fondly described as the Great Silent Majority. Yet for all their much-ballyhooed political conservatism, Midwestern states have consistently elected some of the nation's most liberal politicians. The people tend to be personally frugal yet will spend $50,000 at a drop of a piece of farm equipment. They are practical, "make do" people, whose ancestors lived in sod houses made out of dirt and grass because of the dearth of wood for building.

The very earliest culinary tradition of the Midwest and mountain states goes back to the Indians. Corn was the mainstay of their survival, supplemented by wild grains, fruits and game – when they could get it. Drying was their only means of preservation – when a kill was made the entire tribe gorged themselves on fresh meat. The rest was cut into strips and sun-dried to produce beef jerky. Like the tribes of New England, pemmican – a finely ground paste of beef jerky, suet, marrow and dried fruits – sustained the Indians.

Colorado mountains – for sheep and skiers

White explorers and mountain men relied on their fire power to provide fresh meat for the table. Thick steaks of venison and buffalo, accompanied by hard-tack biscuits or cornbread, was the typical fare. More exotic meals featured beaver, moose, sheep and even rattlesnake.

The immigrants who came to farm brought with them their frugal, no-nonsense culinary traditions from the east and from northern Europe. Sausage, smoked fish, dark breads and cole slaw joined Yankee pot roast. German beef and cheese-making industries were established. Kuchen, tortes, strudels and krumkracker were just a few of the delicate desserts added to the Midwest's recipe bag.

Today the Midwest is "meat and potatoes" country. Most homes and restaurants offer standard American "down home" fare, and the latest west coast or New York food fad makes very little incursion. It is always plain and plentiful, and most Midwestern cooks are insulted if guests refuse a second or third helping – the stated goal being to "get you up to market weight." It is no-frills cooking, but it is delicious.

MICHIGAN YELLOW PEA SOUP

Among Midwesterners, soup is often a meal in itself, served not in a tiny cup, but in huge, old fashioned, soup plates.

Serves 6 as a main course
1 pound yellow split peas
2 pounds smoked pork butt
3 quarts water
2 tablespoons bacon drippings
2 medium-sized onions, finely chopped
1 medium-sized carrot, finely chopped
1 celery stalk, finely chopped
salt to taste
black pepper to taste
¼ teaspoon grated nutmeg

Rinse peas under cold running water. Drain and set aside. ★ Place pork and water in a large pot. Bring to a boil. Lower heat and cover. Simmer over a low heat until pork is tender, about 1½ hours. ★ Remove pork from pot and set aside. Skim cooking water, pour water into a bowl and set aside. ★ In same pot heat bacon drippings. Stir in onions, carrot and celery. Cook for 3 minutes, stirring constantly. Pour reserved water back into pot and add peas. Add salt, pepper and nutmeg. Cover pot and simmer for about 1 hour. ★ Cut pork butt into very small cubes. Add to soup and cook for a further 30 minutes to 1 hour. Serve hot.

CHEDDAR CHEESE SOUP

The Scandinavian and German settlers' cheeses are one of the state's most important commercial producers.

Serves 6 as a first course
3 tablespoons butter
4 tablespoons flour
4 cups chicken broth
2 cups milk
½ onion, finely chopped
¾ pound Cheddar cheese, grated
1 cup half and half
1 teaspoon salt
⅛ teaspoon cayenne pepper

Melt butter in a saucepan. Stir in flour and blend until smooth. Very slowly stir in chicken broth. Continue stirring until mixture is smooth. ★ Add milk and stir. Add onion. Continue cooking over a low heat for 5 minutes. Add cheese and cook until melted. Stir and remove from heat. ★ Stir in half and half, salt and cayenne pepper. Serve hot.

FRUKT SOPPA

The Scandinavian heritage of many Midwesterners is evident in the fruit soups of the region.

Serves 6 to 8 as a first course

- *2 quarts water*
- *1 cinnamon stick*
- *4 cups mixed dried fruits (apricots, prunes and/or raisins)*
- *1 teaspoon water*
- *1 tablespoon cornstarch*
- *1/4 cup quick-cooking tapioca*
- *1/4 cup sugar*
- *1 tablespoon lemon juice*

Place water, cinnamon and dried fruit in a pot. Bring to a boil and boil for 5 minutes. ★ Add 1 teaspoon water to cornstarch and mix well to form a thin paste. Add paste and tapioca to fruit mixture. Stir well and cook for 10 minutes. Add sugar. Stir and cook 2 to 3 minutes longer. Add lemon juice and stir. Remove cinnamon stick and serve hot.

RUTABAGA AND POTATO SOUP

Rutabagas were a staple of the first settlers in the Plains states. They are also called yellow or Swedish turnips, or sometimes just Swedes.

Serves 6 as a first course

- *1 1-pound rutabaga, peeled and cut into small pieces*
- *1 teaspoon salt*
- *1 1/2 cups water*
- *3 medium-sized potatoes, peeled and thinly sliced*
- *2 cups milk*
- *3/4 teaspoon sugar*
- *1 cup chicken broth*
- *2 tablespoons butter*
- *salt to taste*
- *black pepper to taste*

Place rutabaga pieces, salt and water in a saucepan. Cover and cook over a medium heat for 15 to 20 minutes. Add potatoes and cook for a further 10 minutes or until rutabaga and potatoes are tender. ★ Remove saucepan from heat and mash the vegetables. Do not drain. Add milk, sugar, chicken broth, butter, salt and pepper. Return to heat and cook until heated through. Serve hot.

CORN CHOWDER

Chowders have long been associated with New England, where seafood is the dominant ingredient. However, chowders are also popular in the Midwest, where chicken and corn are the typical base for this buttery soup.

Serves 4 to 6 as a first course

- *½ cup finely chopped bacon*
- *1 onion, chopped*
- *½ cup sliced celery*
- *1½ cups diced potatoes*
- *2 cups water*
- *1 bay leaf*
- *1 teaspoon salt*
- *¼ teaspoon black pepper*
- *2 cups milk*
- *½ cup whipping cream*
- *2 cups corn, cut from the cob*

In a saucepan, sauté bacon until well browned. Stir in onion and cook for a further 2 minutes. Add celery, potatoes, water, bay leaf and salt. Simmer gently until potatoes are tender, about 20 to 30 minutes. ★ In a small bowl mix flour with 1 tablespoon of milk. Stir until smooth and add to potato mixture. Add remaining milk and stir. Heat soup until it thickens. ★ Slowly stir in cream and corn. Heat mixture gently but thoroughly. Add black pepper, stir, and serve. *Picture page 189*

BABY CARROTS
WITH PARSLEY AND BUTTER

A simple but delicious way to "get your vegetables."

Serves 4 as a side dish

- *1 pound baby carrots, peeled and trimmed*
- *2 tablespoons butter*
- *2 teaspoons chopped parsley*
- *salt to taste*
- *black pepper to taste*

Cook carrots in boiling water to cover until just tender, about 4 to 6 minutes. Drain well. ★ Melt butter in a saucepan over a moderate heat. Add parsley and stir. Add carrots, toss in butter and parsley until coated, and cook for about 1 or 2 minutes. Season with salt and pepper and serve. *Picture page 188*

CORN ON THE COB

BOILED

Many people add a spoonful of sugar to the water when boiling corn to enhance its flavor. This is not necessary if you are lucky enough to live close enough to a corn field to cook the corn soon after picking. If you must buy supermarket corn, toss 1 tablespoon of sugar into the water just before you add the corn.

Serves 6 as a side dish

6 ears fresh corn on the cob, husked, and stringed

6 tablespoons butter, softened

coarse salt to taste

black pepper to taste

Bring a large pot of water to a full rolling boil. Add corn. Immediately remove pot from heat, cover it and let stand for 8 to 10 minutes, until corn is tender-crisp. ★ Drain corn well. To serve, slather with butter and season to taste with salt and pepper.

FRIED TOMATOES

This recipe is a good way to use up old or soggy tomatoes. Naturally, it's better to use fresh tomatoes.

Serves 4 as a side dish

4 firm, ripe tomatoes, thickly sliced

2 cups yellow cornmeal

salt to taste

black pepper to taste

bacon drippings

sugar

Pour cornmeal on to a plate and season it with salt and pepper. Combine well. Dredge tomato slices in cornmeal mixture until well coated. ★ Heat bacon drippings in a skillet. When hot, add coated tomato slices. Fry tomatoes slowly, turning once, until browned, about 4 to 5 minutes per side. Sprinkle each slice with ½ teaspoon sugar before removing from skillet. Serve at once.

FRENCH FRIES

There's nothing particularly French about fries.

Serves 6 as a side dish	*vegetable oil for deep frying*
6 large Idaho baking potatoes	*salt*

Peel potatoes and cut into strips about 1/4- to 1/2-inch thick. Place strips in a large bowl and cover with cold water. Drain after 30 minutes, cover with fresh cold water, and soak for another 30 minutes. Drain well again and pat dry with paper towels. ★ Fill a large, deep skillet with vegetable oil to a depth of at least 1 inch. Place a frying basket in skillet and heat oil until very hot, 380°F. Remove basket, add only enough french fries to cover bottom of it, and return to skillet. Cook, shaking basket occasionally, until potatoes are golden brown, about 3 to 10 minutes, depending on thickness. Remove potatoes from basket, reheat basket and add more potatoes. Cook as above. Repeat until potatoes are used up. Salt liberally just before serving.

GLAZED ONIONS

Glazed onions are often served as an accompaniment to a pork roast.

Serves 4 to 6 as a side dish	*4 tablespoons butter*
10 medium-sized onions	*salt to taste*
10 teaspoons honey	*black pepper to taste*

Preheat oven to 450°F. Cut onions in half horizontally. Butter each onion and arrange in a buttered baking dish, cut-side up. Sprinkle onions with salt and pepper to taste. Pour 1 teaspoon honey over each onion. Dot with butter. Bake, uncovered, for 45 minutes.

Picture page 192

WILD RICE AND MUSHROOM CASSEROLE

This crop – actually a kind of marsh grass – was a valued food item amongst both the Sioux and Chippewa Indians, to the extent that the two tribes often fought over it. It is still a valued food stuff, as its price reflects.

Serves 6 as a main course

1 cup wild rice

3 cups water

3 tablespoons butter

1 cup almonds, blanched and cut into thick slivers

1 medium-sized onion, coarsely chopped

1 garlic clove, finely chopped

3/4 pound mushrooms, thinly sliced

3/4 cup single cream (can use top of milk)

2 tablespoons brandy

1 teaspoon salt

Put the rice and water in a saucepan over a high heat. Bring to a boil, reduce heat to very low, cover the pan tightly, and cook for 1 to 1½ hours, until grains are tender and fluffy. ★ Meanwhile, melt 2 tablespoons of butter in a medium skillet over moderate heat. Sauté the almonds for 3 to 5 minutes until they begin to turn golden; then add onion, garlic and mushrooms and continue to sauté for a further 3 to 5 minutes until onions are transparent. Remove almonds and vegetables from skillet and reserve. ★ Preheat the oven to 325°F. When rice is done, pour off any excess liquid and combine rice with reserved almonds and vegetables, cream, brandy and salt in a heatproof casserole. Dot the top with remaining 1 tablespoon butter. Cover the casserole and bake for 45 minutes.

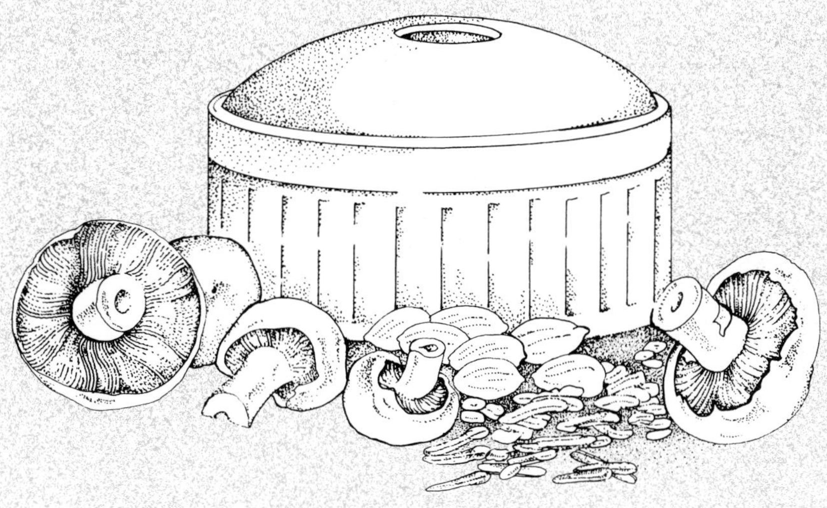

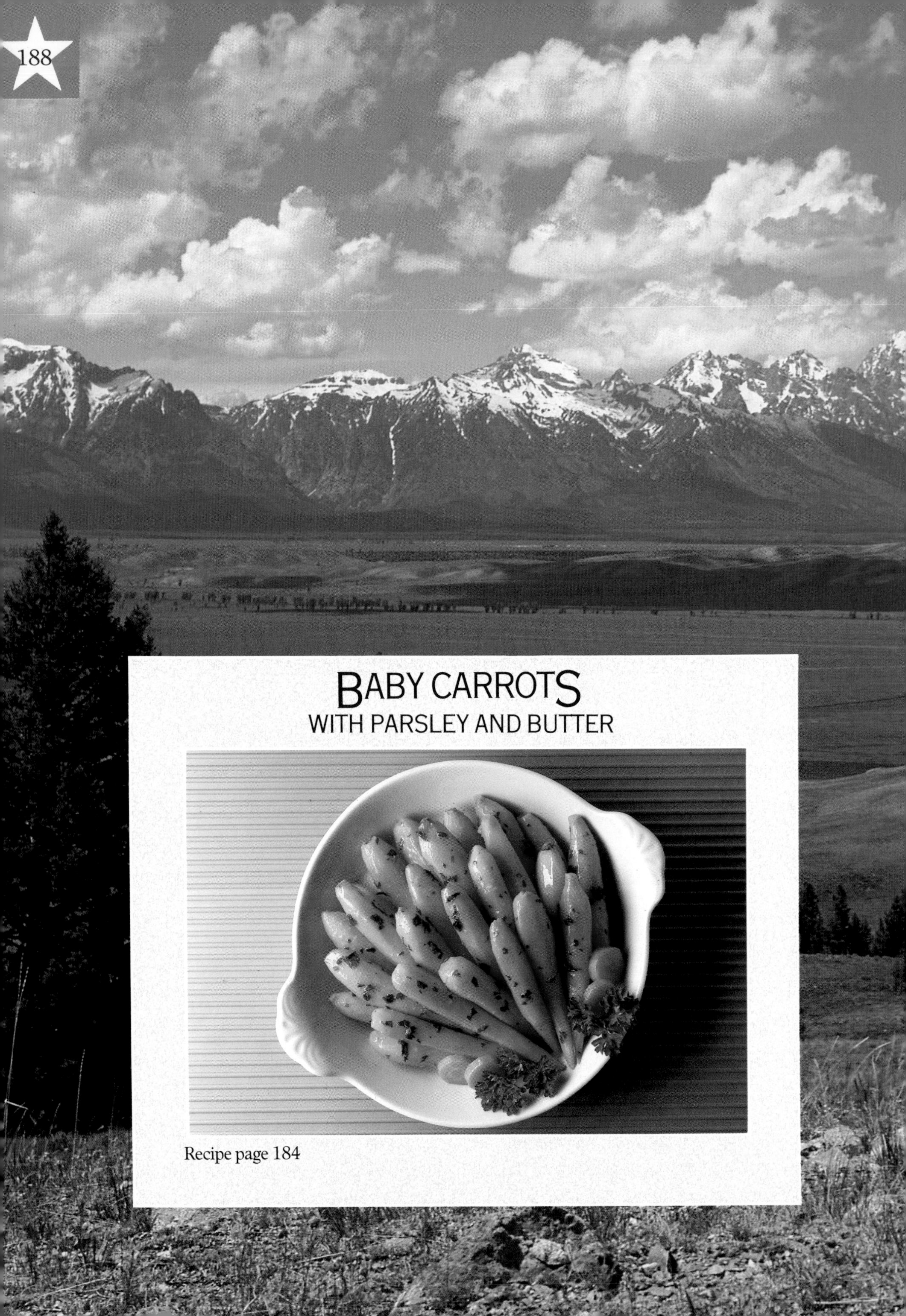

BABY CARROTS
WITH PARSLEY AND BUTTER

Recipe page 184

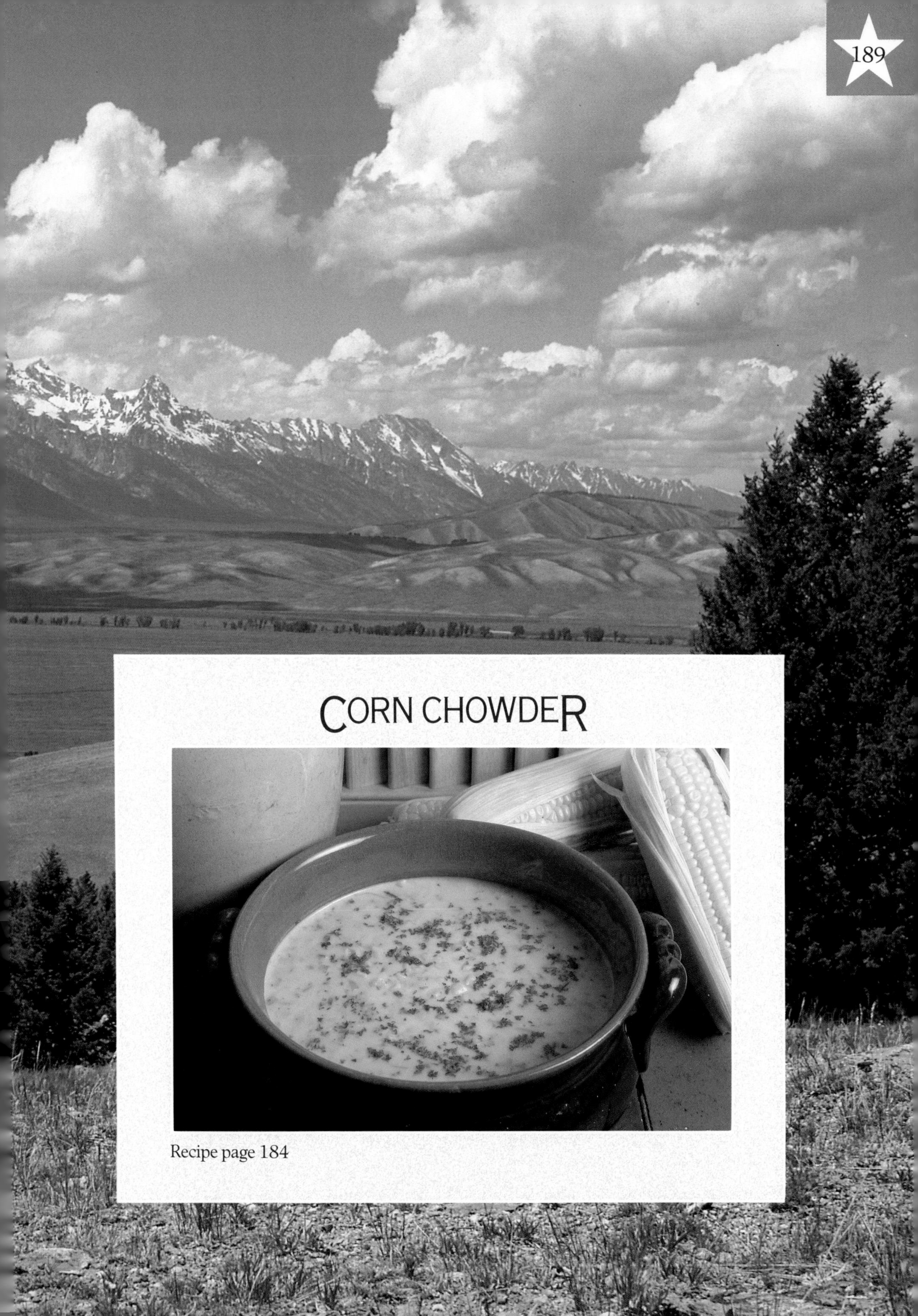

CORN CHOWDER

Recipe page 184

PEA SALAD WITH BOILED DRESSING

More a substantial side dish than a salad, this Midwestern favorite uses old-fashioned boiled dressing.

Serves 6 as a side dish

1 pound frozen peas, thawed and drained
2 celery stalks, finely sliced
4 ounces Cheddar cheese, coarsely grated
1/2 cup diced sweet pickle
2 hard-cooked eggs, chopped
1 teaspoon salt

Boiled dressing:

1 tablespoon flour
1 teaspoon dry mustard
3 tablespoons sugar
2 egg yolks
1/8 teaspoon cayenne pepper
3/4 cup milk
1/4 cup white wine vinegar
1 1/2 tablespoons melted butter, cooled

Combine peas, celery, cheese, pickle, eggs and salt in serving bowl. Toss gently and set aside. ★ To make the boiled dressing, combine flour, mustard and 1 tablespoon sugar in a saucepan. Add egg yolks, cayenne pepper, milk, vinegar and melted butter. Cook over a low heat, stirring constantly, until dressing is thick and smooth, about 20 to 25 minutes. Remove from heat and stir in remaining sugar. ★ When dressing is cool, pour over pea salad. Stir gently. Serve cold.

LETTUCE WEDGE
WITH POPPY SEED DRESSING

This recipe echoes the flavors brought by Eastern European immigrants to Milwaukee and Ohio.

Serves 6 as a side dish or first course

1/3 cup white vinegar
1 1/2 tablespoons onion juice
1/2 cup sugar
1 teaspoon dry mustard
1 teaspoon salt
1 cup vegetable oil
2 tablespoons poppy seeds
1 large head iceberg lettuce

Combine vinegar, onion juice, sugar, mustard and salt in a small mixing bowl. Whisk well. Pour in oil in a slow, steady stream, whisking continuously. Continue to whisk until dressing is thick and smooth. Stir in poppy seeds. ★ Core lettuce and cut into 6 wedges. Arrange a wedge on each plate and spoon some dressing over it.

CELERY SEED COLE SLAW

Combine red and green cabbage in this cole slaw for a colorful effect.

Serves 8 as a side dish

- *1/2 cup cider vinegar*
- *1/2 cup sugar*
- *1 teaspoon caraway seeds*
- *1 teaspoon celery seeds*
- *1/2 teaspoon turmeric*
- *1 teaspoon salt*
- *3 tablespoons light olive oil*
- *3 tablespoons water*
- *1/2 pound fresh green beans, trimmed and cut into 1/2-inch pieces*
- *1 1/2 pound green and/or red cabbage, finely shredded*
- *1 small onion, grated*
- *1 large carrot, grated*

Combine vinegar, sugar, caraway seeds, celery seeds, turmeric, salt, olive oil and water in a saucepan. Cook over a moderate heat until mixture boils, about 2 to 3 minutes. Remove from heat and set aside. ★ Cook green beans in a large pot of boiling salted water until crisp-tender, about 5 minutes. Drain well and rinse under cold water. ★ Combine beans with cabbage, onion and carrot in a large serving bowl. Add dressing and toss well. Cover tightly and refrigerate for 8 hours or overnight.

WILTED LETTUCE SALAD

For the American pioneers in the 1800s, this salad was ideal. It was made from readily available wild salad greens and the omnipresent salt pork. Today, in more settled times, lettuce and bacon have replaced dandelion leaves and salt pork. Serve this salad before simple entrées of roasted meat or poultry.

Serves 4 to 6 as a first course

- *1 head romaine lettuce*
- *4 slices bacon*
- *2 tablespoons sugar*
- *1/4 cup cider vinegar*
- *4 chopped green onions*
- *1/4 teaspoon black pepper*

Tear lettuce into large pieces and put into a salad bowl. ★ Fry bacon in a skillet until crisp. Remove bacon pieces from skillet and add to salad bowl. ★ Add sugar and vinegar to bacon fat remaining in skillet. Stir until sugar dissolves. ★ Pour mixture over lettuce. Add green onions and pepper to salad. Toss well and serve. *Picture page 192*

GLAZED ONIONS

Recipe page 186

WILTED LETTUCE SALAD

Recipe page 191

SHRIMPS DE JONGHE

This dish was created by the de Jonghe brothers, two Belgians who ran a popular Chicago restaurant called "Jacques."

Serves 8 as a first course

3 pounds shrimp, shelled and deveined
3/4 cup butter, softened
1 teaspoon salt
1 garlic clove, finely chopped
1 cup unflavored breadcrumbs
1/4 cup chopped parsley
1/2 cup dry sherry
1/8 teaspoon cayenne pepper
1/8 teaspoon paprika

Cook shrimp in a large pot of boiling water just until they turn pink, about 4 minutes. Drain well and set aside. ★ Combine butter, salt, garlic, breadcrumbs, parsley, sherry, cayenne pepper and paprika in a bowl. Mix well with a wooden spoon until smooth. ★ Preheat oven to 375°F. Lightly butter 8 individual ovenproof serving dishes. Place some of breadcrumb mixture into each serving dish. Top with a layer of shrimp, then a layer of breadcrumb mixture. Bake until nicely browned, about 20 to 25 minutes.

BAKED WHITEFISH FILLETS

Although it is somewhat oily in flavor, a particularly good type of whitefish comes from the Memominee River in Michigan.

Serves 6 as a main course

1 cup fresh coarse breadcrumbs
1 medium-sized onion, finely chopped
1 celery stalk, finely chopped
1 tablespoon chopped parsley
1 teaspoon savory
1 teaspoon salt
1 teaspoon white pepper
3/4 cup butter, melted
2 tablespoons lemon juice
2 1/2 pounds whitefish fillets
1/2 cup slivered almonds

Preheat oven to 475°F. Toss together breadcrumbs, onion, celery, parsley, savory, salt and pepper. ★ Lightly grease a shallow baking dish with a little butter, then toss remaining butter and lemon juice with breadcrumb mixture. ★ Spread half breadcrumb mixture in baking dish. Measure whitefish fillets at their thickest part. Place fillets on top of breadcrumb layer, cover with remaining breadcrumbs, and top with almonds. Bake for 10 minutes per 1-inch thickness of fillet.

FRIED LAKE ERIE SMELTS

These small, silvery fish are best dredged in flour and beaten egg, and pan fried in oil.

Serves 6 as a first course

- *1/2 cup whole wheat flour*
- *1/2 cup yellow cornmeal*
- *1 teaspoon salt*
- *1/2 teaspoon black pepper*
- *2 eggs*
- *2 tablespoons milk*
- *2 pounds cleaned smelts*
- *vegetable oil for deep frying*
- *2 lemons, cut into wedges*

Sift together flour, cornmeal, salt and pepper. In a separate bowl, beat together eggs and milk. ★ Dip smelts one at a time into egg and milk mixture, then coat with flour mixture. ★ Heat oil in a deep-fat fryer or large heavy skillet to a temperature of 375°F on a deep-frying thermometer. Fry smelts for 2 to 3 minutes, or until golden. Drain on paper towels and serve with lemon.

HEARTY BUFFALO STEW

If buffalo is unavailable, use a good cut of stewing beef.

Serves 6 as main course

- *3 pounds buffalo meat, trimmed and cut into 1 1/2-inch cubes*
- *1 teaspoon salt*
- *1 teaspoon black pepper*
- *3 tablespoons flour*
- *3 tablespoons vegetable oil*
- *2 medium-sized carrots, cut into 1-inch pieces*
- *2 large onions, cut into 1-inch pieces*
- *1/2 pound mushrooms, left whole if small or cut in half*
- *1 cup beef broth*
- *1 cup stout or dark beer*
- *2 bay leaves*
- *1/2 teaspoon marjoram*
- *1/2 teaspoon savory*

Season buffalo with salt and pepper and dust with flour. Heat oil in a large, heavy saucepan over a moderate heat. Add buffalo pieces and sauté until well browned, about 10 minutes. Add carrots, onions and mushrooms and sauté for about 5 minutes more. ★ Add broth, stout and herbs. Bring liquid to a boil, reduce heat to a simmer, cover pan and cook stew for about 3 hours, until buffalo is very tender. If sauce is still fairly liquid, strain into another saucepan and boil briskly until it reduces to a consistency thick enough to coat a spoon.

ROAST PORK
WITH WHISKEY FRUIT STUFFING

Bourbon whiskey is distilled from a mash that is 51 percent corn and is aged in charred oak barrels. The process was accidentally discovered in 1789 by the Reverend Elijah Craig of Bourbon County, Kentucky. While heating staves of white oak over a fire to make aging barrels, the minister was called away. When he returned, he found the staves charred, but decided to use them anyway. He later realized that the whiskey from that barrel was far superior to that from uncharred barrels.

Serves 6 to 8 as a main course

- *1 cup pitted prunes, halved*
- *½ cup dried apricots, halved*
- *1 cup Bourbon whiskey*
- *1 teaspoon grated lemon peel*
- *1 teaspoon grated orange peel*
- *½ apple, peeled, cored and diced*
- *1 tablespoon honey*
- *1 5- to 6-pound pork loin roast, boned and butterflied*
- *salt to taste*
- *black pepper to taste*
- *1 garlic clove, cut into slivers*
- *4 tablespoons butter, softened*
- *1 tablespoon dried thyme*
- *2 tablespoons flour*
- *1 cup apple cider*

Put prunes and apricots in a bowl and add whiskey. Soak for 2 to 3 hours. Add lemon peel, orange peel, apple and honey and mix gently. ★ Preheat oven to 325°F. Open out pork roast and sprinkle surface with salt and pepper. Arrange whiskey-soaked fruit in a strip about 3 inches from one end of pork loin (reserve whiskey). Carefully roll meat up around fruit and tie closed with kitchen twine. With a sharp knife, cut deep slits in surface of roast and fill with garlic slivers. Rub surface of roast with butter and sprinkle with thyme. Dust roast with flour. ★ Place roast in a racked roasting pan. Pour cider and reserved whiskey over meat and cover with a sheet of aluminum foil. Roast pork for 25 minutes per pound, about 2½ to 3 hours. At end of first hour, remove foil and raise temperature to 375°F. Baste often with pan juices. Add more cider and/or whiskey as needed. Remove from oven, cover with loose tent of foil and let stand for 15 minutes before slicing. Serve with pan juices spooned over each slice.

CHICKEN-FRIED STEAKS

WITH SPICY GRAVY

With this recipe, the meat is first tenderized by pounding, then dredged in flour and fried to a crisp.

Serves 6 as a main course	**Spicy gravy:**
6 8-ounce steaks, about 1/2 inch thick	pan drippings from steaks
1 1/2 teaspoons salt	3 cups milk
1/2 teaspoon black pepper	6 tablespoons butter
flour	1/4 teaspoon cayenne pepper
milk	2 dashes Tabasco sauce
vegetable shortening	1 1/2 teaspoons salt
	1/2 cup flour

Score steaks crosswise on both sides with a sharp knife. Pound steaks with a mallet until about 1/4 inch thick. ★ Dust steaks with salt and pepper, then dredge each steak in flour. Dip coated steaks in milk, and then dredge again in flour. ★ Melt shortening in a skillet over a medium heat. Add steaks and fry for 3 minutes (less for rare meat) on each side, pressing steaks down on skillet with a spatula from time to time. Remove steaks when done and keep warm. ★ To make the spicy gravy, heat milk in a large saucepan, over a very low heat. Don't let milk boil or form a skin. ★ Reduce heat under skillet containing steak drippings. Add butter, cayenne pepper, Tabasco sauce and salt. Stir for 1 minute. Slowly blend in flour until mixture becomes a roux. ★ Gradually add heated milk to roux, stirring constantly so that it blends evenly. Simmer gravy until it thickens. Serve in a gravy boat.

DAKOTA EGGS

This dish originated with the Indians of the Dakota territories.

Serves 4 as a main breakfast dish	3 eggs, beaten
1/2 pound unsliced bacon, cubed	1 teaspoon salt
2 cups fresh corn kernels	1/2 teaspoon black pepper

Fry bacon cubes in a skillet until brown and crisp. Pour off all but 2 tablespoons of bacon drippings. ★ In a bowl beat together eggs and corn. Add salt and pepper. Pour mixture over bacon cubes and cook until eggs are set and lightly browned underneath.

SLOPPY JOE

A variation of a hamburger, this dish takes its name from a literal truth: it is sloppy to consume.

Serves 6 as a main course
1½ pounds ground beef
1 tablespoon butter
1 medium-sized onion, chopped
1 small green pepper, chopped
1 garlic clove, halved
1½ cups canned tomato paste
½ teaspoon chili powder
¼ teaspoon salt
¼ teaspoon sugar
½ teaspoon Tabasco sauce
⅛ teaspoon ground cumin
6 rolls

Heat butter in a large skillet. Add onion, green pepper and garlic and sauté until golden, about 8 minutes. Stir frequently. Add ground beef and cook, stirring, until browned. Drain off fat from skillet and add tomatoes, chili powder, salt, sugar, Tabasco sauce and cumin. Mix well. Lower heat and simmer for 15 to 20 minutes or until heated through. ★ Split rolls and arrange on serving plates. Spoon sloppy joe mixture over rolls and serve.

STUFFED BEEF BURGERS

For a new variation on an old theme, try this at your next barbecue.

Serves 6 as a main course
3 pounds lean ground beef
1 medium-sized onion, finely chopped
½ cup dry breadcrumbs
½ cup dark beer
1 tablespoon heavy cream
1 teaspoon salt
¾ teaspoon black pepper
6 ounces sharp Cheddar cheese, grated
1 tablespoon prepared mustard

Preheat barbecue or broiler. Mix together beef, onion, breadcrumbs, beer, cream, salt and pepper. Divide mixture into 6 equal-sized balls. Combine cheese and mustard and divide mixture into 6 equal portions. ★ Press a portion of cheese into center of each ball of meat, then flatten meat to seal in cheese and form a thick patty. Place patties on grill or on a racked broiler pan 3 inches from heat. Cook for about 5 minutes per side, until nicely browned. The burgers should be medium rare, with cheese filling just melted.

KANSAS CITY PICKLED BEEF

Kansas City was the jumping off point for the great western migration. This recipe preserved meat for the long overland trek.

Serves 6 to 8 as a main course

2 cups cider vinegar
4 pounds round steak, boned
2 onions, thinly sliced
1 lemon, sliced
1 teaspoon black peppercorns
1 teaspoon juniper berries
1 bay leaf
2 tablespoons butter or olive oil
2 teaspoons salt
1 cup red wine

Place meat in a large glass bowl and pour on vinegar. Add onions, lemon slices, peppercorns, juniper berries and bay leaf. Cover bowl and marinate mixture in refrigerator for 2 days. Turn meat twice a day. ★ Remove meat from marinade. Strain liquid and reserve. Pat meat dry with paper towels. Heat butter or oil in a large skillet. Add meat and brown slowly on all sides, about 3 minutes per side. ★ Add 1 cup of reserved marinade to meat. Add salt and wine. Cover skillet and simmer over a low heat for 2 hours or until meat is tender. ★ Remove meat from skillet and cool slightly before slicing. If desired, thicken pan juices with a little flour and pour over meat. Serve hot.

MICHIGAN BOOYAW

Game is an important component of country fare. This stew combines a domestic meat, pork, with small common game, rabbit.

Serves 6 to 8 as a main course

1 pound pickled pork, cubed
2 2-pound rabbits, cut into serving pieces
1 yellow turnip, cubed
2 large onions, sliced
6 carrots, cut into 1-inch pieces
6 large potatoes, cubed
2 celery stalks, chopped
salt to taste
black pepper to taste

Place pork and rabbit in a large pot. Add enough cold water to cover. Bring to a boil, reduce heat and cover. Simmer until meats are tender, about 1 to 1½ hours. ★ Add vegetables. Cover pot and cook for a further 20 to 30 minutes or until vegetables are tender. Season to taste and serve.

BAKED PRUNE WHIP

A nostalgic treat from before World War II.

Serves 4 as a dessert	*1 teaspoon lemon juice*
1⅓ cups pitted prunes	*1 teaspoon pure vanilla extract*
⅓ cup water	*6 egg whites*
⅓ cup sugar	*¼ teaspoon cream of tartar*

Combine prunes and water in a saucepan and simmer for 10 minutes, stirring constantly, until prunes are soft. Drain well and chop prunes very finely. ★ Combine chopped prunes with sugar and lemon juice in a saucepan. Heat, stirring, until sugar dissolves. ★ Preheat oven to 300°F. Butter a 2-quart baking dish and sprinkle with sugar. Beat egg whites in a bowl until frothy. Add cream of tartar and beat until stiff but not dry. Quickly but gently fold prune mixture into egg whites. ★ Pour into prepared baking dish and bake until golden brown, about 30 minutes. Serve hot with heavy cream or cold with whipped cream.

HEAVENLY HASH

A popular Midwestern dessert. Too much whipped cream is not enough here.

Serves 4 as a dessert	*1 cup whipped cream*
2 eggs	*¾ cup coarsely chopped walnuts*
1 cup confectioner's sugar	*1 large box vanilla wafer cookies*
½ cup butter, softened	

Beat eggs in a bowl with confectioner's sugar and butter until smooth. Fold mixture into whipped cream. Fold in walnuts. ★ Arrange a layer of vanilla wafers in the bottom of a serving dish. Top with whipped cream mixture and another layer of vanilla wafers. Chill until firm and serve with lots of additional whipped cream.

LEMON MERINGUE PIE

Although light in texture with delicate flavoring, this pie is loaded with calories. Its delicacy has always been a test of the true American cook.

Makes 1 dessert pie	*1½ cups hot water*
½ recipe Easy Pie Crust (see page 47)	*1½ cups breadcrumbs*
3 eggs, separated	*1 tablespoon butter*
1 cup sugar	*2 teaspoons grated lemon rind*
2 tablespoons cornstarch	*6 tablespoons lemon juice*
¼ teaspoon salt	*6 tablespoons sugar*
	¼ teaspoon salt

Preheat oven to 400°F. Roll out pie dough on a lightly floured surface. Fit into a 9-inch pie plate and flute edges. Prick pastry all over with a fork and bake for 15 to 20 minutes or until golden brown. Remove from oven and cool. ★ Beat egg yolks in a bowl. Mix sugar, cornstarch and salt together in the top of a double boiler. Add hot water and first stir and then beat mixture until smooth. Add breadcrumbs. Cook over boiling water, stirring constantly, until mixture is thick and smooth. ★ Stir 2 tablespoons of breadcrumb mixture into beaten egg yolks. Add egg yolk mixture to crumb mixture in double boiler. Cook for 2 to 3 minutes. Remove from heat and add butter, lemon rind and lemon juice. Cool slightly. ★ To make the meringue, beat egg whites with ¼ teaspoon salt in a small bowl until foamy. Gradually beat in 6 tablespoons sugar. Beat until whites are stiff but not dry. ★ Pour cooled filling into baked pie shell. Pile meringue lightly on top of filling. Cover filling and edges of pie completely with meringue. ★ Bake for 5 minutes or until lightly browned. Remove from oven and cool completely before serving.

SHAKER SLICED LEMON PIE

Shakers are a spin-off of the Society of Friends (Quakers) and were originally called Shaking Quakers because of their spasm-like movements during services. Because of their vow of celibacy, the group has today nearly died out.

Makes 1 dessert pie

- *2 lemons*
- *2 cups sugar*
- *4 eggs*
- *1 recipe Easy Pie Crust (see page 47)*

Preheat oven to 450°F. Slice lemons into very thin rounds. Remove pits and put slices into a bowl. Add sugar and mix well. Let stand for 2 to 3 hours. ★ Roll out half pie dough on to a lightly floured surface. Fit pastry into a 9-inch pie plate. Roll out remaining pastry for a top crust, cut a slit in it and set aside. ★ In a small bowl beat eggs until foamy. Add eggs to bowl with lemon slices and mix well. Pour mixture into prepared pie shell. Cover with top crust, fit well and seal edges well. ★ Bake pie for 15 minutes. Reduce oven temperature to 350°F and bake for a further 45 minutes. Remove from oven and serve warm.

CORN OYSTERS

Not an oyster anywhere to be found in this recipe. The name is based on the premise that the end result, mild and creamy, tastes something like an oyster.

Serves 6 as a side dish

- *2 eggs, separated*
- *2 cups fresh corn kernels*
- *3 tablespoons whipping cream*
- *1¼ cups all-purpose flour*
- *1 teaspoon baking powder*
- *1 teaspoon salt*
- *1 teaspoon sugar*
- *vegetable oil for deep frying*

Beat egg yolks until light and lemon-colored. Stir in corn and cream. Beat egg whites until they form soft peaks. ★ Sift together flour, baking powder, salt and sugar. Gradually stir them into corn mixture. Then fold in egg whites. ★ Heat oil to 375°F on a deep-frying thermometer. Drop batter into oil by tablespoons and fry, turning once, for about 5 minutes, until golden. Drain fritters well on paper towels.

OHIO PUDDING

Although the ingredients of this recipe would have you believe it's a savory pudding, in fact it is a sweet dessert.

Serves 6 as a dessert
4 eggs
1/4 cup brown sugar
1/2 cup mashed cooked sweet potatoes
1/2 cup grated carrot
1/2 cup diced yellow squash
1 teaspoon salt
1/4 teaspoon black pepper
1 cup unflavored breadcrumbs
4 cups half and half
1 teaspoon pure vanilla extract
Sauce:
1/4 pound butter, softened
1 1/2 cups confectioner's sugar
1/2 cup heavy cream
1 tablespoon lemon juice

Preheat oven to 350°F. Butter a medium-sized baking pan. ★ Combine eggs, brown sugar, sweet potatoes, carrot, squash, salt, pepper, breadcrumbs, half and half, and vanilla extract in a mixing bowl. Mix well and pour into baking pan. Bake for 1 1/4 hours. ★ To make the sauce, combine butter, confectioner's sugar, heavy cream and lemon juice in a bowl. Beat well until smooth.

DRIED FRUIT COMPOTE

Drying fruit prevents the growth of bacteria. Pioneer cooks showed a great deal of creativity with this dried food source. Use any combination of dried fruits you like. The small quantity of sugar here gives it a tart flavor that goes well with meats. Add more sugar to taste if you plan to serve the compote for dessert, accompanied by heavy cream.

Serves 6 as a relish or dessert
1/2 cup prunes
1/2 cup dried apples
1/2 cup dried apricots
1/2 cup seedless raisins
1/4 cup brown sugar
1 teaspoon grated lemon rind
2 2-inch pieces of cinnamon
1/4 teaspoon whole cloves
1/4 teaspoon nutmeg

Rinse fruit well, put in a bowl, cover with water and leave to soak overnight. ★ Put soaked fruits and soaking water in a saucepan with remaining ingredients. Add enough extra water just barely to cover fruit. Bring to a boil over a moderate heat, then simmer gently for about 30 minutes, until fruit is almost meltingly tender. Serve hot or chilled.

INDEX

Page numbers in italic refer to illustrations

ACKNOWLEDGMENTS

The pictures on these pages were produced by courtesy of the following:

2/3 (b) Michael Freeman; 6/7 Michael Freeman; 14/15 New Zealand Meat Producers Board; 30 Walter Rawlings; 32 Ian Howes; 33 Ian Howes; 40/1 (b) Ian Howes; 44/5 (b) Ian Howes; 50/1 (b) Michael Freeman; 58/9 (b) Ian Howes; 63 Walter Rawlings; 70/1 (b) Walter Rawlings; 78/9 (b) Michael Freeman; 84 Michael Freeman; 85 Michael Freeman; 104/5 (b) Michael Freeman; 112/3 (b) Ian Howes; 117 Walter Rawlings; 124/5 (b) Walter Rawlings; 135 Walter Rawlings; 138/9 (b) Michael Freeman; 146/7 (b) Walter Rawlings; 154/5 (b) Trevor Wood; 162/3 Walter Rawlings; 170/1 (b) Michael Freeman; 174/5 (b) Trevor Wood; 181 Walter Rawlings; 188/9 (b) Walter Rawlings; 192/3 (b) Walter Rawlings

All other photographs are the property of Quarto Publishing Ltd.

Key: (b) background

Quarto would like to extend thanks to Frank Odell Ltd, 70 High Street, Teddington, Middlesex, TW11 8JD, England, for the loan of outdoor cooking equipment.

While every effort has been made to acknowledge all copyright holders, we apologize if any omissions have been made.